# Crime
# and Culture in
# America

**Recent Titles in Contributions in Criminology and Penology**

# CRIME AND CULTURE IN AMERICA

## A COMPARATIVE PERSPECTIVE

Parviz Saney

CONTRIBUTIONS IN CRIMINOLOGY AND PENOLOGY, NUMBER 11

Greenwood Press

NEW YORK • WESTPORT, CONNECTICUT • LONDON

HV
6789
.S27
1986

**Library of Congress Cataloging-in-Publication Data**

Saney, Parviz.
  Crime and culture in America.

  (Contributions in criminology and penology,
ISSN 0732-4464 ; no. 11)
  Bibliography: p.
  Includes index.
  1. Crime and criminals—United States.   2. Criminal
behavior—United States.   3. Criminal justice, Adminis-
tration of—United States.   I. Title.   II. Series.
HV6789.S27     1986        364'.973        86-3594
ISBN 0-313-24340-9

Library of Congress Catalog Card Number: 86-3594
ISBN: 0-313-24340-9
ISSN: 0732-4464

First published in 1986

Greenwood Press, Inc.
88 Post Road West, Westport, Connecticut 06881

Printed in the United States of America

The paper used in this book complies with the
Permanent Paper Standard issued by the National
Information Standards Organization (Z39.48-1984).

10  9  8  7  6  5  4  3  2  1

This book is dedicated in the spirit of friendship and gratitude to Walter Gellhorn of Columbia Law School: a superb scholar, a concerned individual, and a true friend.

# Contents

# Part I
# Facts and Figures

# Introduction

Twenty minutes after 3 A.M., on March 13, 1964, a twenty-eight-year-old bar manager named Catherine Genovese was stabbed to death near her Queens neighborhood apartment. She was repeatedly stabbed for more than half an hour while thirty-eight respectable, law-abiding citizens stood by and heard her screams and horrified pleas for help. They turned their lights on—some watched the gruesome scene—but not one did anything to save her life. No one made a timely telephone call to the police. The story shocked the nation. Since that time more than 1,000 articles and books have been written to fathom and explain the psychological and sociological factors that could have caused such a callous disregard for life in the cold-blooded apathy of the thirty-eight bystanders.[1]

The story is by no means unique. Almost every day we read about numerous incidents where people could have intervened, without risking too much, to save someone else's life or to stop a rape or mugging, but who did nothing, letting it all happen and going their way as if nothing serious had taken place. We have read or heard about forcible rapes being committed in broad daylight, in public places, in schools and streets, while the victim's cry for help fell on the deaf ears of the passersby who did not want to become involved. The same has happened with murders, muggings, burglaries, and others; the apathy in the Genovese case certainly was not an exception. It is rather widespread. But why? one might ask. What factors make certain people so insensitive to other people's pain and suffering, discourage the public from getting "involved," having sympathy for others?

On December 22, 1984, on a New York subway, Bernhard H. Goetz shot four teenagers who had accosted him and asked him for some money. At the time nobody knew his identity; he disappeared from the scene but later decided to give himself up. He was brought back to New York from New Hampshire to face possible trial. While he was gone, people started to talk about the man who had shot the teenagers as if he were a national hero, a vigilante who had done something praiseworthy not only to defend himself against an undeserved attack, but also to help make the subways a less threatening place for everybody, something police and other city authorities had apparently failed to do. When he identified himself, a wave of enthusiastic support greeted him; countless people donated more than enough money to bail him out of jail. It seemed that everybody was grateful for his courageous stand in performing an uplifting social deed. Bernhard Goetz was eventually cleared by a grand jury of attempted murder charges, accused only of illegal weapons possession.

The media and the public were keenly interested in Bernhard Goetz's case. Most people praised and supported him. Typical of the mood and perception of the public and indicative of how people felt about the whole problem of crime and official reaction to it are the following opinions as expressed in many letters written to Sydney H. Schanberg of the *New York Times* in response to an article he had written on the subject:

"Me, I'll take the wild west any day. At least it had a certain wholesomeness, a thrust toward decency and order. True, bystanders might get hurt in confrontations, but suffering from an exchange of bullets is better than suffering at the hands of subway sadists."

"Thank God for that vigilante. Bernhard Goetz for Mayor."

"People have been running scared. Here's someone who struck back."

"They used to hang people for stealing horses. It worked!"

"Why have you not written again and again and again about the utter failure of the police and the courts to protect the ordinary citizen?"

"I, too, blanch at the concept of vigilantism, but I, too, as a generally law-abiding citizen, would feel safer with vigilantes roaming the streets in place of the muggers that are out there now."

"One problem is that the subways are used only by the little, unimportant, uninfluential people. We really don't count much to politicians. The mayor, council president, governor all have big autos supplied at our expense. They don't have to use subways to be at work on time. Our local government is not doing the job; that's why the guy with the gun is a hero."[2]

In 1984 the SmithKline Beckman Corporation was brought to trial for having failed to disclose the serious ailments that resulted from one of its products, a blood-pressure drug call Selacryn. The drug was linked to thirty-six deaths and more than 500 cases of liver and kidney damage. The company was quite aware of these ill effects and was required by law to disclose the facts; it never did so, and the drug was for sale until it was withdrawn from the U.S. market in January 1980.

The Food and Drug Administration had recommended felony charges, but the Justice Department decided on misdemeanor charges, arguing that it was difficult to prove that the company's failure to disclose was intentional. The company was fined $100,000, which in all likelihood will be collected from the same public who suffered from the drug, by increasing the price of the company's products. What about the managers of the company who had committed the offense? The three who pleaded no contest to misdemeanor charges were placed on probation and sentenced to perform 200 hours of community service!

One may wonder why on earth I have chosen these episodes as my introductory remarks, events that do not superficially represent any of the basic concerns regarding the crime problem in America. Couldn't we more appropriately discuss some of the more salient features of the nature and scope of crime in this country? To portray a more representative picture of crime, shouldn't we be talking about facts of murder, rape, mugging, or burglary in different cities?

The choice of these apparently unrelated incidents has been deliberate. The goal is to stress the possible role of certain aspects of American culture that may have a great deal to do with the crime problem in this country, but for whatever reason have not been widely studied by criminologists. To be sure, there are various aspects of culture which have a direct bearing on the problem. As we shall see later, for instance, the emphasis on personal achievement and material success—dominant values in American culture—cannot help, other facts being equal, but to reinforce tendencies toward criminal behavior. The fact remains, however, that other, seemingly irrelevant aspects of the American culture may also affect the crime picture, albeit in an indirect way. If, to take the Genovese case as an example, the deplorable perception in the public is that for whatever reasons—heterogeneous population, diversity of subcultures, or an individualistic world outlook—people living in big urban centers do not have any moral or social obligation to risk their necks to save someone else's life, then the would-be mugger would have an amorphous but reliable feeling that, at least in the absence of police, he should not fear any obstacle in the way of his antisocial behavior. In a different sociocultural setting, such as in many African or Middle Eastern countries where people almost instinctively swarm around anyone in distress in no time, a potential offender with a similar design in mind thinks twice before starting on his course of action.

To take the Goetz case, if it signifies a deeply felt perception that people living in big cities like New York do not receive any real protection from the police and the criminal justice system, that they are all likely prey to violent crime, that "there is a jungle out there" where each person is for himself and should take the initiative to protect his own interests, then the incentive to cooperate with the police and other agents of the criminal justice system will be at best only minimal. Also, with such a negative social outlook, more people would be prone to cross the boundary lines of legal permissibility, to gain some highly desired but undeserved privilege.

Finally, what does the SmithKline case say about the quality of justice in American courts and the economic system? What is the public perception of the power of big corporations to influence not only the legislature to enact laws that are most favorable to their interests, but also the whole criminal justice system, which seemingly accords them almost complete personal immunity for crimes which, when committed by the average citizen, are most severely punished? What does it say about the question of legitimacy of the sociopolitical system? Lack of concern for the plight of other human beings, the public's distrust of the criminal justice system in providing adequate protection for the average citizen, and a pervasive feeling that the criminal justice system mostly works against the poor and the underprivileged, may seem unrelated—at least directly—to the problem of crime in the United States. The fact is, however, that if we want to have a meaningful understanding of the various factors that can influence or encourage criminal behavior, then the way the public feels and responds to the incidence of crime—before, during, and after it is committed—and what it feels about the sociopolitical system and the direct or indirect effect of the criminal justice process in fighting crimes of various sorts—as exemplified by the rate of arrest, conviction, and punishment of offenders—should also be definitely taken into account as most relevant indeed.

Of the various factors that have been deemed responsible for the high rate of crime in America, I have selected the cultural: the norms and values that comprise the contemporary American world outlook and directly or indirectly influence the nature of the social structure and individual behavior in all life situations. To be sure, in a heterogeneous society like America, we have a cluster of value systems, each pushing the individual members of a different subculture to engage in certain type of behavior. A distinction should be also made between the officially expressed ideologies and values of the criminal justice system as expressed in the Constitution and other relevant documents and the actual perceptions and thought processes that guide the behavior of the police, the public prosecutor, judges, juries, and prison authorities in practice. To distinguish these two aspects, Herbert L. Packer uses the expression "the Due Process Model" and "the Crime Control Model." Underlying each model is a system of interrelated norms and values that may be in conflict with those of the other model; the actual outcome of the criminal law process is determined in each individual case by the practical compromises reached between the often conflicting requirements of the two models. Packer explains:

Each of the two models we are about to examine is an attempt to give operational content to a complex of values underlying the criminal law. As I have suggested earlier, it is possible to identify two competing systems of values, the tension between which accounts for the intense activity now observable in the development of the criminal process.[3]

With due regard for the reality of the two-model value systems that dominate the actual behavior of officials responsible for the administration of criminal law, it is nevertheless possible, at least theoretically, to discover what kind of values—or what combination of value systems—do in fact motivate and guide the actors—police, public prosecutor, and others—in the criminal justice system to adopt particular modes of behavior as appropriate in dealing with the crime problem at each of the various stages. As Packer has noted, "The kind of criminal process we have depends importantly on certain value choices that are reflected, explicitly or implicitly, in its habitual functioning."[4]

Another point to be noted is that the explicit or implicit ideology adopted by any of the institutions involved in the criminal justice process necessarily affects the functioning and outcome of the other relevant institutions. A diligent and conscientious police force that brings more offenders to trial creates a heavier load for the public prosecutor and the courts. A strict court system that sends most convicted offenders to jail helps create prison overcrowding, which in turn may result in easier parole standards or a cyclical return to leniency by the court itself. On the other hand, a court that is, or seems to be, lenient to offenders can create apathy and indifference in the police, who will instinctively realize that their tireless effort in detecting and apprehending criminals is a thankless and indeed wasted job in the face of the court's lax stand in the fight against crime. It may also alert the public that the system has failed in providing protection and security for the average citizen.

We will discuss the concept of culture in more detail in chapter 3. Here, to complete the introductory picture, suffice it to say that my assumption is that the offender acts in reaction to sociocultural forces dominant in his society, that he somehow consciously or unconsciously must justify or rationalize his antilegal behavior by reference to certain dominant norms and values not only in his particular social group(s), but most probably also in the whole society. If the criminal justice system has failed to provide peace and security for the average American as many have repeatedly stated,[5] then the system may be acting—again consciously or more probably under the pressure of blind and unquestioned force of tradition—in accordance with criminal law ideologies and policies which are no longer effective, if in fact they ever were, in achieving the proclaimed objectives of the criminal justice system.

If the average urban American has become indifferent to the plight of other human beings, if he normally prefers not to cooperate with police in preventing and detecting crime because he has lost confidence in the criminal justice system or because he feels that if he does intervene he will not receive adequate protection from the police, these and similar attitudes, which are culturally determined, will have a great deal of impact—directly or indirectly—on the scope of criminal activity in society. Thus, unless these perceptions and the social forces that cause them are properly studied and understood, any hope of significantly reducing the incidence of crime in society would be illusory. As Herbert Packer has put it, "If the laws go unenforced—which is to say, if it is perceived that there is a high percentage of failure to apprehend and convict in the criminal process—a general disregard for legal controls tends to develop."[6]

My assumption, in short, is that before we can draw a meaningful picture of crime in society—and find possible solutions for it—we should seriously probe the nature of present-day American values and their impact on both the socialization process, which determines how the individual is raised to view and react to his social world, and the social control processes, especially the criminal justice system. If this is the case, then the nature of the values and thought processes which motivate the police, the judge, and the prison authorities in their daily confrontations with offenders also has a very significant bearing on how the individual offender—and the rest of the public, including potential offenders—view and react to the restrictive commands of penal laws.

The influence of culture on social life is of course quite pervasive; it encompasses all aspects of social life and human experience. One of the most significant ways that sociocultural forces affect our perceptions of and our reactions to criminal behavior is the process by which certain acts are chosen to be defined as criminal. Durkheim was the first to note that what is considered criminal is not by nature either good or bad. The decision of the people in authority to call an act a crime gives it this particular quality. To quote him:

Since there cannot be a society in which the individuals do not differ more or less from the collective type, it is also inevitable that, among these divergences, there are some with a criminal character. What confers this character upon them is not the intrinsic quality of a given act but that definition which the collective conscience lends them.[7]

At times when the concept of crime was synonymous with that of religious sin, all sorts of cruelty were inflicted on the offender in the name of expiating his soul from the clutch of evil spirits. When the founders of the Italian School of Criminology and other humanitarian thinkers redefined crime as a basically social and psychological problem, offenders were viewed and treated in a more humane fashion. Thus the definition of crime, which in a pluralistic society is the outcome of constant clashes and compromises among different interest groups and their respective ideologies, is also an important element to be scrupulously analyzed before one can begin to grasp the nature of forces that may encourage criminal activity.

In more recent times, other sociologists have tried to analyze and identify the process by which certain acts are designated crimes by law. Howard S. Becker, for instance, focusing on the interactive nature of deviance and its definition, refers to the social processes involved in intergroup rivalries and the resulting labeling of certain acts deemed contrary to the interest of the dominant political group(s) as deviant and, in the case of criminal behavior, as officially punishable. "(Social) groups create deviance by making the rules whose infraction constitutes deviance, and by applying those rules to particular people and labeling them as outsiders. From this point of view, deviance is not a quality of the act the person commits, but rather a consequence of the application by others of rules and sanctions to an 'offender.' "[8]

The important factor in the conceptual creation of crimes and the application of punitive sanctions to those who violate penal codes and statutes is the structure of the political system and the distribution of power in society. What Durkheim uncritically called "collective conscience" is really nothing more than the outcome of the ongoing clash of interests among various social groups which struggle with each other for the acquisition of power and other social values.

It is true that in Western democracies—in contrast with totalitarian regimes—the public makes decisions about the distribution of social values among different classes by casting votes. The fact remains, however, that people are not initially equal when they enter the democratic process; they are differentially endowed with their share of social values and their ability to influence others. Certain classes have almost exclusive control over the mass media; naturally they can influence public opinion and the law-making process more effectively than the interested but unorganized individual or even organized groups that, due to financial and other limitations, do not possess a comparable amount of power and influence. The result of these differential possibilities and opportunities among various social groups is a social order that represents and protects the rights and privileges of the members of the ruling class. In such a setting any act that is considered seriously inimical to the interests of the dominant groups presented and advocated through the use of the democratic process of government by representation is defined and punished as a crime. At least theoretically, anyone who commits the forbidden act will be treated as the enemy of the social order and subjected to specific punishments. Thus, the way Americans define and view illegal activity obviously has a direct bearing on how they react to it. In other words, values that dominate the world outlook and behavior of officials involved in the criminal justice process are relevant to how they react to an offender, and in turn also to how the public, through formal and informal education, views their practices. An example from a different cultural setting will clarify the issue. In China crime is explained as a manifestation of the still existing contradictions between social forces—

the so-called "residuals" of the former capitalistic society—in the present Communist order. According to the late Chairman Mao's major address in 1957, "On the Correct Handling of Contradictions Among the People," such contradictions are of two kinds: those that materialize "among the people," and "those between the enemy and ourselves." Contradictions among the people, including almost all minor offenses except those committed against "public" properties, should be resolved through "persuasion-education." This has meant reliance on nonprofessional bodies, chiefly the primary units of work or residence, that should sanction deviants and handle disputes in an informal and flexible fashion.[9] On the other hand, contradictions between the people and the enemy, which are at times expressed in the commission of offenses against state organs and the Communist economic system, "are to be handled by the organs of dictatorship," for example, regular courts of law led by the Communist Party.[10]

In brief, culture is a dominant factor in the whole crime process—in its influence in encouraging certain types of antisocial behavior, in how we treat convicted felons, and in promoting the types of attitudes and perceptions in the public that either directly or indirectly influence the spread or restriction of criminal behavior in society.

As we have noted, the essence of the social processes that create crimes is also an important factor in causing specific perceptions in the public. Thus, to have a complete picture of crime in society, such social processes should be studied, along with processes and institutions that apply criminal sanctions to various offenders. However, due to limitations of time and space, we shall not deal with that subject in this book, except indirectly. The perceptions people have, consciously or subconsciously, about the justness of the existing societal arrangements for the distribution of wealth, power, and other social values in society will inevitably affect their perceptions about the criminal justice system and the possible existence of any moral obligation to obey the enacted penal laws. We will address these issues later under the title of "legitimacy."

As indicated before, I have chosen the study of American cultural values as important factors affecting criminal behavior. These values shape the common mood and mentality of the people, encouraging certain types of behavior. Cultural factors, however, are not the only forces responsible for the behavior patterns of individual actors. Thus, the emphasis I have put on cultural forces, which I consider to be the most important determining factors because they are very basic and powerful on account of their unconscious sway over social settings and human behavior, does not in any manner negate the significance of other, sociopsychological studies. Our study will hopefully complement them. Crime, like other social problems, can be studied from three distinctive and equally valid perspectives: individual, sociological, and cultural.

## THE INDIVIDUAL PERSPECTIVE

Any study using this approach would focus on the effect of innate or acquired individual potentialities. Under the influence of outside pressures, which in the process of growing up become ingrained in the human psyche, such potentialities may result in criminal activity. Some criminologists, both past and present, have claimed that the propensity to commit crimes is inborn. The majority of experts, however, have rejected the idea. One can of course accept the fact that individual human beings are endowed with different innate qualities; some are physically stronger, taller, or more intelligent than others. Some may by nature be more aggressive than others. However, being physically strong or weak, being more or less intelligent, or having other hereditary qualities does not by itself determine the nature of human reaction in different social positions. The social and cultural forces shape these inborn qualities and tendencies, and when they are expressed either approve or condemn the action. Even being constitutionally aggressive will not by itself result in socially disapproved violent acts. A man with an aggressive nature, if cultivated according to dominant norms and values of Western cultures, can become a war hero, a champion boxer, a successful business executive, or a respected lawyer. What is important, therefore, is the learning or conditioning processes and the underlying sociocultural forces, which can make a criminal out of a morally neutral human infant. However, the focus of attention in such personality studies is the process of criminalization that produces the individual offender, not the nature of the outside forces that create or reinforce criminal tendencies in a particular individual.

## THE SOCIOLOGICAL PERSPECTIVE

Many criminologists have studied the impact of various social phenomena—family, poverty, slum areas, drugs, alcoholism, and others—on criminal behavior. If we review the vast body of such studies, the accepted conclusion is that no single social factor can be considered to be the definite cause of criminal activity. It is all well and good to investigate the nature of social institutions that can in conjunction with other social forces lead to illegal behavior. However, when we view the processes of human interaction that determine how real human beings interact with each other under various conditions, it is logically necessary to study and understand the meaning of these interactions, the mental outlook, the ideology, and the cultural values that condition the people to think and behave in particular ways as well.

## THE CULTURAL PERSPECTIVE

This approach is based on the self-evident truths that human beings, unlike animals, which are guided and controlled by instincts and conditional reflexes, learn to act in accordance with social norms and standards of behavior. These standards and values, which provide moral support for them, do not emanate from the individual actor but are imposed from outside. In the final analysis, therefore, it is the perception and belief of the individual about what is right or wrong, what is proper or improper, that motivate him to engage in certain types of behavior. And it is certainly the culture that provides the social standards, norms, and values. In certain societies, for instance, the individual is taught to accept his social position and "destiny" as god-given and thus inevitable. This cultural perception produces a set of expectations for the individual quite different from what is true in American culture, which consciously preaches that everyone is entitled to shape his own destiny, to choose his life-style. It is, therefore, the cumulative effect of the interaction of various social values in American society today that we should study as the ideological basis of all social problems including crime as well as some of the great achievements of this society, not only in material terms, but in intellectual, artistic, and scientific fields as well.

One final note. I shall not repeat in this book the outcome of studies made on the basis of psychological and sociological outlooks on crime. I shall limit my work to the cultural influences on criminal behavior. It should be noted, however, that I use cultural influences as a comprehensive concept. Thus, aside from values ordinarily associated with the American culture, we will be studying some political issues and other values that specifically affect the behavior of police, public prosecutor, prison authorities, and other agencies involved in the fight against crime. Before we start on that main theme of this book, we should put the American crime picture in a proper comparative perspective to see whether there is anything very different about the scope or nature of crime in this country. I will try to show in the following chapter that in comparison with certain other countries, the extent and nature of criminal behavior in the United States is indeed excessive.

## NOTES

1. On the second weekend in March 1984 experts from the field of law, psychology, and sociology joined government officials at Fordham University for a three-day Catherine Genovese Memorial Conference on Bad Samaritanism to review once more the facts and conceivable explanations for the dreadful lack of concern shown by the witnesses to the crime.

2. Sydney H. Schanberg, "The Bernhard Goetz Mailbag," *New York Times*, January 19, 1985, p. 21.

3. Herbert L. Packer, *The Limits of the Criminal Sanction* (Stanford, Calif.: Stanford University Press, 1968, 1979), p. 154.

4. Ibid., pp. 152–153.

5. Typical of such a view is *Fair and Certain Punishment: Report of the Twentieth Century Fund Task Force on Criminal Sentencing*, (New York: McGraw-Hill, 1976), p. 3, where it is said:

> The greatest indictment of the criminal justice system in the United States is simply that it fails in providing equitable justice    Lacking credibility, it also fails in its essential purpose of protecting society by deterring criminal and violent actions. . . . By failing to administer either equitable or sure punishment, the sentencing system . . . undermines the entire criminal justice structure.

6. Packer, *The Limits of Criminal Sanction*, p. 158.

7. Emile Durkheim, *The Rules of Sociological Method*, trans. Sarah A. Salovay and John H. Mueller, 8th ed. (New York: The Free Press, 1966), p. 70.

8. Howard S. Becker, *Outsiders: Studies in the Sociology of Deviance*, (New York: The Free Press, 1973), p. 9.

9. Mao Tse-Tung, "On Contradictions," in *Selected Works of Mao Tse-Tung*, vol. 1 of 5 vols. (Peking: Foreign Languages Press, 1967), p. 311f.

10. See sources cited in J. Cohen, *The Criminal Process in the People's Republic of China, 1949–1963: An Introduction* (Cambridge: Harvard University Press, 1968); see also, Randle Edwards, "Reflections on Crime and Punishment in China, with Appended Sentencing Documents," *Columbia Journal of Transnational Law* 16 (1977), pp. 45–103; Mao declared in his speech of February 27, 1957, that law is not always a suitable means for resolving different disputes. There are two ways to solve the contradictions that still plague the Communist order.

> "One is the appeal to the use of law and its sanctions, and this is a method of dictatorship. It was formerly thought suitable to apply law to barbarians; today it will be applied to counter-revolutionaries when all hope for their reform is abandoned. But law is not, on the other hand, suitable to resolve merely internal, rather than antagonistic, social contradictions. . . . If a citizen commits some wrongdoing, there is no need to treat him as a criminal, cite him before a court for judgment and punishment. . . . It is more appropriate to undertake his education and apply persuasion rather than subject him to the indignity represented by a civil or criminal condemnation."

Rene David and John E. C. Brierly, *Major Legal Systems in the World Today: An Introduction to the Comparative Study of Law*, 2d ed. (New York: The Free Press, 1978), p. 488.

# The Crime Problem in a Proper Context

Concern about crime in the United States has risen sharply in the last two decades. Not only has the crime rate increased continuously, but the nature of criminal acts committed has also changed. On the whole, crimes have become more vicious, impersonal, "senseless," and hence more alarming. As an official response to public outcry over the widespread feeling of insecurity and uncertainty, President Johnson signed an executive order establishing the President's Commission on Law Enforcement and Administration of Justice to "deepen our understanding on the causes of crime and how society should respond to the challenge of the present levels of crime."

The report of this commission came out in 1967. Other commissions were established and their respective reports were published in the following chronological order:

1968. National Advisory Commission on Civil Disorders, known also as the Kerner Commission or the Riot Commission.

1969. National Advisory Commission on the Causes and Prevention of Violence, known as the Eisenhower Commission, or the Violence Commission.

1970. National Commission on Obscenity and Pornography.

1972. U.S. Commission on Marijuana and Drug Abuse.

1973. National Advisory Commission on Criminal Justice Standards and Goals.

Reports submitted by these commissions and other reliable sources all indicate that the rate of increase in criminal activity in the United States as compared with corresponding rates in other Western democracies is alarming indeed.

The Eisenhower Commission, named after its chairman Milton S. Eisenhower, observed in its final report:

Violence in the United States has risen to alarmingly high levels. Whether one considers assassination, group violence, or individual acts of violence, the decade of the 1960s was considerably more violent than the several decades preceding it and ranks among the most violent in our history. The United States is the clear leader among modern, stable democratic nations in its rates of homicide, assault, rape, and robbery, and it is at least among the highest in incidence of group violence and assassination.

This high level of violence is dangerous to our society. It is disfiguring our society—making fortresses of portions of our cities and dividing our people into armed camps. It is jeopardizing some of our most precious institutions, among them our schools and universities—poisoning the spirit of trust and cooperation that is essential to their proper functioning. It is corroding the central political processes of our democratic society—substituting force and fear for argument and accommodation.[1]

The President's Crime Commission had a similar message to convey to the American people:

The fear [of crime] leads many people to give up activities they would normally undertake particularly when it may involve going out on the street or into parks or other public places at night. The costs of this fear are not only economic, though a burdensome price may be paid by many poor people in high crime rate areas who feel compelled to purchase protective locks, bars, alarms, who reject an attractive night job because of fear of traversing the streets or who pay the expense of taxi transportation under the same circumstances. In the long run more damaging than costs are the loss of opportunities for pleasure and cultural enrichment, the reduction of the level of sociability and mutual trust, and perhaps even more important, the possibility that people will come to lose faith in the trustworthiness and stability of the social and moral order of society.[2]

A national Gallup Poll survey conducted in February 1983 confirmed the existence of fear, concern, and worry about crimes committed in the streets. Among the findings were that:

1. Fifty-four percent of Americans said the number of crimes in their neighborhoods is more than the preceding year. Three out of four respondents believed that crimes committed at the time were more violent than they were five years before.

2. People living in cities considered crime to be the top problem facing their neighborhoods. Twenty-five years ago crime was not mentioned among the top ten urban problems.

3. Almost half the people interviewed said that they were afraid to walk alone at night in their neighborhoods. In smaller communities such fears were more pronounced: 32 percent of people living in small towns or villages were afraid

to stay out after dark even within their own communities. One in every six admitted to being afraid even behind the locked doors of his or her home at night.

4. In the twelve months preceding the survey one in every four households in America was hit at least once by either burglary or theft, or a household member was victimized by physical assault.[3]

Incidentally, the findings also confirmed the result of victimization studies that show, as we noted before, that the actual number of crimes committed is much larger than the official data collected and published by the Federal Bureau of Investigation would indicate.[4]

The question remains whether the American crime rate, even though on the increase, is still a natural consequence of unavoidable social changes and hence should be considered as inevitable. Some authorities have argued that American society has always been beset by violence, that if we review the history of this society from its early days, violence has always been a feature of social interaction among people. We have become more alarmed today, they would say, because we have much more effective systems of communication. Because of the aroused level of consciousness, we have learned to view crime as a social problem.

No doubt if we come to the conclusion that crime is the unavoidable price that more developed countries have had to pay for their advanced state of existence, that it is the unavoidable consequence of alienating forces in all progressive industrial societies, then any search for possible solutions—or partial solutions—to the problem would seem to be a futile exercise. The fact is, however, that not all industrial societies suffer from crime to the same extent. And some societies like Japan have even shown a consistent decline in their crime rates. The relevant question, then, is whether American crime rates are significantly higher than in other socially comparable societies, and if so, what may be the reason(s) for the difference. Of course, before we can make any comparison, we should have a reliable method of determining the real scope of criminal activity in the several societies we are interested in. Our perceptions and information about crime come from different sources.

## MEDIA COVERAGE

The accounts we read in newspapers or see on television provide us with our basic but usually noncritical information on the subject of crime. The nature, space, and location of coverage a news item gets in the media depends on the owners' and managers' points of view and their perception of what their particular audience wants to read or hear about. Thus, depending on the type of paper we read or television channel we watch, we may get a more accurate or a distorted picture of crime in our society. If we read the *New York Post* or the *Daily News*, which usually fill their covers and pages with sensational stories, we may get the feeling that the amount of crime committed in the city has surpassed the limits of our tolerance. On the other hand, if the *New York Times* or the *Wall Street Journal* is our favorite paper, we will learn about crime in the context and in conjunction with other, more constructive activities, and our surrounding environment will not seem as threatening or dangerous. In any event, the information we usually receive from the media is rather impressionistic; it does not always stand the exacting test of scientific scrutiny. This information is nevertheless significant in many ways.

To begin with, it shapes the perceptions and reaction tendencies of the average citizen. The actual context of social life includes a multitude of activities, many of which are affirmative and constructive. If violent and gruesome crimes, such as murder, rape, and muggings are chosen for reporting and presented with exaggerated sensationalism in the press or on television, then the feelings developed on the basis of such selective and lopsided coverage will be anger, fear, insecurity, and dissatisfaction with the criminal justice system.

Perhaps American news media are more open than their European counterparts in their coverage of news and other social events. Freedom of expression is a highly valued right in American society, and American media have refused to accept any measure of self-censure. Perhaps they feel that the proper role of the media in a free society is not to educate the public, an accepted concept in many other societies, but to inform, to amuse, and of course, also to sell. In any event, the net result is that American news media have a significant role to play in shaping public perceptions and attitudes toward crime and the criminal justice system.

## PERSONAL REPORTS

Many people who have been involved in various capacities in the criminal justice process—as judges, scholars, practicing attorneys, convicts, and victims of crime—have written about their personal experiences in their particular social settings, as well as their contacts with the police, criminal courts, the jury system, prison conditions, and so on. Such personal, detailed accounts can provide valuable and realistic impressions of the personal dramas that engulf the lives of offenders, victims, and prison inmates.

A less detailed but more systematic personal account of various aspects of crime can be obtained by the interview technique, which is widely used by social scientists as a reliable research method. For instance, we can interview a representative sample of offenders to learn about the social conditions and the motivating forces that have driven them to criminal behavior—not only their economic and social status, but also their feelings and perceptions about the whole social structure, the political system, criminal court procedures, police, prosecutors, and the prison community. Since by definition offenders have had firsthand contact with criminogenic factors and/or were less able than the average law-abiding citizen to control their desires and tendencies, their experiences can be highly valuable in indicating the nature of the sociocultural forces that can cause criminal behavior. We can also interview a sample group of nonoffenders, asking comparable questions to learn what factors can be singled out for their staying within the legal boundaries. We can try to establish whether they, too, have committed illegal acts that were not noticed but would have been punishable if detected. We can interview the actual and potential victims to learn what they have to say about our laws, the Supreme Court decisions stressing the rights of the accused, about judges, the police, and the rest of the criminal justice system. We can ask the general public about their impressions regarding the quality of life in big urban centers and particular neighborhoods. We can learn about their fears, complaints, and hopes as well as their possible suggestions as to how to fight the crime problem.

Again, the information we gather may be unscientific in the strict sense of the word. Nevertheless, such studies can be very useful especially when we are concerned with the seemingly irrelevant but highly significant role of such institutions as the criminal court system, the political structure, and the distribution of wealth in American society.

## CRIME STATISTICS

The third source of information, and perhaps the most reliable, is criminal statistics. Such data are collected at three different levels: crimes reported to and/or detected by the police, number of convictions in criminal courts, and the number of inmates in prisons. As we move from police records to court convictions and inmate population, criminal statistics become less reliable as true indices of actual numbers of crimes committed in society. But even police records do not accurately reflect the true magnitude of criminal activity. As victimization surveys and other studies of hidden criminality have shown, a vast number of crimes are never detected, and therefore do not appear on official records.

The President's Crime Commission conducted the first crime victimization survey in 1966. The study involved 10,000 households (containing 33,000 people). The people were asked whether they had been victims of some serious crime during the preceding year and whether such crimes were reported to the police. To provide a more representative picture of crime victimization, the National Crime Survey has increased the number of households and individuals covered since 1973 to 60,000 and 132,000 respectively. Futhermore, interviews are now conducted twice a year.

Victimization surveys have shown that for various reasons many crimes are not reported by the victims to the police; hence no action is brought against the offender. As a matter of fact these surveys showed that less than

50 percent of all crimes were reported to the police. The rate of reporting varied with different crimes and in different situations. For example, 84 percent of rapes committed by a stranger were reported as compared to 54 percent committed by a person known to the victim. Larceny is the crime least reported and car theft the most reported to the police, in the latter case undoubtedly because such reporting is mandatory for claims against insurance companies. At any rate, victimization surveys indicate that police statistics cannot be taken at face value.[5]

This conclusion has been supported by other studies as well. For instance, a large number of self-report studies have indicated that close to 100 percent of all people have committed some sort of punishable offense, even though only a few were actually arrested.[6]

A significant study of the youth in the United States confirmed the same conclusion. The study involved 847 representative thirteen- to sixteen-year-old boys and girls nationwide who voluntarily reported the delinquent acts they had committed. The results were analyzed for differences in sex, age, race, and socioeconomic status and were afterwards checked and compared with police records and court files.

Of the total sample, 88 percent confessed to having committed at least one offense for which they could have been adjudicated delinquent. In contrast, only 9 percent had been detected by the police, only 4 percent received police records, and less than 2 percent were judged delinquent. Offenses committed by the 9 percent who were caught represented less than 3 percent of all the acts that could be charged as delinquent.[7]

A large number of visible and detectable crimes are not reported to the police for various reasons. Some victims prefer not to press charges because they have lost confidence in the efficacy of the criminal justice system; they feel it will be a further waste of time if they decide to pursue the matter through the slow, cumbersome process of criminal adjudication. In certain crimes, such as rape, the incentive not to report is even stronger. In addition to the suffering already experienced, the victim does not wish to go through the excruciating trauma of being subjected to all sorts of ordeals by the defense attorney, including the accusation of having wished and asked for the violent and humiliating act as well as having other moral depravities and flaws of character.

When the police receive crime reports, they have discretion in a great number of cases not to pursue the matter any further, to drop the case. This happens mostly in the so-called victimless crimes and also in minor infractions involving public peace and order.

From cases that are entered in police books, a large proportion are dropped later due to lack of sufficient evidence. And among the cases that eventually reach the courts, a great many are dismissed before trial or end in acquittal. Still, in not all cases that result in conviction will the offender necessarily end up in jail. There are a number of alternatives available to the judge when he decides on the sentence.

In short, out of 2,000 known crimes, police are notified in only about 50 percent of the cases; when notified they come to the scene about three-fourths of the time; and in four out of five times no arrest is made. Of the 20 percent of offenders who are arrested, more than half are released without trial; of the 40 percent who are tried, about one-half are convicted, and some serve some kind of sentence.[8] Thus, none of the available statistics accurately reflect the reality of crime and its magnitude.

The problem becomes even more complicated when one decides to compare the crime rates of different societies. Notwithstanding the many problems this society faces today, the United States is unique among nations in that the citizens here discuss the most unsavory social problems with utmost openness and candor. Problems that are routinely swept under the rug in other countries are revealed and openly discussed in America. Here one hears more about homosexuality, drug abuse, prostitution, the threat of herpes and AIDS developing in epidemic proportions, not necessarily because America has more of these problems, but because, unlike many other peoples, Americans are more willing to face the bitter truth more openly.

Most countries are reluctant to reveal any facts they deem damaging to their national self-image or their international standing. This is certainly true of many Communist countries. The Soviet Union, for instance, does not publish any crime statistics. However, Soviet officials frequently claim without offering any concrete evidence that the rate of crime in that country has dropped, percentagewise, compared with figures for a particular year in the past. They also claim that crime is a passing problem in the socialist world. Lenin had confidently stated, "We know that the fundamental social cause of violations of the rules of society is the exploitation of the masses, their want and their poverty. With the removal of this chief cause, excesses will inevitably begin to 'wither away.' We do not know how quickly and in what order, but we do know they will wither away."[9]

Criminologists from East Germany, like those of other Communist countries, make the same claim today, even though the socialist order has existed, at least in the Soviet Union, for well over half a century, and crime is still a problem in that country. According to East German authorities: "Criminality . . . under the conditions in the GDR . . . is a relatively 'superficial' phenomenon which is totally alien to the core or the inner nature of our society."[10]

Communists claim that whatever crime still exists in the socialist world is mainly due to "survivals" of capitalist modes of thought and provocation by Western countries. According to V. S. Orlov, a Soviet authority on criminology, "survivals" include all phenomena "contrary to socialism but rooted in the ideology and morality of presocialist economic and social groups, and, in particular, of present-day capitalism, the pernicious influence of which gives rise to alien views and ideas within our socialist society."[11]

In the face of the relentless persistence of the crime problem in Communist countries, some criminologists have recently felt compelled to admit that aside from other usual explanations, some inherent factors in the socialist mode of life could be at least partially responsible for the existence of crime in such societies.[12] Nevertheless, the prevailing tendency is still to deny the importance of the problem in Communist countries and to blame it mostly on the "residues" of Western, capitalistic ideologies.

The tendency to downplay the significance of the crime problem is not confined to Communist societies. Many developing countries also feel that an admission of the existence of any social problem, including high crime rates, would be taken as a definite sign of backwardness and lack of civilization. This seemingly irrational reaction is of course rooted in the historical experiences of these countries. Many were colonized by Western powers and remained under foreign domination for long periods of time. Hence the sensitivity about the admission of any fault and the exaggerated desire to look "civilized" by ignoring their existing social problems.

And then, of course, there are other dictatorial regimes where any admission of flaw or mistake is unthinkable. Such an admission would destroy the dictator's bloated self-image, which helps him keep his basically shaky psychological equilibrium. He can never admit that crime is a serious problem under his rule. He has assumed personal responsibility for whatever goes on in his country, and he needs to pretend that everything is working well.

Another difficulty in obtaining reliable comparative statistics is that countries differ as to what they define and punish as criminal acts and how they classify them. An act—say, drug trafficking and use—may be a crime in one society, thus inflating that country's national crime rates, while in another country it may be considered an innocent act. There may also be a discrepancy between the legal ideals as expressed in statutes and the actual behavior of the people. When a custom is widespread in a society, it will resist the oppressive force of the law. A statute that runs against such a custom is doomed to failure unless it is buttressed by well-planned educational programs for the public. Thus, there may be numerous violations of the law which are actually condoned by the public and the official representatives of the criminal justice system; they are not reflected in the overall criminal statistics. A good example of such a situation in the United States was Prohibition of the 1920s. During that period, certain activities, such as the importation, production, sale, and consumption of alcoholic beverages, were legally prohibited, while in practice, in conformity with long-established social customs, many people freely engaged in those activities. In most countries, bribery is defined as a crime in the statute books. Nevertheless, giving and receiving money in return for personal favors is quite common in many places. And since it has become an accepted and very functional practice, nobody, except in very rare cases, bothers to bring charges against the offenders. On their face, crime statistics would show low rates for bribery in such countries, in the same way official rates for the detection and conviction of alcohol-related crimes were relatively low during Prohibition in the United States.

Statistical shortcomings may be due to innocent lack of know-how on the part of the officials responsible for compiling and recording the relevant facts. Even among competent social scientists, it is not always easy to keep personal biases and preferences out of the research project and the interpretation of the collected data.

Finally, there is also the risk of irresponsible or even dishonest reporting of the facts. We know that statistics can be manipulated to give whatever impression one wants them to give. Thus, police may try to exaggerate their own efficiency and competence by presenting the type of data that would indicate that they have solved more crimes than the facts could support; the judge may wish to give the impression that he is overburdened with a heavy load of cases and still capable of processing and finalizing them. The prison warden likewise may wish to emphasize the significance of his role and hence may overstress those aspects of his job that are likely to convey such a message. For instance, he may stress only the aggressive tendencies of the inmates, thus portraying a distorted image of the prison population.

Notwithstanding all these limitations, we can still get a relatively accurate picture of crime if we use a combination of different sources and impressions, trying to keep our objectivity as much as possible. And it is with these reservations in mind that we view the following international statistics.

Except for a handful of countries, most of which are not among the advanced industrial nations, the crime rate has been increasing constantly during the past decades around the world. The available data indicate that in the decade between 1955 and 1964, the rate of increase per 100,000 population for different countries was as follows:[13]

| Country | Percentage |
|---|---|
| France | 70 percent |
| Netherlands | 54 percent |
| Sweden | 44 percent |
| Italy | 40 percent |
| Denmark | 27 percent |
| Germany | 26 percent |
| Austria | 25 percent |

In the next four years crimes committed per 100,000 population increased again: in England a little more than 10 percent; in Germany, Austria, Denmark, and the Netherlands, each 20 percent. In the same period, the crime increase rate in France was 40 percent.[14]

In the United States, the rate of increase was even more rapid. If we do a little comparing, the result will reveal the alarming scope of crimes committed in big American cities. For instance, the number of murders in Manhattan roughly equals that of England and Wales combined. In Detroit, which has the same population as Northern Ireland, the number of murders is five times as great as in that country. The National Advisory Commission on Criminal Justice Standards and Goals summed up the facts and the related concern:

If New York has 31 times as many robberies as London, if Philadelphia has 44 times as many criminal homicides as Vienna, if Chicago has more burglaries than all of Japan, if Los Angeles has more drug addiction than the whole of Western Europe, then we must concentrate on the social and economic ills of New York, Philadelphia, Chicago, Los Angeles and America.[15]

In the years between 1973 and 1977, the number of homicides, rapes, robberies, and serious wounding in the United States increased 40 percent, twice as fast as crimes committed against property. An average resident of New York City has six chances in ten during his or her life-time of being a victim of murder, rape, assault, or robbery.

All this alarming information about the crime rate in the United States becomes even more significant when we notice that in some other countries crime is not a serious problem; in still others, the crime rate has actually been decreasing in recent decades. Some of these countries cannot serve as a basis for comparison because their standards of living and quality of life are drastically incompatible with American ideals and values. Saudi Arabia, for instance, claims to have a very low crime rate. The claim may be justified, but the low degree of criminality there has been possible at a very high price people are paying in terms of individual rights and growth potentials. With the threatened and actual use of severe and inhuman punishments—cutting off the hand, stoning the offender to death, and others—the oppressive politico-religious system of government has been able to suppress not only most criminal tendencies but also any other manifestation of human creativity and industry. A low crime rate, therefore, has been possible in that society at a cost that is practically unimaginable in a country like the United States.

Communist countries also claim low crime rates. But as pointed out, no reliable statistics are ever published for these countries. We cannot know for sure the extent of criminal activity in such societies. However, we can say with certainty that a very low level of expectation about life opportunities, which is endemic in Communist countries, including very restricted freedom of expression and movement as well as a harsh and uncompromising system of punishment, could act as possible deterrents to criminal activity.

A country whose crime rate can be logically compared with the United States is Japan. Japan is a highly industrialized society with overpopulated cities and a slow decline in traditional social bonds. Nevertheless, it shows a relatively low crime rate. Japan is also an appropriate case for comparison with the Western world because it, too, has a free economic system. In addition, the formal structure and content of Japanese laws and political institutions resemble those of Western democracies. For our present purpose, a brief look at the general crime picture in Japan will suffice. According to a recent study:

In all of Japan in 1979 the number of crimes involving the use of handguns totaled only 171—a figure that would be incredibly low for some individual police precincts in the United States. And a comparative study of crime rates made in 1978 revealed that for every 100,000 inhabitants New York had eight times as many rapes as Tokyo, ten times as many murders—and 225 times as many armed robberies. More remarkable yet, the per capita incidence of violent crime, which has been skyrocketing almost everywhere else in the industrialized world, has actually declined somewhat in Japan over the past twenty years.[16]

Aside from the disturbing impression one gets from comparing traditional crime rates in the United States with some other comparable societies, a more comprehensive picture of the crime problem will have to include many other relevant facts. For instance, in addition to the commonly recognized property crimes, there are other illegal acts which rarely come to public attention, even though they are at least as serious as any other property crime. Based on estimates provided by the U.S. Department of Commerce, Charles Silberman gives the following account:

Stealing from employers is [quite] prevalent. What retailers euphemistically call "inventory shrinkage"—and is mostly theft by employees—came to $5.3 billion in 1974. Shoplifting accounts for only 20 to 25 percent of that missing inventory; while some of the remaining "shrinkage" undoubtedly was due to honest mistakes in record-keeping, the great bulk was the result of employee theft of merchandise and fraudulent manipulation of inventory records. And retailers were not the only ones victimized by employee theft. The Commerce Department estimated wholesalers' 1974 inventory losses at $2.1 billion and manufacturers' losses at $2.8 billion.[17]

Another fact about the U.S. crime problem is the drastic change in the nature of and motives for the illegal acts committed. We can safely say that on the whole crimes against the person have become more vicious, "senseless," and impersonal. Let us take two examples, that of murder and rape. Traditionally, murder was mostly a crime of passion, committed against people personally known to the offender. One result was that if a person was more cautious about people with whom one had to deal, he or she could be relatively safe from murder. The picture has changed now. At present, most murders and other violent acts are committed by people who do not have any personal knowledge of or emotional attachment to their victims. Sometimes there is no rational reason to kill; the victim has handed over his purse or wallet without resistance, and there is no way he could recognize the mugger-murderer. Since the 1960s, murder in the hands of total strangers has increased twice as fast as the traditional cases of murder committed against hated relatives, estranged lovers, or despised enemies. Available statistics for murder in Chicago are also revealing. In that city in the period between 1965 and 1973, the rate of murders committed by people known to the victim increased 31 percent, whereas murders committed by total strangers more than tripled.[18]

The same observation is applicable to rape. In the past, women were raped by jealous former husbands, lovers, or other people known to the victim. At present most rapes are committed by total strangers who suddenly appear in just any place: street corners, subways, deserted school yards, and neighborhoods. In 1967 people known to the victim were responsible for about half of all the rapes committed. In 1975 two-thirds of rapes were committed by total strangers. The strong emotions generated by such violent acts as stranger homicides or stranger rapes—aside from causing personal injury or death of the victim—are those of total bewilderment, disbelief, mental dislocation, and oppressive anxiety. In both these stranger crimes, there is usually no clue to help the police or the victim to solve the perplexity and shock. This additional factor makes such crimes even more heinous, more scary. The fear created by senseless crimes, often committed under the influence of drugs or severe emotional stress, then spreads and engulfs the whole nation. It affects the public's perceptions about all aspects of life in contemporary society. It influences social relations and contacts. It is small wonder, then, that according to public opinion polls, two Americans in five are scared to go out alone at night. The figure is one in two for large cities. At a news conference to launch a $1.8 million project to finance a study in Newark on crime fears (as a sample of American cities so affected) the United States attorney general said at City Hall in January 1983, "The fear of crime had virtually paralyzed residents of neighborhoods across the country." He also quoted a recent Gallup Poll showing that almost half the people surveyed were afraid to walk alone at night near their homes. For women, the elderly, and inner-city residents the figure was almost two-thirds. He said that according to another poll, "40 percent of the people had changed their daily habits to avoid potential violence."[19]

These facts and figures seem sufficient to show that the increase in American crime rates when compared with available data on some socially comparable countries and also America's own crime rates in the past is alarming indeed. It has become a serious social problem, which requires more comprehensive concern about the deeper roots of criminal behavior, in other words, the cultural values. But before we move on to the discussion of the possible role of culture in causing criminal behavior, another point should be noted.

When we talk about the "average" man of the statistics and his chances of becoming a crime victim, we should not forget the substantial differences that exist between various social groups in their enjoyment of life privileges and their chances of being victimized. A person living in the affluent and well-protected Upper East Side in New York City obviously has a much better chance to be relatively immune from criminal behavior than someone who lives in a poor, crime-infested neighborhood. The same observation also applies to every other situation where we deal only with numbers and averages and not with actual human beings who live under different social conditions. Class and status differences and the power that socially dominant groups enjoy also influence the types of behavior that official law-makers select and define as criminal. They affect a person's chances of being caught and punished by the criminal justice system. Whereas, for instance, shop-lifting of even a trifle item from a supermarket may lead to criminal in-vestigation, social stigma, and perhaps a prison sentence, every year hundreds of millions of dollars are taken, in fact stolen from the average citizen by big businesses without being characterized or punished as such. The public is not yet willing to view many socially harmful acts, such as price fixing in an actual state of monopoly or the types of behavior that Edwin Sutherland calls "white-collar crimes,"[20] as reprehensible enough to be characterized and treated as criminal. Neither is the public yet disposed to look at some even more dangerous acts, such as the illegal dumping of toxic waste which poisons our environment and causes many serious ill-nesses, as something that should be punished—when committed knowingly or recklessly—at least as severely as killing an individual human being.

## NOTES

1. Final Report of the National Commission on the Causes and Prevention of Violence, *To Establish Justice, To Insure Domestic Tranquility*, (Washington, D.C.: U.S. Government Printing Office, 1969, New York: Bantam Books, 1970), p. xxv.

2. President's Commission on Law Enforcement and Administration of Justice, *Task Force Report: Crime and Its Impact—An Assessment* (Washington, D.C.: U.S. Government Printing Office, 1967), p. 94.

3. Charles F. Silberman, writing about the pervasive fear of crime in America, gives the following account in his book, *Criminal Violence, Criminal Justice* (New York: Vintage Books, 1980), p. 6: "Fortunately, my own family has escaped violent crime until now, but my home was burglarized, as was my son and daughter-in-law's, while I was writing this book."

4. See Harold J. Vetter and Leonard Territo, *Crime and Justice in America: A Human Perspective* (St. Paul, Minn.: West Publishing Co., 1984), p. 2.

5. See in general Al Paez and Fred Shenk, *Criminal Victimization in the United States* (Washington, D.C.: Bureau of Justice Statistics, 1983); Wesley G. Skogan, *Issues in the Measurement of Criminal Victimization* (Washington, D.C.: U.S. Government Printing Office, 1981).

6. See Eugene Doleschal, "Hidden Crime," *Crime and Delinquency Literature* 2, no. 5, (1970): 546–572.

7. Jay R. Williams and Martin Gold, "From Delinquent Behavior to Official Delinquency," *Social Problems*, 20, no. 2 (1972), 209–229.

8. See Philip H. Ennis, "Crime Victims and the Police," *Trans-Action*, 4, no. 7 (June 1967): 39–40.

9. Lenin, *Works*, Vol. 25 (3rd Russian ed.), p. 436, quoted in Valery Chalidze, *Criminal Russia: Essays on Crime in the Soviet Union*, trans. P. S. Falla (New York: Random House, 1977), p. 204.

10. Erich Buchholz, Richard Hartmann, John Lekschas, and Gerhard Stiller, *Soviet Criminology: Theoretical and Methodical Foundations* (London: Saxon House; Lexington, Mass.: Lexington Books, 1974), p. 171.

11. Quoted in Chalidze, *Criminal Russia*, p. 206.

12. See for example Buchholz et al., *Soviet Criminology*, especially pp. 172–173.

13. See Sir Leon Radzinowicz and Joan King, "The Growth of Crime: The International Experience," in Sir Leon Radzinowicz and Marvin E. Wolfgang, *Crime and Justice*, vol. 1, *The Criminal in Society*, 2d rev. ed. (New York: Basic Books, Inc. 1977), pp. 3–24.

14. Ibid., p. 4.

15. National Advisory Commission on Criminal Justice Standards and Goals, *Task Force Report: Correction* (Washington, D.C., U.S. Government Printing Office, 1973), p. 352.

16. Robert C. Christopher, *The Japanese Mind: The Goliath Explained* (New York: Linden Press/Simon & Schuster, 1983), pp. 163–164.

17. Silberman, *Criminal Violence, Criminal Justice*, p. 56.

18. See Richard Block, "Homicide in Chicago: A Nine-Year Study (1965–1973)," *Journal of Crime and Criminology* 66, no. 4 (December 1976): 496–510.

19. See *New York Times*, January 11, 1983, p. B1.

20. For an early statement, see Edwin H. Sutherland, "White Collar Criminality," *American Sociological Review* 5 (1940): 1–12.

# Part II
# The Cultural Dimension

# 3

# The Role of Culture in Shaping Human Behavior

Human life in society is composed of a series of complex, interconnected, and constantly changing patterns of interaction among individuals in identifiable social settings. The human infant is born into a particular society and raised to internalize and act in accordance with particular sets of norms, values, and expectations. He or she learns to speak a special language ("the mother tongue"), develop a particular world outlook, believe in certain religious or moral precepts, like or dislike unique art styles, and react to various social stimuli with calm, anxiety, or even violence, as the case may require.

Human society is related to its past and its future by certain factors which have been defined by some anthropologists and sociologists as "culture." The unique historical experiences of every nation are summarized and preserved for posterity in the capsulated form of ideas, traditions, appropriate emotions, and symbols. Every society has its own vast reservoir of folklore, norms, music, and other art forms which give it a distinctive quality. It is through culture that the basic characteristics of every human society are preserved and transmitted to succeeding generations. Thus, for instance, to appreciate the nature of life in the Soviet Union today, one must also study the distinctive features of Russian society under the autocratic rule of the czars. Likewise, what makes a Latin American country like Mexico what it is today has a great deal to do with that society's past history: lack of real democratic experiences in its political past, the exaggerated cultural emphasis on the reality and reliability of sensate feelings, and so on. In a similar vein, to know the reasons for many of the substantive and procedural rules of criminal trials in the United States, we must study not only the capitalistic ideology, which as we shall see has had certain negative implications in this society, but also the strong suspicion and fear of organized government and centralized power and control, which stem from the unique life experiences of this nation as expressed in various cultural phenomena, including the Constitution, statutes, and other legal documents.

We shall elaborate on these points later in this chapter. But first it is appropriate to say what we mean by the concept of culture as defined by social scientists.

Culture has been defined differently by various anthropologists and sociologists. Some have been content to define it simply as anything and everything that is transmitted from one generation to the next by means other than human genes. In the 1920s and 1930s a general concept such as "culture is learned behavior" seemed quite sufficient. Others, however, have tried to give culture a more precise meaning. A. L. Kroeber and Clyde Kluckhohn, after reviewing several hundred definitions of the word, came up with the following, which they thought incorporates the basic features of the concept and would be acceptable to most social scientists:

Culture consists of patterns, explicit and implicit, of and for behavior acquired and transmitted by symbols, constituting the distinctive achievement of human groups, including their embodiments in articrafts; the essential core of culture consists of traditional (i.e. historically derived and selected) ideas and especially their attached values; culture systems may, on the one hand, be considered as products of action, on the other as conditioning elements of future action.[1]

It should be noted that in this definition the patterning or regulating aspect of culture is emphasized. The point is that human needs, both biological and social, can be fulfilled in an infinite number of ways. Hunger, for instance, can be satisfied by eating meat, vegetables, dairy products, and many other things. Food can be consumed raw or cooked; other items can be added to the basic ingredients to enhance their flavor. Certain sources of nutrition are taboo in some religions. Food can be eaten at the table, or on the floor, with knife and fork, with one's own fingers, or in other ways. Out of these endless possibilities and other equally endless possibilities related to the satisfaction of other human drives and needs (for example, sexual drive, need for protection against excessive heat or cold, and others) certain types of behavior have been selected on the basis of geographical requirements, historical events, and chance occurrences and presented through the culture as appropriate reaction to specific conditions. As Melford E. Spiro has observed:

Culture, as a normative system, is a functional requirement of a human social order. Because of the enormous degrees of biological plasticity and cognitive ingenuity that, together, produce the broad variability characteristic of human behavior, the absence of this normative dimension would render human social systems impossible. The range of behavior patterns potential in any individual is much broader than the limited range required for the performance of any custom or set of customs. Beyond a certain critical point, whose limits are still unknown, variability in behavior precludes the very possibility of custom. In other words, human societies have had to set limits (by means of prescriptive and proscriptive norms, and of rules) to the range of permitted variability in customary behavior.[2]

Thus, culture by necessity regulates and patterns human behavior, and of course this is one of its most important aspects. Irrespective of the contents and quality of human interaction, it had to be limited and patterned before human beings could develop civilization. The emphasis on the patterning function of culture, however, seems to make it a static concept, somehow incapable of portraying the dynamics of change in social action.

To stress the everchanging nature of life in human society, some social scientists have used the concept of social structure. Radcliffe-Brown, for instance, defined the concept as a network of social relations, including social classes, groups, and roles. In this theory, every structural system is assumed to be a functional unity in which all the component parts act and react with each other in such a way that the system's existence and continuity are preserved. Of course, social structure is not an objective reality to be directly observed. It is an abstract concept that is useful in analyzing actual social phenomena. However, even observable social relations cannot be properly understood unless we visualize them in the context of the existing cultural patterns and the motivating forces behind them. Thus, as can be noted, the concept of patterning in culture is not contradictory, but indeed complementary to that of the social structure. As Radcliffe-Brown has pointed out, "Social relations are only observed, and can only be described, by reference to the reciprocal behaviour of the persons related. The form of a social structure has therefore to be described by the patterns of behaviour to which individuals and groups conform in their dealings with one another."[3]

Patterning or regulating social relations is achieved through a series of rules. Depending on the type and strata of society, these rules may be based on morality, etiquette, or law. The point, however, is that compliance with the social rules is assured, in the last analysis, by the inculcation in the public of the perception that it is more pleasurable or less painful to observe the customary and/or enacted rules. In other words, the public gradually learns through the medium of culture to favor certain types of behavior and to condemn others. Again, as Radcliffe-Brown has observed, "Whenever we say that a subject has a certain interest in an object we can state the same thing by saying that the object has a certain value for the subject. Interests and values are correlative terms, which refer to the two sides of an asymmetrical relation."[4]

The concept of value as an object of interest derived from the work of the American philosopher, R. B. Perry, is thus extended by Radcliffe-

Brown and others to include the definition of a social value as the object of a common interest. And this leads him to the position that values, which are defined and transmitted by culture, are the motivating force and therefore the determinants of social relations, hence of social structure.

Granted that people are motivated to act by their desire to obtain various interests, or more precisely, by their conception of what those interests are—and these conceptions or "values" are culturally determined—the question is still whether cultural values are authentic or independent variables or changing consequences of actual social relations, in other words, a mere reflection of what is essential, that is the socioeconomic structure of life in any given society. If the second assumption is valid, then it would be a waste of time to study the cultural; we would be better off limiting our concerns to the study of socioeconomic conditions of life and perhaps certain psychological factors to find out what causes criminal behavior.

The question is of course an old one; it has been raised time and again by moral philosophers in the form of the controversy over the relative significance of "mind" or "matter," the "spiritual" or the "material," in shaping individual and social events. In more recent times, a similar controversy has been rekindled by the teachings of Karl Marx on the one hand and Max Weber on the other. To Marx, the significant element in shaping all aspects of social life is the quality and structure of economic relations. According to him, every other social phenomenon, including the arts, sciences, law, politics, systems of religion, and morality is based on the quality of economic relations and accurately reflects the nature of those same relations. To understand the working of social institutions and human behavior, including criminal activity, we need only to analyze and comprehend the underlying economic factors, which in fact create, in their own image, the cultural values and modes of thought that correspond closely with the particular mode of production in any given society. Incidentally, it is in this frame of reference that Communist criminologists always view the crime problem in the Western world. They argue that crime is the natural and inevitable consequence of the underlying capitalistic mode of production and its corresponding value system. Roots of crime should be sought in

laws of human society and of the dominant social behavior of productive forces and production relations—and thus ultimately in the socio-economic or property ownership structure. . . . The basic pattern of social behavior in capitalism . . . is individualism and selfishness, the isolation and alienation of the individual, the conflict between individual and society.[5]

Max Weber, on the other hand, tried to refute Marx's thesis about the exclusive role of economic factors in shaping human society by pointing out in his study of several religions that Marx had overlooked the role of ideas in creating particular social arrangements. In fact, he argued, it was the transformation of Christian ideals and the advent of Protestant ethics that gave rise to the spirit and practice of capitalism, a spiritual event changing the economic order.[6] In Weber's analysis, religious values, themselves an important part of the cultural traditions, have a tremendous impact on the structure of social life, on man's patterns of relationship with other human beings.

For our purpose, it is not necessary to seek a solution for the controversy. Actually, it is a neverending problem. Marx chose to disregard the possible impact of spiritual or cultural values on the modes of economic production, and Weber could not prove convincingly that the advent of Protestant ethics was not itself the consequence of some preceding developments in economic relations. We can be sure, however, that once a set of cultural values is created and established—either because of economic factors or intellectual or moral transformations—they tend to become autonomous in their impact. From that point on, they can influence human relations independently of their original sources. And since they are, as a rule, accepted uncritically and through the mostly inadvertent process of socialization, they are regarded as normal and inevitable within each cultural system. Thus, they may continue to shape human relations even long after they have become dysfunctional or disruptive. A sad example of the unquestioned effect of cultural values is the sometimes relentless efforts at modernization in developing countries that have been defeated by ossified religious beliefs.

We know that our patterns of behavior as well as our perceptions, ideas, emotions, likes, and dislikes are shaped by the type of environment in which we live and grow up. Aside from our physical potentials and tendencies that are determined by hereditary factors, we become what we are, and we behave as we do because we happen to have been raised in a particular society and as a member of various social groups. These groups exposed us to certain norms and values that were prevalent in our sociocultural milieu. It is true, of course, that different members of the same social group (for example a family) may act differently from one another. The disparity may be partly due to the members' varied innate potentials and partly to some social factors. Members of a family, for instance, all belong to the same membership group but most likely have different reference groups. In such a case the behavior patterns of each member may be shaped, at least partly, by the different perceptions, ideas, or emotions that are prevalent outside the membership group. Of course, the process is much more complicated; everyone is exposed to a myriad of sociocultural phenomena, including chance encounters with other people and events, which may have a lasting effect on his or her life.

Nevertheless, although it is difficult to specify accurately how a particular individual would normally react in the face of various social stimuli, given the uniqueness of each person's background it is fairly easy to see that our behavior patterns will generally conform to the requirements of our environment and upbringing. At the same time we know that the norms and values that are internalized by the individual in the process of growth are not created at random by social groups or institutions; they are the embodiments of societal needs and expectations as perceived and translated in response to the unique historical experiences of a nation into cultural norms and values.

Cultural values are of two kinds in their scope of coverage: the more general, which influence whole populations like the concept of economic freedom and initiative in the United States, and the more limited, which may affect only a particular segment of the population. The concept of subculture, for instance, explains a set of values and norms that belongs to particular groups in a society. The important point is, of course, that cultural norms and values are transmitted to individual human beings by means of the various social institutions. And the complex experiences that the individual has with these norms and institutions and his internalization of the subjective meaning of these experiences, shape his particular behavior patterns, including antisocial or criminal acts. It is obvious, therefore, that criminal behavior, like "normal" behavior, is learned. And since it is learned, there must be certain elements in the subculture of special groups or in the more general cultural heritage of the whole society that encourage and motivate some individuals to engage in criminal activity. As we shall see later, even a severe deprivation of basic human needs does not by itself frustrate and motivate the individual to commit aggressive acts. Rather, it is the way the individual views such deprivational situations and on a more conscious level, his perceptions about his chances of success in the face of various official restrictions, that determine the nature of his reaction to such deprivations. On the other hand, what causes him to view such outside factors or even the fact of deprivation itself in a particular vein are the cultural values of the larger society and the subculture of the group to which he happens to belong.

It should also be noted that since every type of learned behavior is accompanied by a value judgment, individuals learn to judge everything they see or do according to the yardsticks provided by their particular cultural traditions. It becomes almost impossible for most people to be objective about the validity or effectiveness of the predominant norms and values in society. As a matter of fact, our standards of objectivity, like the ones of good, bad, short, long, and others are also provided and imposed by the culture. The end result is that while many social practices and concepts may be dysfunctional and even harmful to individual and social interests, they may seem quite natural to the people involved, simply because as members of the culture they have internalized the relevant yardsticks for judgment without ever questioning them. In a way, most people hardly ever become aware that particular practices or belief systems are actually dysfunctional. Unless we train ourselves to develop a more objective perspective by analyzing our beliefs and practices in a comparative context, we will not be intellectually and emotionally able to question their validity or to visualize the possibility of better alternatives. It is in fact this impermeability of cultural values and norms to conscious and objective analysis that makes them even more powerful as determinants of social behavior. This same quality prompts the suggestion that we study our cultural values more systematically as major causes of all human action, including criminal behavior.

Social interaction among human beings can be studied as reflections of the intricate interplay of three distinct but closely interrelated systems: the psychological, the social, and the cultural.[7] The psychological system or personality takes shape gradually through the interaction of the child with other human beings, especially the significant ones who are biologically and emotionally close to him and who by force of blood or convention provide for him. The child progressively learns that his or her parents have certain expectations about behavior. From day one they start to teach the child all sorts of social habits. First, he or she learns to take in food. In many cultures, the mother breast-feeds the child; in others, the child learns to eat other kinds of food. Then, there is toilet training, speaking the language, doing different chores, and so on. The child learns that certain acts on his part make the parents happy, and they show their approval and contentment by giving him love, compliments, or desired objects. He notices that certain other types of behavior arouse their displeasure and anger, perhaps also a temporary withdrawal of love or even punishment. These experiences, which are repeated over and over again, are gradually introjected and form part of the child's personality. Call it "conditioning," learning, or whatever else we want, the fact remains that these internalized patterns of interaction, first with parents and siblings, and then with other significant persons or events in the child's world—like teachers, playmates, and even passive reception of television programs—form the basis of future behavior. If a child has learned especially from a personal experience, that lying or stealing will be always met with unpleasant consequences, he will, as a rule, abstain from doing such things when he grows up and is faced with tempting opportunities. And should he commit such acts as an adult, the unconscious expectation of punishment, which is developed in his mind on the basis of the actual or vicarious experience of punishment in childhood, will cause a related feeling of guilt and anxiety. This feeling of guilt, which is the unconscious alarm system for the expected punishment, or a person's desire to avoid it, can act as an important factor in deterring people from committing crimes or in fact, any other forbidden act. This is possible, however, only when the internalized crime-punishment sequence has been consistent, inevitable, and continuous.

Let us think for a moment about the dolphins in Florida's Sea World or for that matter any other animal that learns to respond to cues provided by its trainer. We know that the dolphins react positively to certain signals given by the trainer. They jump through a hoop held in the air, play with balls, swim backward, and do other tricks. Every act they perform is followed by a related reaction; the trainer rewards them with extra food. In a long process of conditioning, the dolphins develop certain "conditional reflexes," in other words, they react to "conditional stimuli," which in this case are the gestures of the trainer. The process of interaction between the animal and the trainer has proved time and again to be a pleasurable experience to the animal; the dolphin receives a reward after each act of compliance with the trainer's wishes. The conditional reflex, however, is created in the animal only if certain prerequisites are met regarding the conditional stimulus: that the quality of the signal given by the trainer is always the same, that it is repeated a sufficient number of times, and that it always results in the same outcome if it is responded to.

A similar psychological process takes place and motivates certain types of behavior in the human child. Parents can succeed in training their children to behave in certain ways only if, and to the extent that, they reward or punish (which sometimes may simply mean a slight showing of displeasure and withdrawal of privileges) particular types of behavior, and do so consistently and as an inevitable consequence of certain acts, for a relatively long period of time.

The important fact is that the child internalizes not only the contents of the parents' teachings, but also the strength or weakness of the emotional charge his interaction with the parents generates. In other words, if the reaction of the parents to violations of their expectations has been mild, half-hearted, or inconsistent, the child gets the message that breaking the rules does not result in serious consequences. Thus, the feeling of guilt experienced by the individual adult when committing similar violations will be also mild and noneffective. On the other hand, if parents are firm and consistent in punishing certain acts, or rewarding others, the individual will definitely and strongly experience a feeling of guilt or elation as the circumstances of his behavior would require. Likewise, if parents are firm and consistent in their interaction with the child, they help him develop strong self-discipline and control. If, on the other hand, they fail to establish strong emotional ties with the child, either because they themselves lack emotional stability (for instance, they are divorced or in constant conflict with one another) or for any other reason, the child, when he grows up, will likewise lack strong emotional attachments, ethical convictions, and self-discipline. Such an individual, if faced with strong incentives to break the law, is much more likely to do so than a well-adjusted, emotionally secure person.

We learn to behave in particular ways by growing up as members of different social groups. Groups, however, do not initiate or invent the norms, values, and rules that their members learn. They simply transfer to their members the dominant values and types of relationships that have become patterned, established, and accepted in society. Relationships that have acquired specific forms and persist, unaltered, for a relatively long period of time among large segments of the population are called "social institutions," or taken as a whole, the "social system."

Social institutions have several common characteristics.

### External Existence

Institutions exist independently of our will or wishes. They exist whether or not particular individuals come into being. The human family, for instance, has been around for millennia and will continue in existence after all members of particular families pass away.

### Coerciveness

Through the process of socialization we learn to adapt our desires and wishes to the requirements of social life, that is, social institutions. If we want to be accepted in our community, we have to follow certain rules and procedures that were established long before we came into being. If, for instance, we want to earn the respect and trust of our fellow human beings, most societies normally expect us to attend the church, synagogue, or mosque regularly and in the company of other believers, or otherwise follow commonly accepted rules of social decorum and concern.

### Moral Authority

Institutions have moral authority over our lives because we grow up in them and get used to their requirements and because they have existed for a relatively long time and shaped the lives and relations of our ancestors, too. The American forms of economy, government, or court system, for instance, are accepted, usually without much questioning, not necessarily because we are convinced of their usefulness or efficiency, but mostly because they have existed as social institutions without any drastic change for a long period of time.

In every society, institutions determine how people should act in order to achieve certain objectives. In many societies, for instance, sexual gratification is permitted exclusively through marriage and formation of a family. In addition to this traditional mode of gratification, in certain other cultures extramarital or even homosexual relations have been accepted.

In the past, to become a lawyer, one could read law or work as an apprentice to a practicing attorney for a number of years. As a rule in the United States today, one has to graduate from a law school and pass the bar exam before being permitted to practice law.

Likewise, around every other significant human concern a cluster of patterns has developed that determines how the individual should achieve certain social values. Obviously, the most important institutions or types of stable, patterned interaction are the family, educational system, economics, political system, work, and leisure time. However, almost any type of human relationship can become a social institution, provided it develops the required qualities.

As we have noted, the psychological system (or personality) is shaped by the social system (or institutions); on the foundation of our innate qualities, the social system makes us what we are as members of a particular society. Our ideas, convictions and emotions gradually take shape, in the long process of socialization and under the pressure of various social institutions. Social institutions, however, are in turn maintained and reinforced by the cultural system. Upon every institution, a cluster of value judgments is superimposed. The message they usually give is that what we are required to do in various social situations is "good" or proper, and what others who do not belong to our culture do is wrong or "bad." Our system of government is "good"; communism is "bad."[8] Monogamous marriages are good, polygamous relations, uncivilized; the free enterprise system is good because it encourages individual initiative and industry (which is, of course, true for people who have the needed opportunity to develop their potentials); a controlled or planned economy is bad because it stifles the profit-seeking, creative urge of the individual. This may be true from one perspective, but it does not adequately show the other side of the picture, which is the equitable provision by government in such systems of the basic needs of the underprivileged classes.

Ideas, norms, and values in a culture were not created or adopted by deliberate, rational choice for their usefulness or positive effects. Rather, for the most part, they have emerged as natural consequences of the complex interaction among various environmental phenomena, historical realities, and chance occurrences. Agriculture developed in ancient Egypt and Mesopotamia partly because plenty of water existed in these regions. Venice could not have become a world trade center if it were not located near the ocean. The Russian Revolution, which was caused by numerous socio-historical phenomena, in turn became a powerful force in shaping modern history and people's perception about many social events. And then, of course, there is the element of pure chance or historical accidents that also affect human life and the way people perceive it. If America had been discovered at an earlier or later date by a different explorer; if the first immigrants to this country had not left their own homeland to escape religious and political persecution ... if many other chance accidents had occurred differently, then possibly quite different sets of values and ideals might have become dominant in America.

The important point is that when and for whatever reasons cultural values become established in a society, they become a powerful driving force in shaping social and individual life. They support and justify the existing social institutions. And since, through the process of socialization, the individual learns not only the norms of social behavior, but also the perception that whatever he is supposed to do is the "proper" and the "best" way of doing it, cultural values become ingrained in his total outlook. The individual accepts them; he unconsciously and consciously follows them and rarely questions their validity or propriety. If fact, he grows to see and judge everything through the prism of his society's cultural values.

The psychological, the social, and the cultural systems are not, of course, static. They keep changing and affecting one another, mainly through interaction with other individuals, societies, and cultures. Sometimes the change is affected first in the social system, which in turn causes corresponding changes in the other two. Even individuals have been able at times to cause significant changes in their society. This has been possible mainly by the innovators's creative adoption of a different perspective, which he acquired through exposure to different sociocultural environments. Zarathustra, Moses, Jesus, Muhammad, and Gandhi, among others, come to mind as having revolutionized the social system, ethical beliefs and other widespread perceptions of their respective societies. Nevertheless, because of the interdependence and constant reinforcement of each system by the other two and the forceful properties of the sociocultural phenomena, as a rule cultures, social institutions, and individual personalities resist change. In reality, the "national character" of the French, Germans, English, and Americans has not changed very much over the centuries.

Studies conducted mainly by anthropologists on primitive tribes and other people have shown more specifically how culture affects human behavior. Ruth Benedict studied the culture of three Indian tribes: the Zuñi, the Dobuans, and the Kwakiutl.[9] She found that among the Zuñi, a Pueblo Indian tribe, rites and rituals were socially very important, so important in fact that they stifled individual initiative. In Zuñi culture the "ideal" person is the one who is quite serious, is friendly toward everyone, and follows tribal customs unfailingly. Any deviation from the tribal convictions and customs is condemned. Persons who are moderate, mild-mannered, and industrious enjoy the respect of others. Conflict and feelings of guilt exist to the lowest possible degree.

The Dobuans, on the contrary, are violent, competitive, and mean. They believe in sorcery and cheat each other. It seems there is deep enmity between individuals and villages. A mother who has a daughter of marriage age will try to find her in bed with a man and thus force him to marry her. Every married man is supposed to live every other year among his wife's relatives and suffer the terrible treatment that is accorded to all foreigners. In return, the wife goes to her husband's tribe the following year and is likewise mistreated. Cut-throat competition characterizes economic and other relations in this society. Every success is achieved at the price of someone else's downfall. Betrayal and secrecy are widespread. Suspicion and ill feeling dominate all social relations, even between husband and wife. Illegitimate sex is also common among the Dobuans.

The Kwakiutl Indians are very individualistic and competitive. Private ownership encompasses not only tracts of land but also beaches, underwater surfaces, and even poetry, folktales, and titles of respect. It is very important for these people to gain social recognition. For this purpose, they give a party whenever necessary and either destroy or give away blankets, canoes, copper, or precious oils. If they give these items to others, the recipient has to return them with a very high interest payment, which he normally can't afford. Every occasion is seized by the individual to show off and impress others with his wealth and ability. People make fun of each other, but they are afraid to be laughed at. If a man hurts himself with an axe, if he falls down, or if his canoe turns over, he is worried that he will be mocked and humiliated. He feels ashamed and tries to wipe out this feeling by giving away some personal property.

In another classic work, Margaret Mead studied and compared the dominant cultural values and perceptions about sex in three primitive societies: the Arapesh, the Mundugumor, and the Tchambuli.[10] The first tribe, the Arapesh, had a very cooperative social system. Kindness, gentle behavior, sensitivity to the needs of others, and mutual assistance were important cultural values in their society. They believed in the goodness of human nature. The difference between the social roles of men and women, old and young, were at the lowest possible level in this society. The "ideal" personality type among the Arapesh was someone who was warm and sociable, sensitive and peaceful.

The Mundugumor, who had been cannibals earlier, were aggressive and belligerent. Bravery and violence were important to them, and they tried to develop the same traits in their children. The ideal personality type for this tribe was the same for both men and women: violent and competitive, sexually aggressive and jealous, a person who sensed an insult quickly and reacted to it violently, who enjoyed showing off and fighting others. Mild-mannered, easy-going people had no place in this society.

Finally, the Tchambuli had a very elaborate and artistic culture. For them, ceremonies were very important events, and everybody was expected to master a special skill or art. Men had a leisurely life; women, on the other hand, worked hard; they fished, made various artifacts, and traded. They also wielded the real power in the community. Women initiated the act of lovemaking; they also took the initiative in choosing their husbands. Men mixed with other men. They were aggressive, coquettish, sneaky, and suspicious.

Many of these studies have been criticized for various reasons. Most of the findings, however, have remained valid. One thing is certain; these studies have convincingly shown the effect of cultural values on human behavior. This impact has also been confirmed by, among others, psychiatrists and psychoanalysts. For instance, Abram Kardier, a psychiatrist, and Ralph Linton, an anthropologist, have analyzed the influence of children's early training on their future development and the emergence of the basic personality type, which corresponds with the requirements of each given culture.[11] These interests had been already pursued by the same authors in another work, *The Individual and His Society*.[12] In this book, Kardiner and Linton published the results of their extensive studies on childrearing practices of the Marquises Islanders. In this society, for unspecified reasons, the number of females was much lower than the number of males. This fact produced intense competition among men for possession of women. Perhaps also for the same reason, married women had many extramarital sexual affairs at the expense of neglecting their maternal responsibilities. Mothers as a rule did not breast-feed their babies, or did so for only a short period of time. Instead, they prepared a special kind of dough, and laying the infant on its back, put some of it on its mouth. The infant, without help from the mother, would try to get as much dough in its mouth as it could and swallow it. Other needs of the infant were satisfied by other men, who were in reality the mother's secondary husbands. Lack of physical and emotional contact with the mother caused the children to be ridden with anxiety and insecurity. The child could not understand why he was so nervous, but his anxiety would be projected onto outside forces and surround the whole spectrum of folklore, religious beliefs, and other manifestations of social life.

Kardiner and Linton concluded that if parents do not have a loving and orderly marital life themselves and if they do not show enough care, love, and discipline in their training of the child, the child will develop a weak ego. A proportionate combination of love and discipline employed consistently in parental interaction with the child, on the other hand, will make a strong ego and a secure, strong-willed personality.

Karen Horney, another noted psychiatrist, has argued convincingly that even mental illness is caused by values and expectations nurtured in a culture. Neurosis, for instance, is caused by the internalization of conflicting life experiences. The individual is faced with conflicting cultural values which cannot be reconciled. This in turn makes social adjustment a painful process; one cannot easily adjust to conflicting and inconsistent demands. The individual then becomes neurotic, or as Horney calls him, "the stepson of our culture."[13]

Such examples of the effect of culture on personality and human behavior can be duplicated indefinitely from scientific literature in different fields. For our purposes, however, the relevant facts are quite clear. Because of particular historical and chance occurrences that take place in special environments, certain norms and values have become dominant in a given culture. These norms and values, in turn, help shape the mentality of the people, their ideas, perceptions, emotions, and also their reactions. In many Third World countries, the scarcity of food and other resources has been translated into cultural values that teach the inevitability of human fate and the absolute necessity of submissively accepting whatever one's fate brings. People living in such societies do not have a real choice; they have to obey cultural imperatives. No matter how desperately the individual may try, his chances of modifying his life situation or of changing the cultural values that are dominant in the society are almost nonexistent. Hence, fatalistic world outlooks have emerged in certain societies. As Henry A. Murray and Clyde Kluckhohn have explained:

> The yogi whose discipline leads him to the attainment of a passive state, devoid of all needs and claims, whose goal is to have no external goals, would be an extreme case in point. Possibly one of the determinants of this philosophy was an environment in which the ratio of gratification to frustration was, for many people, very low. By voluntarily attaining the state of Nirvana, a man deprives the environment of its power to move or frustrate him. This aspect of the state of Nirvana would constitute the defensive triumph of an introvert living in a repellent world.[14]

By contrast the culture of the United States is filled with positive, individualistic, and aggressive values. America has been the land of vast opportunities. To reach its high level of progress and affluence, American culture has encouraged industry, innovation, ambition, individuality, and the willingness to take high risks, to be able to persevere in the face of dire defeat. These same ideals are expressed in America's fundamental political documents. Recognition of the right of every citizen to "life, liberty, and the pursuit of happiness," for instance, is simply another expression of these same dominant values, the same ideals that have made possible the present high standards not only in material achievements but also in individual freedoms and privileges. The point is, however, that these same cultural values may be responsible, at least partially in the context of present-day social conditions, for some of the more serious social problems, including a high rate of criminal activity, as I shall try to show in the following chapters.

## NOTES

1. Alfred L. Kroeber and Clyde Kluckhohn, *Culture: A Critical Review of Concepts and Definitions* vol. 47, no. 1 (Cambridge, Mass, Harvard University Peabody Museum of American Archeology and Ethnology Papers, 1952), p. 181.

2. Melford E. Spiro, "Culture and Personality," in *International Encyclopaedia of the Social Sciences*, 17 vols. (New York: Macmillan and Free Press, 1968), 3: 560.

3. A. R. Radcliffe-Brown, *Structure and Function in Primitive Society: Essays and Addresses* (Glencoe, Ill.: The Free Press, 1952), p. 198.

4. Ibid., p. 199.

5. See Erich Buchholz, Richard Hartmann, John Lekschas, and Gerhard Stiller, *Soviet Criminology: Theoretical and Methodical Foundations* (London: Saxon House; Lexington, Mass.: Lexington Books, 1974), pp. 139–140.

6. Max Weber, *The Protestant Ethic and the Spirit of Capitalism*, trans. Talcott Parsons (New York: Charles Scribner's Sons, 1958).

7. See Talcott Parsons, "The Action Frame of Reference and the General Theory of Action Systems: Culture, Personality and the Place of Social Systems," in Talcott Parsons, *The Social System* (New York: The Free Press, 1951), pp. 3–23.

8. Soviet citizens, of course, hold the opposite view.

9. Ruth Benedict, *Patterns of Culture* (Boston and New York: Houghton Mifflin Co., 1934).

10. Margaret Mead, *Sex and Temperament in Three Primitive Societies* (New York: William Morrow and Co., 1935, 1963 edition).

11. Abram Kardiner, *The Psychological Frontiers of Society* (New York: Columbia University Press, 1946).

12. Abram Kardiner and Ralph Linton, *The Individual and His Society* (New York: Columbia University Press, 1936).

13. See Karen Horney, *The Neurotic Personality of Our Time* (New York: W. W. Norton and Co., 1937).

14. Henry A. Murray and Clyde Kluckhohn, "Outline of a Conception of Personality," in Clyde Kluckhohn and Henry A. Murray, *Personality in Nature, Society and Culture* (New York: Alfred A. Knopf, 1949), p. 20.

# 4

# American Culture and the Crime Problem

In the last chapter I explained that our behavior, including criminal behavior, is shaped by cultural values, judgments about what is proper or improper in various social situations. In this chapter I will argue that there are certain fundamental values in the American culture that, taken together in the face of present social conditions, may lead to criminal behavior.

We should recall that like every other animal, man is guided by the pleasure-pain principle. We are naturally driven to seek pleasurable experiences and avoid painful situations. The natural urge to satisfy our needs, which is pleasurable, however, is gradually restricted and brought under control. The restrictions are imposed, initially from outside, but then become gradually internalized in the process of growing up; they form part of our "ego," or social self, and the "superego" which consists of the "ego-ideal"—what we expect to become—and the "conscience," that part of the personality that judges our behavior and gives us a feeling of elation or guilt as the judgment about our behavior would require. As can be seen from this rather simplified description of personality components, an important factor in controlling human behavior is the structure and contents of both the ego and superego. I will point out in this chapter that the currently dominant American values lead to intensification of the natural desires and interests created by society at the same time that they weaken the controlling elements of the ego and the superego. We shall also see, in later chapters, that the same mechanisms, that is, those that encourage deviant acts and discourage self-restraint and discipline, are applied also to the actual working of the criminal justice system, thus, in fact nullifying the possible effect of the fear of punishment, which otherwise could act as an effective deterrent in many cases.

Before we get into these issues, I would like to emphasize that most of the values that may, under present social conditions, lead certain people to criminal activity are at the same time at least partially responsible for America's great achievements, both in material and spiritual realms. To take just one example, Americans develop much higher expectations than most other nations. When our expectations are not fulfilled, we may get a feeling of frustration, which depending on other factors, can lead to criminal activity. The point is that these same high expectations have engendered in most Americans not only a strong urge to work hard and succeed in material terms, but also a perception of individual worth and social equality that is unsurpassed in any other country. For our purpose however, which is to discover any possible link between cultural values and crime in America, the attention will be focused only on the negative, crimogenic effects of such phenomena.

For the sake of consistency in analysis, I shall divide the values which may have a significant impact on the problem of crime into the "deviance-inducing" and "control-reducing" categories. We will be using the same concepts later when we deal with the possible effect of the criminal justice system on the crime problem.

## DEVIANCE-INDUCING VALUES

By definition, these values are the perceptions and value judgments that can act as strong stimuli in encouraging the individual to be active and under certain conditions to engage in criminal activity. The most important of such values and their possible results are the following.

### High Expectations

*Political (the right to the pursuit of happiness).* In no other country are the sociopolitical hopes, expectations, and wants of the people raised to such a high level as in the United States. Of course, a lot of rhetoric is used everywhere to praise the bright possibilities to be realized in the future, but in no other country are the political promises taken as practical plans of action. The Declaration of Independence contains the following language, which sets the tone for the public's officially endorsed expectations and dreams:

We hold these Truths to be self-evident, that all Men are created equal, that they are endowed by their Creator with certain unalienable Rights, that among these are Life, Liberty, and the Pursuit of Happiness.

These same lofty ideals are mirrored, directly or indirectly, in many other cultural phenomena. They are repeated almost daily in history books, folklore, movies, television programs and games, lotteries, and elsewhere. They become part of every American's psyche and affect the way the average person perceives and reacts to reality. America, of course, is no utopia; the right to life, liberty, and the pursuit of happiness is more real for some than for others. Some people start life with deep-rooted disadvantages that make the achievement of the enumerated "unalienable" rights extremely difficult. Nevertheless, the expression of these aspirations in various formal documents of the country has been no idle effort; these expressions form the outer boundaries of everybody's hopes and expectations. As a keen European observer of American society has remarked:

America . . . has the most explicitly expressed system of general ideals in reference to human interrelations. This body of ideals is more widely understood and appreciated than similar ideals are anywhere else. The American Creed is not merely—as in some other countries—the implicit background of the nation's political and judicial order as it functions. . . . These principles of social ethics have been hammered into easily remembered formula. All means of intellectual communication are utilized to stamp them into everybody's mind. The schools teach them, the churches preach them. The courts pronounce their judicial decisions in their terms.[1]

*Judicial (the civil liberties).* Through a series of judicial decisions, the Supreme Court of the United States has interpreted the several constitutional amendments to guarantee the most comprehensive rights and protections for the accused. As James Wilson, among others, has noted, "We have preserved and even extended the most comprehensive array of civil liberties found in any nation on earth despite rising crime rates and (in the 1960s) massive civil disorder."[2]

In this respect, it is interesting to note that in England, where the Common Law system originated and developed and which is considered by many to be a bastion of democracy and individual freedom, some of the safeguards that are routinely taken for granted in this country do not exist. A person can be arrested in England on mere suspicion. He can be interrogated by the police without any warning and in fact against his protestations and request for the presence of a lawyer. The only test criminal courts apply to determine the validity of a confession is that it should have been made voluntarily, that is, without physical or psychological compulsion. Otherwise, if the police violate any of the enumerated rights of the accused, the only way to redress would be to file an official complaint against the individual officer, a possibility that will not be taken very seriously, given the overall ideology of the criminal justice system and the public opinion realities, which put a very high premium on maintaining peace and order.

In a comprehensive report on an actual English case, Michael Graham explains how the accused was arrested at the airport on mere suspicion and simply because he had $1,358.07 in his possession and, after questioning, was found to be unemployed. During the period between arrest and charge, the police kept questioning him without any warning that he could use the services of an attorney. Actually, they continued their interrogation in spite of the fact that the arrested man insisted on seeing a solicitor before he would answer them; the only reaction he received was sarcastic laughter and further questioning by the police until he confessed to having committed a bank robbery.[3]

The point is that the British judiciary accepts these serious restrictions on individual freedoms and somehow ignores various violations of the rule of law by the police as a necessary price to be willingly paid to keep peace and order in society. As a recent survey of the English system makes clear: "The unlawfulness of the arrest for any reason has no effect . . . upon the introduction of evidence derived from the accused at his trial. The English do not employ concepts like the exclusionary rule or the 'fruit of the poisonous tree.' "[4]

The English approach has been summarized in the case of *Kuruma Son of Kaniu v. Reginam*, in the following language: "In their Lordships' opinion, the test to be applied in considering whether evidence is admissible is whether it is relevant to the matters at issue. If it is, it is admissible and the court is not concerned with how the evidence was obtained."[5]

The significant fact is that official condoning of police violations of individual freedoms is equaled, if not surpassed, by the expectations of the public concerning similar acts which are restrictive of individual liberties. In May 1966 a social survey poll conducted in Britain included the following statement addressed to the public:

The Home Office is examining a scheme to introduce compulsory fingerprinting of adults as a method of combating crime. Do you think this is a good idea or a bad idea? The result of the survey indicated that 64 percent of the respondents thought it was a good idea, as against 23 percent who thought it a bad idea. Furthermore, 72 percent responded that if the program was voluntary, they would submit to fingerprinting. Only 19 percent said they would not volunteer.[6]

It seems that in general Europeans are much more willing than U.S. citizens to accept official restrictions on their freedoms. Many European democracies, including West Germany and France, use national registration, systems of registration of movements, and various other citizen intelligence and bookkeeping techniques to provide information on the whereabouts and movements of every individual, practices that certainly would not be tolerated in this country.

The emphasis in the United States on civil liberties and protections, including those accorded the accused, naturally raises the expectations of the public, especially concerned lawyers, as to how criminal prosecutions and trials should be conducted. The result is a much keener sensitivity in this country to official violations of procedural rules and standards, and hence a greater likelihood of criticism and frustration with the criminal justice system. The same sensitivity and awareness also put serious restrictions on the ability of the police, public prosecutors, and the courts to apprehend and convict the offender, thus causing a deeply felt frustration in the public that the system has failed in providing protection against unjustified harm to their life, liberty, or property. To the average citizen the release of a real murderer on the grounds that his conviction was partly based on a confession obtained by the police without first giving him the Miranda warning or in the absence of a lawyer (which is quite commonplace in many countries, including, as we saw, England) symbolizes only the insensitivity and failure of the criminal justice system in protecting his or her legitimate rights. On the other hand, the spread of such perceptions and frustrations in the public can lead as we shall see at least to apathy and indifference toward the legal system and other institutional arrangements, if not indeed to a conscious determination to violate official norms of behavior.

*Material (incessant needs, strong desires).* The American free enterprise system thrives on the ability and willingness of the public to buy and consume products that are made and sold by various companies. In many other societies the highest aspiration of the masses is still to provide only the most basic needs for their families. In America, however, numerous social needs have been added to the basic biological requirements; their satisfaction is deemed necessary, almost like a legal right. Furthermore, the economic system depends on the creation of ever newer needs and desires in the public. If the factories are to keep working, if the economy is to grow continuously, then the public must feel a strong urge to buy newer products while the older ones are still usable and useful. Possession of a new car, refrigerator, television set, and stereo system becomes a must to anybody who is incessantly subjected to the powerful influence of big advertising companies. Only the disillusioned exclude themselves from the experience of the happy masses who are shown to enjoy the alleged pleasures of the new product. Advertising has become a highly developed art in America, capable of strongly influencing public opinion and reaction in various fields. It is accepted practice to employ public relations firms not only to sell products even to people who may be indifferent or even negatively inclined toward them, but also to sell public images, to get people elected as presidents, senators, and other officials. Advertising also sells perceptions supporting the interests of various social groups to Congress, to win enactment of a particular piece of legislation or rejection of a given proposal, to serve the interests of those organizations and individuals who have the financial capacity to pay for such campaigns. As Jules Henry has argued:

In America there is an asymmetry and imbalance among products, machines, wants, consumers, workers, and resources. It is never certain in our culture that a new product will be wanted or that an old one will continue in demand; on the other hand, there are always some economic wants that are unfulfilled. There is a continuous race between consumers and products. Consumers must buy or the economy will suffer, and there must always be enough products to satisfy consumer demand. There must always be enough workers to man the machines, and there must always be just enough machines turning to absorb enough workers. Finally, there must always be enough raw materials to manufacture the needed goods, and the proper instruments must be produced in order to provide the raw materials necessary for manufacture.[7]

The public's strong and lasting desire to consume is so necessary for the continuous functioning of the economic system that the appetite for the consumption of new products must frequently be whetted by various means and the desire artificially created and intensified. Henry quotes from a full-page advertisement in the New York Times, "Now, as always, profit and growth stem directly from the ability of salesmanship to create more desire. . . . To create more desire . . . will take more dissatisfaction with time-worn methods and a restless quest of better methods! It might even take a penchant for breaking precedents."[8]

This concern with creating new material desires and reinforcing the old in the public has, of course, significant consequences and implications. As Henry sees it:

The second modern commandment, "Thou shalt consume!" is the natural complement of the first—"Create more desire!" Together they lead the attack on the key bastion of the Indo-European, Islamic, and Hebrew traditions—the impluse control system—for the desire for a million things cannot be created without stimulating a craving for everything.[9]

If Jules Henry is right in stating that the American socioeconomic system is necessarily geared to producing ever more and newer products and that the conditional response of the public in such a system is constant craving for more goods and products, then it is obvious that the nonfulfillment of the great number of artificially created desires can engender an equally large amount of frustration. In the context of American cultural emphasis on individual rights and privileges in the absence of corresponding duties and responsibilities and the belief in free expression of emotions and the strong urge to achieve and succeed, such frustration can result in deviant and criminal behavior. The aggregate culture has a great deal to do not only with the raising (or lowering) of public expectations, but also with how the individual members of society are supposed to behave in the face of the raised expectations or desires and of strong frustrations caused by non-satisfaction of those desires. To Jules Henry's reasoning, the loosening of internal control mechanisms in the individual is a necessary condition for the continuous functioning of the American economic system. Discussing the inner transformation of the American psyche caused by the necessities of the consumer economy, Henry refers to the resultant "unhinging of the old impulse controls,"[10] and goes on to state that "for most Americans, self-denial seems to lead nowhere any longer, for heaven has become detached from society, and for most people work is merely a dreary interlude between nourishing hours with one's family."[11]

We shall see that the loosening of the inner control systems is also encouraged by certain other transformations in the American educational ideology and world outlook.

### Individual Need For Achievement

America has been a land of vast opportunities. To master its extensive terrain, to capture its hidden resources and fight its severe and varied climate, strong human will was always needed. The functioning of the huge economic system and the mushrooming of numerous industries also required rugged individualism and courageous risk-taking. Another basic element in the formation of American culture was a strong desire to get away from religious and political persecution, which initially brought the people together and reinforced their will and determination to build a rigorous democracy on the foundations of human dignity and personal freedom. The result was the American culture's emphasis on and love for independence of thought, freedom of the will, and unbending individualism. These cultural traits make the average individual more concerned with personal success, less responsive to group pressures, and more inclined to break the law when the transgression can be justified on the basis of individualistic considerations.

## THE CRISIS OF LEGITIMACY

One particular aspect of the discrepancy between the raised level of expectations and the actual scope of their fulfillment requires special attention. This is what I call the crisis of legitimacy. It is my assumption that the expectation of the American public concerning the quality and validity of their social system has been raised to a level well beyond the possibilities of the system; in other words the basic American ideals about democracy and equal rights of the citizens can no longer be fulfilled. This fact can act as a strong source of dissatisfaction among the people.

Some legal philosophers have examined what they have called the "sense of injustice," that is, the perception that the enacted norms of society are not fairly and evenly applied to individual cases. They have pointed out that such a perception is quite detrimental to the proper functioning of the legal system. It creates a feeling of indifference or even disrespect for the whole system and a tendency to violate the official norms of the country without feeling much guilt or remorse.

Legitimacy, however, is a much more comprehensive concept, which is applicable to the whole spectrum of social life. It implies that the public considers the social system (in a sociological sense, which includes the political and economic, as well as the legal system) to be legitimate or valid. If so, the social system works much more smoothly, and the need for the threat or actual application of physical force to insure compliance with social norms will be minimal.

The observation concerning the perception of legitimacy among group members is of course true for any kind of social arrangement. The intellectual and emotional acceptance of a given arrangement by group members as valid or legitimate makes the compliance with the related rules almost automatic. On the other hand, when such a perception is lacking, the group, or for that matter the society at large, would have to depend on the use of external forces for the continued existence of the social system. As Max Weber points out, "A system of order which is guaranteed by external sanctions may at the same time be guaranteed by interested subjective attitudes. . . . It is possible for ethically normative beliefs of this kind to have profound influence on action in the absence of any sort of external guarantee."[12]

In cases where, as in the United States among certain groups, the social system is considered to be unjust or illegitimate, and furthermore, the criminal justice system is for a variety of reasons incapable of creating the necessary fear or reprisal when a penal law provision is violated, the incentive to commit crimes, which aside from satisfying certain desires, also implies a challenge against a presumed unjust system, would be quite strong. The legitimacy ascribed to the social system may be any or the combination of the following.

### Traditional

A system may be considered valid simply because it has existed for a long period of time. As Weber points out, "The derivation of the legitimacy of an order from a belief in the sanctity of tradition is the most universal and most primitive case. The fear of magical penalties confirms the general psychological inhibitions against any sort of change in customary modes of action."[13] The British monarchy is an example of a legitimate order based on traditional perceptions.

### Emotional

Traditional orders have been replaced at times by a new, mostly religious order due to the believers' emotional attachment and strong conviction as regards the sanctity and supernatural qualities of an oracle or a prophet. The present regimes in Saudi Arabia and Morocco, for instance, are considered legitimate on the basis of the assumed descendance of the ruler from the prophet Muhammad. Thus, whatever the ruler does or decides for the people is accepted without reservation or questioning; according to dominant beliefs, he is properly vested with religious authority.

### Rational

A social system may be considered legitimate "by virtue of a rational belief in its absolute value."[14] The example Weber gives of such an intellectual justification of a social order is the Natural Law tradition. The concept that man is born free, for instance, or that he should enjoy certain freedoms, including freedom of expression and freedom of movement, gives validity and legitimacy to these aspirations, which in most Western democracies have become actual realities because they are rationally accepted as inevitable for human welfare and dignity.

### Legal

Finally, a social system may receive its attribute of validity and legitimacy from the fact that it has been created and is maintained by rules and decisions made in accordance with the fundamental political documents of the country. "To-day," notes Weber, "the most usual basis of legitimacy is the belief in legality, the readiness to conform with rules which are formally correct and have been imposed by accepted procedure."[15] This fact is certainly true in the case of the United States where for various reasons, the reliance on the rule of law for legitimizing the social order is much more emphatic than in many other societies. This country enforces a complete separation of religion and state. Furthermore, the dynamic nature of the American society, which encourages innovative productivity, cannot tolerate and does not stress strong reliance on the role of tradition in maintaining the social system. Thus, the sources of the legitimacy of the American social order are essentially and almost exclusively rational-legal. This fact, of course, is responsible for the creative and productive nature of life in this society. At the same time, however, it makes governance that much more difficult. No action can be justified in this society only because it is backed by tradition; no social issue is immune to change or revision solely because there is a particular religious command on the subject. No person is above the law because he is the descendant of a tribal chief or a prophet. The only valid criteria applicable in judging official action—economic arrangements, political activity, court decisions, redistribution of social values, or anything else—are the provisions of the Constitution and other legal documents. Therefore, a perception that the laws, judicial decisions, or executive orders are not just, that they are contrary to the letter or spirit of the Constitution or against the legitimate interests of certain classes of people, unjustly favoring others, will cause much deeper frustrations and adverse reactions in the American public than it would in another society where the expressed wishes of the ruler are unquestionably accepted as legitimate manifestation of respected traditional or religious beliefs.

The question of legitimacy is still more significant in American society, because, unlike any other country in the world, Americans have formally advocated the right of the citizen, if unjustly deprived by his government of his basic rights, to rise in revolution and replace the political system. The 1776 Declaration of Independence states in part:

We hold these truths to be self-evident, that all men are created equal, that they are endowed by their Creator with certain inalienable Rights, that among these are Life, Liberty and the pursuit of Happiness—that to secure these rights, Governments are instituted among Men, deriving their just powers from the consent of the governed—that whenever any Form of Government becomes destructive of these ends, it is the Right of the People to alter or to abolish it, and to institute new Government, laying its foundations on such principles and organizing its powers in such form, as to them shall seem most likely to effect their Safety and Happiness. Prudence, indeed, will dictate that Governments long established should not be changed for light and transient causes; and accordingly all experience hath shown, that mankind are more disposed to suffer, while evils are sufferable, than to right themselves by abolishing the forms to which they are accustomed. But when a long train of abuses and usurpations, pursuing invariably the same Object evinces a design to reduce them under absolute Despotism, it is their right, it is their duty, to throw off such Government, and provide new Guards for their future security.

It can be argued that the "right to abolish the existing government" as provided in the Declaration of Independence is limited in coverage to the historical circumstances that induced the American people to sever their political ties with their ruling land. The document is mainly an attempt to enumerate the excessive abuses of the king of England, which justified breaking off the bonds between the then American colonies and the British government. It can be also argued that the right to revolt against the existing government is mainly a symbolic confirmation of the will of the people as the only foundation of the political government; to state otherwise would be to justify a revolution any time people are dissatisfied with the way their government has provided them with one of their basic rights such as "the right to the pursuit of happiness." Then, of course, there remains the question of how and when the citizen may be said to have withdrawn consent from the government.

The fact is that the concept of the right of the citizen to rise against unjust government has a long history in the United States and has been confirmed time and again in various sources. It is a fact that many of the original founders of this society, and other social thinkers of seventeenth-century America were quite familiar with and influenced by John Locke's ideas as expressed especially in his Second Essay Concerning Civil Government (1690).

Following Hobbes and unlike Rousseau, who had envisioned a social contract between the people on the one side and their government on the other, Locke had argued that the social contract is made only among the people themselves, who then choose a government as their representative or their trustee. In Locke's theory, then, the people do not have any obligations toward their government; they simply entrust it with the power to govern the society. As long as the chosen government functions for the good of the people, it remains in power; if the trust vested in the government is violated, however, the people have the right to depose it and replace it with another government of their choice. As to the question of who decides whether that trust has been violated Locke makes it clear that only the people themselves possess the right to judge. To quote from Locke directly, "Whosoever uses force without Right, as every one does in Society, who does it without Law, puts himself into a state of War with those, against whom he so uses it, and in that state all former Ties are cancelled, all other Rights cease, and every one has a Right to defend himself, and to resist the Aggressor."[16]

Here, 'tis like, the common Question will be made, who shall be judge whether the Prince or Legislative act contrary to their trust? This, perhaps, ill affected and factious Men may spread amongst the People, when the Prince only makes use of his due Prerogative. To this I reply, The People shall be judge; for who shall be judge whether his Trustee or Deputy acts well, and according to the Trust reposed in him, but he who deputes him, and must, by having deputed him have still a Power to discard him, when he fails in his Trust? If this be reasonable in particular Cases of Private Men, why should it be otherwise in that of the greatest moment; where the Welfare of Millions is concerned, and also where the evil, if not prevented, is greater, and Redress very difficult, dear and dangerous?"[17]

The basic theme, namely the right of the people to depose their government whenever it consistently acts against their interests, and which was known through Locke also to the drafters of the Constitution and often quoted by them, had already appeared independently in the writings of other American thinkers. To give just a couple of examples, John Winthrop had declared in 1637 that "no commonwealth can be founded but by free consent."[18] In 1682 William Penn had put the concept more graphically: "Governments, like clocks, go from the motion men give them; and as governments are made and moved by men, so by them they are ruined too. Wherefore, governments rather depend upon men than men upon government."[19]

In any event the theme has been solemnly stated in many historical documents. The Virginia Declaration of Rights upon which Jefferson drew for the opening paragraphs of the Declaration of Independence, became the basis of the Bill of Rights in the Constitution and had a significant impact on the French Revolution. It was written by George Mason and adopted by the Virginia Constitutional Convention on June 12, 1776. It already provided in pertinent parts:

Section 1. That all men are by nature equally free and independent and have certain inherent rights, of which, when they enter into a state of society, they cannot, by any compact, deprive or divest their posterity; namely, the enjoyment of life and liberty, with the means of acquiring and possessing property, and pursuing and obtaining happiness and safety.

Section 2. That all power is vested in, and consequently derived from, the people, that magistrates are their trustees and servants and at all times amenable to them.

Section 3. That government is, or ought to be, instituted for the common benefit, protection, and security of the people, nation, or community; of all the various modes and forms of government, that is best which is capable of producing the greatest degree of happiness and safety and is most effectually secured against the danger of maladministration. And, that, when any government shall be found inadequately or contrary to these purposes, a majority of the community has an indubitable, inalienable, and indefeasible right to reform, alter or abolish it, in such manner as shall be judged most conducive to the public weal.[20]

Abraham Lincoln in his First Inaugural Address, which was delivered in front of a large crowd in Washington on March 4, 1861, emphasized the same theme by declaring:

If by the mere force of numbers a majority should deprive a minority of any clearly written constitutional right, it might in a moral point of view justify revolution—certainly would if such right were a vital one. ... this country, with its institutions, belongs to the people who inhabit it. Whenever they shall grow weary of the existing government, they can exercise their constitutional right of amending it or their revolutionary right to dismember or overthrow it.[21]

Here, then, we have a formal political ideology that justifies and in fact encourages opposition to and revolt against unjust government. Furthermore, there are various instances in American history where actual protest and civil disorder against excesses of government have been condoned and even recommended. Writing to Edward Carrington from Paris on January 16, 1787, Jefferson discussed the Shays' Rebellion, which took place in the summer of 1786 in Massachusetts and disturbed many of the political thinkers of the time:

I am persuaded myself that the good sense of the people will always be found to be the best army. They may be led astray for a moment, but will soon correct themselves. The people are the only censors of their governors; and even their errors will tend to keep these to the true principles of their institution. To punish these errors severely would be to suppress the only safeguard of the public liberty."[22]

In the same letter, Jefferson confirmed his belief in the desirability of the right to protest against government in a more instructive language. He wrote:

I hold it that a little rebellion now and then is a good thing, and as necessary in the political world as storms in the physical. Unsuccessful rebellions, indeed, generally establish the encroachments on the rights of the people which have produced them. An observation of this truth should render honest republican governors so mild in their punishment of rebellions as not to discourage them too much. It is a medicine necessary for the sound health of government.[23]

It is this same spirit of sportsmanship and tolerance for adversity that Henry David Thoreau expressed in his "Resistance to Civil Government" (1849); it is the same spirit that has inspired several protest movements against government actions such as the American government's involvement in the Vietnam War and the most recent campus protests (at Columbia, Rutgers, Cornell, and elsewhere) against these universities' financial involvement in companies that deal with the racist South African regime. It is also the same spirit that has produced, on the whole, relatively mild reactions by organized government in the face of these civil disturbances.

The pertinent fact remains, then, that Americans (1) have much higher expectations of their government, and (2) deem it a right, if not indeed a duty, to fight against any nonlegitimate rule. These political perceptions, which are theoretically and practically much stronger in America than in other societies, make the average American much more sensitive about what he or she considers to be an injustice. Therefore, the high expectations of the people about the proper functioning of government and indeed about the whole question of its legitimacy can produce strong feelings of frustration, even though the institutionalized tolerance for adversity makes the pressure more bearable, at least when opposition is expressed formally, directly, and openly, than it would be otherwise. Let us now review, with this background picture of the average American's expectations of legitimacy, the rather widespread existence of inequality, poverty, and corruption in America, which are certainly inimical to the ideals Americans value most, to see what possible effect they may have on the crime problem.

## INEQUALITY

Human beings are endowed with unequal talents and qualities. To this innate and inevitable inequality is added, in most human societies, yet another kind of inequality—social inequality—which is caused by initially different opportunities for enjoyment of social values among the people. The difference in life's opportunities is itself the cumulative effect of the successes or failures of one's parents and ancestors in achieving their material objectives. Utopians have theorized about the possibility of diminishing or even completely eradicating the sources of inequality by making various recommendations for a more equitable distribution of wealth. Communist countries have supposedly made an actual attempt to create a just and egalitarian society. We know, however, that these efforts to a large extent have either failed or have been only partially successful.[24] And they have paid a very high price in widespread public apathy, indifference, and cynicism.

Because of its promises, the failure to create equality of opportunity looms greater in capitalist societies. Here the basic assumption is that the individual's pursuit of his own self-interests, if unfettered by the state, will result not only in his or her personal success, but in the process will also benefit the society at large. And if this is the basic premise—as it indeed is in all capitalist societies—then it does not make sense to take away too much of what the creative, hard-working individual makes, thus weakening his productive incentives, to give to people who have had fewer opportunities or less willpower to succeed. It follows that no truly capitalist society can honestly claim to try to make people equal or even to provide equal opportunity for everyone. Within the range of this basic limitation, however, various capitalist societies have tried to equalize, to the extent possible, the possibilities available to every citizen. A valid distinction can thus be made between different sociopolitical systems on the basis of how and to what extent they have minimized the inevitable class differences by such measures as higher tax rates for the rich and proper and efficient social services (inexpensive or free food, shelter, and medical treatment) for the poor and the underprivileged.

With this background in mind, let us now look at some of the facts and figures pertaining to American society. According to the U.S. Census statistics, in 1968 about one-fifth of 1 percent of the American public, the so-called "superrich," owned almost 60 percent of the corporate wealth in this country. Approximately 1.6 percent of the population owned 80 percent of all stock, 100 percent of all state and municipal bonds, and 88.5 percent of corporate bonds.[25] In the same year, the top fifth received 43 percent of the total money income; the top tenth received 27 percent and the top 5 percent received 17 percent. In contrast, the bottom half of the population earned only 22 percent. "In slightly more graphic terms, the top one percent of the American population got more money in one year than all the men, women, and children the government defined as poor; in fact the top one percent of the American population received in one year more money than the poorest 50 million Americans."[26]

The number of American families who own 1 billion dollars or more was sixty in 1977, and over 100,000 were millionaires. Today in just about every industry, 60 to 98 percent of all business is handled by a few giant companies. "The wealth of America is not in the hands of a broadly based 'middle-class ownership.' " [27]

The problem is that the tremendous economic disparity among different classes of people is self-perpetuating and irreversible. The concentration of huge riches in the hands of relatively few people makes it possible for them not only to increase their wealth incessantly, but also to use their economic power to obtain other social values. Wealth, for instance, can be used to obtain political power, and political power, in turn, can be employed to influence the enactment of laws and executive orders that support the economically advantageous position of the rich. Lobbying is accepted as a legitimate vehicle for influencing legislation and policy decisions. And there is no limit on how much money different groups of people can spend to lobby for any socioeconomic cause. Some powerful lobbies like the American Medical Association and the American Rifle Association wield great power in American society. The latter has managed, for instance, to obstruct the passage of laws that would seriously limit the sale and use of firearms, even though various authoritative sources have strongly argued that the easy access to such weapons is an important factor in a large number of the murders and other fatal shootings that take place in this country. Of course, lobbying requires large amounts of money, and the poor, the average, and the middle-income citizen do not have the needed financial ability or the necessary organization to use the available channels of communication to shape public opinion.

A related fact is that people can also influence legislation and other policy decisions by contributing either directly to the individual candidate running for office or to the party that claims to support the cause in which they may have an interest. Again, although theoretically everyone has the same opportunity to influence the outcome of an election by making financial contributions, it is obvious that in practice, the chances of the rich and the poor to affect public policy are widely discrepant. Someone who can contribute $1 million to a political campaign is much more likely to receive considerable favors that are normally denied an equally qualified but non-affluent citizen. As an acute observer has remarked:

George Meany of the AFL–CIO is fawned over in Washington but not entirely for his intellectual brilliance. And not because he can deliver labor's votes. He can't. What he can deliver and does deliver is political money.

The present U.S. Ambassador to Great Britain was not appointed for his contributions to creative foreign policy and diplomacy but for his contribution of political money. This is not new. Back in the fifties, the President appointed one of his big contributors ambassador to a country, then it was found he didn't even know where the country was.

So, jobs like that, and Washington influence, are in effect for sale. All it takes is money, political contributions in election years. [28]

Then, of course, there is inequality of people and groups before the law, both in adoption of legal norms (passage of laws more favorable to special interests) and in practice. I have already referred to the SmithKline case. The company pleaded guilty to fourteen misdemeanor counts of failing to notify the Food and Drug Administration about the adverse effects of the drug it had produced. It also pleaded guilty to twenty counts of falsely labeling the drug Selacryn with a statement that there was no causal link between it and liver damage. The company, we remember, was fined $100,000; its three managers were only put on probation and sentenced to perform 200 hours of community service.

Another typical case that surfaced in 1985 involved E. F. Hutton, the famous New York brokerage firm. In early May 1985, it pleaded guilty to federal charges of having defrauded numerous small banks of millions of dollars by means of a check-writing system that gave it interest-free loans. Obviously, these offenses were committed by real human beings. The Justice Department had also indicated, without naming any particular person, that some senior executives had been involved in the frauds. Nevertheless, no charges were brought against any executive, a decision that touched off sharp criticism and a letter of complaint by fifteen senators to the attorney general.[29] In his essay "For Whom the Bell Toils (A Felonless Felony at E.F. Hutton)" William Safire of the *New York Times* discussed the inappropriate handling of the case that resulted in the conviction of the firm but of no individual, stating, "The story is not so much Hutton, but prosecutorial misjudgment that let a company pay for the crimes its officers committed."[30]

Referring to the manner in which the Justice Department had handled cases against several corporations, including SmithKline, Eli Lilly & Company, and E. F. Hutton, a member of the Senate Judiciary Committee, Senator Howard M. Metzenbaum, Democrat of Ohio, said, "The Justice Department has let down the American people. . . . Even though 36 people died due to corporate irresponsibility, the Department let SmithKline off the hook."[31]

## POVERTY

Poverty in America, the land of plenty, is a shocking example of social inequality. The problem is still more alarming because in this country, the gap between the rich and the poor has become much wider than in most other Western democracies, and the country does possess the material means and the needed know-how to eradicate poverty altogether if it sets its mind to it. The problem, however, has not received the necessary attention it deserves, and the number of poor people in this most affluent society is increasing.

Poverty has been defined as the status of a person or a family (of various sizes) whose income falls below a certain level, called the poverty line. The figures defining the line are adjusted every year, taking into consideration the rate of inflation. For a three-member family, for instance, the figures were $3,099, $4,293, $5,784, $6,565 and $7,938 for the years 1970, 1975, 1979, 1980 and 1983, respectively.[32]

Taking these base standards, it is estimated that the number of poor people in America has risen from 26,072,000 in 1979 to 35,266,000 in 1983. The rate of poverty has increased from 11.7 percent in 1979 to 13.0 percent in 1980, 14.0 in 1981, 15.0 in 1982, and 15.2 in 1983.[33] If we include noncash benefits given to the poor, the number will be somewhat reduced. But this is of course true every year; the fact is that the increase in the number of the poor in this country has been steady and alarming.[34]

According to the latest data published by two government agencies, the Congressional Research Service and the Congressional Budget Office, the incidence of poverty among American children is also increasing at an alarming rate. According to these studies, in 1983, the last year for which complete data were available, about 13.8 million children, representing 22.2 percent of Americans under the age of eighteen, came from poor families. Children make up 26.8 percent of the American population, but 39.2 percent of the poor people are children, which makes the child poverty rate for 1983 at "the highest level since the mid–1960's."[35] There is of course a basic difference between various groups of Americans in their extent of poverty. Statistics show that Blacks, Hispanics, and households headed by women are economically the hardest hit.

In the back of these official data on poverty also lies the disturbing fact that the problem is almost totally ignored by the average citizen and most social institutions. In his classic study of the American poor, Michael Harrington has explained that for various reasons poverty has become "invisible"—the poor are isolated and mostly confined to special sections of cities and towns—and thus easily ignored by most people.[36]

Another disturbing fact about poverty in the United States is that it develops its own subculture, its pessimistic world outlook, which aside from being a serious problem in itself, can also lead to other social ills. "[The other America] is populated by the failures, by those driven from the land and bewildered by the city, the old people suddenly confronted with the torments of loneliness and poverty, and by minorities facing a wall of prejudice."[37]

Because of these shattering experiences which they share with few other groups, the poor become pessimistic, apathetic, and fatalistic in their outlook. As Harrington has noted, "the outrage of want, and even hunger, in the richest society in the world is rooted in our structure, our institutions, our normal way of doing things."[38] Consequently, the poor cannot be realistically helped out of their abject misery unless some basic sociocultural changes are effected to give them, before anything else, a reasonable hope that their lives can indeed be improved, that they can gain a certain minimum measure of decency, respect, and recognition in their society.

Poverty, in the meantime, subsists in America, and frustrations associated with desiring things and not being able to get them can lead to various negative or antisocial reactions, which we shall discuss separately. What should be noted is that a by-product of acute poverty is the development, at least among certain groups that are conscious of the social roots of the problem, of a feeling of distrust and disrespect, perhaps eventually the withdrawal of the attribute of legitimacy from the sociopolitical system, because despite its massive wealth and possibilities, it does not seriously try to solve this inexcusable problem. In the words of a keen observer, "The existence of hungry and abused men, women, and children in the midst of what is supposed to be the most prosperous and humane country on earth makes a mockery of American claims to 'liberty and justice for all.' "[39]

## CORRUPTION

As noted before, lobbying and contributions for political campaigns are accepted practices for influencing public opinion and legislative action; these practices, at times, lead to corruption. The American political system does not make any distinction between "good" and "bad" money. Money derived from lawful activity or illicit acts is treated alike if it can help achieve certain political objectives. Anyone who can contribute is welcome to join the bandwagon and in return reap the privileges offered by the system. Thus, corruption has been a constant feature of American politics, Americans have always considered politicians to be crooks and politics to be dirty. Throughout the years, there has been talk about the unholy alliance between organized crime and public officials. The National Commission on Law Observance and Enforcement, after completing its inquiry into police practices in 1931, concluded:

Nearly all of the large cities suffer from an alliance between politicians and criminals. For example, Los Angeles was controlled by a few gamblers for a number of years. San Francisco suffered similarly some years ago and at one period in its history was so completely dominated by the gamblers that three prominent gamblers who were in control of the politics of the city and who quarrelled about the appointment of the police chief settled their quarrel by shaking dice to determine who would name the chief for the first two years, who for the second two years, and who for the third.[40]

This statement was made more than half a century ago. Today no dice are cast to decide who appoints the next mayor. Nevertheless, the principle of political influence and illegal exchange of favors between criminals and politicians is as widespread today as it was then. So is corruption in general, even though some of the practices are made to seem quite normal to average Americans.

In recent history, Donald Dawson, a close aide of President Truman, was implicated in a scandal involving the misuse of public funds. Truman's former appointments secretary was also involved in a tax scandal.

Sherman Adams, a close Eisenhower associate, was found to have accepted numerous personal gifts from Bernard Goldfine, who was trying to buy favors with the Federal Trade Commission. When Nixon was in power, the textile industry contributed over $400,000 to his reelection campaign, and in return, won a tariff on textile imports from Japan. The measure assured a high and stable price for American textiles for many years. This contribution and the oil industry contribution of more than $5 million, which likewise was certainly made for "consideration," were effected just one day before the law requiring disclosure of campaign contributions went into force. According to Jack Anderson, the president of the McDonald's hamburger chain contributed $250,000 to Nixon's reelection campaign and won in return an exemption from the minimum wage law for high school students which was personally written by President Nixon. This exemption gave McDonald's a very strong edge over regular restaurants across the country.[41]

The milk industry contributed $1 million and was awarded with a boost in milk prices at the same time that other prices were frozen to curb inflation. ITT promised a $400,000 contribution to underwrite the expenses of the Republican National Convention. The Department of Justice later dropped an antitrust suit against the company.

Nixon also initiated an effective campaign to curb the influence of the Democrats with labor unions and the mob and to bring them over to his side and the Republican party.

Widespread fight against the influential mobster, Myer Lansky, was engaged in several fronts, and the booty of the victories distributed among various Nixon and Republican party elements. For example, the control of a Miami-based bank shifted from Lansky to Nixon's close friend Bebe Rebozo. Union funds which were invested through Lansky's banks were transferred to the Republican side. Law firms that had lucrative union contracts lost them to firms which were owned and controlled by Republicans; the Teamsters hired Nixon's own firm.[42]

Naturally all this was done for consideration, and Nixon did indeed deliver on his pledge. He granted Jimmy Hoffa, the former head of the Teamsters Union, executive clemency, and he was released from prison. The new head, Frank Fitzsimmons, was treated as an old intimate friend. He was publicly acknowledged by the president as being "welcome in my office any time; the door is always open to Frank Fitzsimmons." The leverage that the head of the Teamsters Union had with the president and other high officials around him helped him to stop the FBI's continued attempt to establish his and the union's illegal involvement with the Mafia and investigation of other criminal acts he was suspected of committing.[43]

The involvement of high public officials in corrupt and corrupting practices is not, of course, limited to the president, the men around him, or the party machine. Such involvement on the part of people so high in government, however, has a much stronger impact on the perception of the public; it symbolizes the nature of the whole political process and implicates the highest office in the United States as having at least indirectly justified such dubious deals and practices. The sad fact is, of course, that such practices, repeated over and over again, have become acceptable to the public; nobody seem to be outraged enough to do something about them. This lack of shock and angered reaction, however, also indicates that the sensitivity of the public has dulled, and this dulling of our social awareness surely affects our total disposition and reaction to social ills and problems, including crime.

If we study the problem more closely and do not write it off simply as a traditional American practice as many tend to do, it becomes clear that lobbying as it is conducted today in fact implies at least a partial negation of democracy. By allowing the rich and the influential to make massive campaign contributions and thus directly or indirectly influence decisions in Washington, we have made it much more difficult for the average citizen to have a meaningful voice in the affairs of the state. Even though we have chosen not to admit it, this is in reality a de facto abrogation of representative government. Theoretically, everybody has the same right to free expression, to assemble, and to influence public opinion. But how could the average citizen, who has all the usual financial worries of making a living, realistically compete with huge interest groups and politicians who can spend millions of dollars to influence legislation and other policy decisions?

Recently John B. Oakes, a former senior editor of the New York Times, wrote an article discussing how, in his words, big money "prostitutes" Washington.[44] He stated that the various political action committees (PAC), which have large sums of money at their disposal, actually bribe the legislators and buy their votes on different issues. Today there are 3,600 such registered and "independent" PACs, and they spend some $120 million buying votes from members of the Congress.

The PAC handouts on a newly gigantic scale are only the most spectacular form of bribery of members of Congress. The "honorarium," which should be called "dishonorarium," is another.

It is commonplace for a member of Congress to rent himself out to a lobbyist for up to $2,000 a throw to sit around a luncheon or dinner table in Washington as a so-called guest for an intimate chat with a few of the lobbyist's prestigious clients.

Some $4.5 million in "honorariums" for this and fancier kinds of private services, such as visits to arms plants, were paid to members of Congress in election year 1982 by special interests.[45]

Representative Leon E. Panetta, Democrat of California has stated, "Congress is literally bought and sold by PAC contributions." Is this true? Oakes gives several examples that confirm the allegation. I have chosen only a few of those examples for quotation here:

The champion PAC donor of all time is the A.M.A., which has handed out at least $10 million over the years to Congressional incumbents and candidates. Together with the American Dental Association, it gave more than $3 million in the House prior to a vote to exempt doctors and dentists from federal regulatory jurisdiction.

The United Automobile Workers paid out nearly $2 million in the 1982 Congressional election when domestic-content legislation was becoming a hot issue. It still is, and the PAC is going stronger than ever.

The House vote overturning a ruling to protect used-car buyers from unscrupulous dealers followed a $1 million distribution by the dealers' PAC.

The 12 members of a House subcommittee who voted to weaken the Clean Air Act got $200,000 from seven major industries that thought they would benefit thereby.[46]

Oakes states in his opening paragraph that "money power poses an immediate and growing threat to the American representative system." He ends his article by saying that the power of money " 'undermines party discipline and control.' Worst of all, it erodes public confidence in the integrity of the Congressional system." The fact is that such commonly accepted practices undermine the whole foundation of political legitimacy. They imply an all-out war, waged in a subtle and covert manner, by the rich and influential against the rights of the public. If the dairy industry can spend $1 million through its PAC to maintain the price support the industry enjoys, it can only mean that consumers must pay a higher price for their dairy needs. And if the same thing can happen in successfully fighting measures that would stop air pollution and other kinds of contamination, which have become major health hazards in many American cities, how can we expect the average citizen to trust the system and consider it legitimate? If people, animals, and vegetation must die because it is more profitable for big chemical or pharmaceutical concerns to dump their dioxide or other poisonous waste in public lands, rivers, and lakes as they seem to be doing with the help of political influence, how would it be possible for the average citizen to believe in the representative nature of the government or its legitimacy? Is it any wonder, then, that the average individual should feel, consciously or subconsciously, that he is surrounded by ominous forces trying to rob and exploit him even if they have to sacrifice his well-being or life and that he should try to protect himself or get back at the system, if necessary by illegal activity? Is there a fundamental difference except for magnitude and comprehensiveness between the crime committed by a big industrial concern in gradually killing people by dumping dioxide all around and actually not being punished for it and a single case of murder, rape, or mugging? If anything, the first should be considered much more serious and punished more severely. However, we know that this is not the case. Neither are hundreds of other violations of human life, liberty, and dignity which are regularly committed by big concerns ever punished properly. The public, of course, senses the facts, and the widespread perception of "illegitimacy" makes it much easier for the individual, emotionally and mentally, to engage in criminal acts, which are really not any more serious than the callous acts perpetrated regularly against him on a much larger scale by the rich and powerful who incidentally seem to be immune from proportionate responsibility.

Corruption, of course, is not confined to professional politicians alone; it exists in all levels of government. Almost every day we read about corrupt mayors, congressmen, senators, judges, police, and other public officials. In the absence of reliable data for many European countries, which, being fearful of the adverse effects of publicity, do not usually advertise their examples of corruption as much, it is difficult to say whether the incidence of corruption in the United States is higher than it is in other Western democracies. Nevertheless, the impression one gets from the American mass media somehow indicates that it is.

To give other examples of the deeply entrenched corruption in American politics, Michael Parenti, beneath the caption "Corruption as an American Way of Life," has the following to say:

In recent years there have been reports on corruption involving federal, state and local officials in every state of the Union. In Congress 'Corruption is so endemic that it's scandalous. Even the honest men are corrupted—usually by and for the major economic interest groups and the wealthy individuals who together largely dominate campaign financing. In some states—Louisiana for instance—scandals are so prolific that exposure of them has absolutely no impact,' reports one observer. A Republican member of the Illinois state legislature estimated that one-third of his legislative colleagues accepted payoffs. In 1970–1971, officials in seven of New Jersey's eleven urban counties were indicted or convicted for graft and corruption, along with the mayors of the two largest cities, the minority leader of the state assembly, the former speaker of the state assembly, a prominent state senator, a state prosecutor, a former secretary of state, and a Port Authority Commissioner. At about the same time, major scandals were occurring in Texas, Illinois, West Virginia, Maryland and New York. In New York City alone half the Police Department was reported by the Knapp Commission to be accepting payoffs. In 1974 widespread corruption was found in the police forces of Chicago, Philadelphia, Indianapolis, Cleveland, Houston, Denver and New York, involving gambling, prostitution, narcotics and stolen goods. In Albany, N.Y., according to a state commission, policemen in every precinct of the city were involved in one or more of the following practices: burglarizing stores (or covering up burglaries), looting parking meters, accepting bribes, protecting narcotics dealers, shaking down prostitutes and intimidating witnesses who attempted to testify against police crime. In 1976 it was revealed that FBI leaders had used Bureau funds for personal purposes and the FBI agents routinely accepted unsecured loans at preferred rates of interest from a bank in New Jersey. Municipal and federal narcotics agents were found 'to be some of the mob's most successful pushers.' Doctors were cheating the government out of 'a billion dollars a year and all their patients much more,' reported health officials, by falsifying health insurance claims, padding bills, participating in kickbacks and overcharging for often unnecessary laboratory tests by as much as 100 to 400 percent.[47]

Campaigning for President in 1976, Jimmy Carter made a plea for honesty in government at a $100-a-plate dinner in Miami while beside him on the dais sat a mayor recently imprisoned for tax evasion, a couple of Florida state senators who had just pleaded guilty to conflict of interest, a commissioner facing trial for bribery, and three other commissioners charged with fraud.[48]

Parenti goes on to explain at least his personal impression of the cheating environment:

Corruption in America is so wide-spread that, as Lincoln Stefens pointed out long ago, throwing the rascals out only means bringing more rascals in. Through all this, the public looks on with growing cynicism, uttering jokes about the habits of politicians and sometime failing to appreciate how the corrupt officeholder is part of the same individual acquisitive system that includes the plundering corporate manager, the lying advertiser, the rent-gouging landlord, the price-fixing merchant, the cheating lawyer, the fee-gouging doctor and at a more modest level, the pilfering auto mechanic and television repairman.[49]

The existence of inequality, poverty, and corruption should be viewed in the context of American ideals and basic values. Obviously, other Western democracies and of course most of the developing countries are also plagued by the same social problems. The issue, however, becomes much more serious in America for the following reasons:

1. Whereas in most other countries, the media are pressured by official policy and/or self-imposed censorship to be more restrictive in their portrayal and criticism of the evil aspects of life in society, the American media are defiantly determined to inform the public not only about heartening and glorious events, but also about the sleazy side of the social life and politics. As a matter of fact, some of the mass media put the emphasis on the negative and the gory as an effective means of selling their products. In any event, compared with Europeans, the American public is more aware

of the widespread existence of social ills in this country. The perception of mismanagement and corruption even though at times unfounded or highly exaggerated when we look at the issues in a comparative context is much stronger and more evident among the intellectuals in this society.

2. In many countries, the facts of inequality, poverty, and corruption are accepted as inevitable. Among Muslims, for instance, it is earnestly believed that poverty and wealth of the people are willed by God. As we read in the Koran:

> Say: 'O God, Master of the Kingdom,
> Thou givest the Kingdom to whom Thou wilt,
> and seizest the Kingdom from whom Thou wilt.
> Thou exaltest whom Thou wilt,
> and Thou
> abasest whom Thou wilt;
> in Thy hand
> is the good;
> Thou art powerful
> over everything.[50]

There are of course similar pronouncements in all other major religions. The difference is, however, that in the West, because of the industrial revolution and other social developments on the one side, and the gradual acceptance of the teachings of the social sciences on the other, people have come to regard themselves as masters of their destiny. Among Muslims and many other people in developing countries, the words of the Koran are taken literally to mean that irrespective of man's individual and joint efforts, only the will of God, which manifests itself in the minutest affairs of this world, will be actualized. Thus, nothing can be done, nothing can be reversed, nothing can be corrected, except through prayer and a hope for God's change of will.

The acceptance of inequality, corruption, and other social ills is further facilitated to an extent unthinkable in the West by Muslims' sincere belief that as God has repeatedly promised, the evildoer shall be definitely and severely punished in the other world, if not necessarily here and now. A similar fatalistic perception exists, perhaps to a lesser degree, also among certain classes of people in less developed European countries. Americans, however, have come a long way in terms of social awareness or secularization of the roots of social injustice. They put the responsibility in the sociopolitical structure. The sense of frustration, therefore, is much stronger among average Americans when they are faced with what they consider to be a social problem.

3. The issue becomes even more serious in American society because unlike any other society on earth, the American political ideology, as discussed before, explicitly advocates the right of the citizen to revolt against

the established government when that government acts in ways contrary to the interests of the people. This, on the one hand, raises the level of public expectations and, on the other, raises the feeling of frustration to a much higher level than is true for many other societies.

In a very interesting study based on data collected from American schools and a sample of students from other cultures (Denmark, Greece, India, Italy, and Japan), June Tapp and Lawrence Kohlberg found that at the highest level of education, in college, a large number of students stated that if the rules were immoral, they could be broken. Students at lower levels were more absolutist, perhaps because the older ones were more sophisticated and could analyze facts more objectively. To quote the results of the study:

Although significantly more preadolescents than primary-schoolers felt that an immoral rule provides a justifiable reason for violation, by college this motive increased significantly (54%). These students argued that expected compliance must be weighed against the inherent rightness or morality of the rule, independent of circumstances. Rather than hardship justifying deviation (which was the reason accepted by middle-school students) the justice of the rule was the primary condition for disobedience. A college female's comment was typical: "When the rule is immoral or unjust because I believe that people are morally accountable for their actions, and this is above the law or rules.[sic]"[51]

What is significant from the perspective of cultural values and the actual conditioning of attitudes is that the cross-cultural sample did not respond in the same fashion as American students. In other words they did not say that if the rule was immoral, they would have the right to break it.

In five out of seven cultures there was strong support for the conventional notion that rules can be broken under certain circumstances; also, older preadolescents more willingly maintained that rules or laws are breakable. They increasingly adopted a conventional posture. The post-conventional focus on the morality of the rule, which strongly emerged by college in the developmental study was not a dominant cross-cultural justification for rule violation.[52]

We shall see in the next chapter that frustration can lead to aggression, and aggression, in turn, can be canalized, under appropriate conditions, into criminal activity. Given the fact that frustration, for reasons discussed above, is much more widespread and activated in American society, the question of its dissipation becomes a central issue. There are various institutionalized vehicles for the purpose. In practice, much frustration is discharged through direct or vicarious sports. Theoretically, the deep-seated American sense of freedom and the avowed right to rise against any injustice should also make it possible for many people in ordinary situations to voice their grievances or actively influence public action and thus to discharge more of their frustrations. For various reasons, however, these channels are not always available to the average citizen. Therefore, the remaining sense of frustration will gradually accumulate and search for possible outlets. And since the legitimacy of the sociopolitical system is questioned in various instances, the aggressive tendencies of the discontented citizen will be directed at times toward institutions and values that represent the established political structure. Lack of trust in the criminal justice system and courts in general, a strong belief that the system works for the benefit of the few and in disregard for the majority's interests, and a growing cynicism that there is no real possibility to rectify the unjust social system will reinforce the feeling among many citizens that they are in fact engaged in a total war against the usurpers of wealth, power, and other social values. With such an emotional outlook, which is also constantly fanned by radical leftist groups, the logical conclusion reached by many dissatisfied citizens is that whatever they can do to weaken and harm the system will be justified. As a keen observer of the crime problem has remarked:

The moral bind of law is loosened whenever a sense of injustice prevails. Law, whatever its guiding principle, trial by ordeal or due process, binds members of society to the extent that it maintains a semblance of even-handed administration. Guiding principles may vary but, whatever their substance, persistent violation of their spirit occurs at the peril of alienating the subjects of law and order. A legal system based on trial by ordeal is tenable, but one in which the internal logic of that system is regularly violated would to that extent lose the loyalty of its subjects. The legitimacy granted to law would be withdrawn.

Legal order is not simply a system of coercion. The maintenance of law depends partly on its legitimacy. Among the basic elements of legitimate order is the belief on the part of the subjects that some semblance of justice prevails. The common sense of Western traditions was well formulated in Augustine's rhetorical question, "What are states without justice but robber bands enlarged?" The cry of injustice is among the most fateful utterances of which man is capable—and no less consequential when expressed by schoolboys. It is tantamount to asserting that chaos or tyranny reign instead of order and society.[53]

When the public feels cheated and victimized, it is only natural that it should resort to illegal practices, especially when the fear of punishment is minimal, to try and supposedly rectify the wrong, to get something which in this kind of outlook already belongs to it and has been taken away from it by unjust and irregular methods. Every day brings news of corruption and abuse of power in high places, giving the impression that the powerful and the rich can engage in illegal and/or unethical practices with total immunity while the poor and ignorant shoplifter who may have been forced by socialization or necessity to steal is severely punished. Naturally many elect to commit crimes especially when the chances of being caught are relatively negligible. Others simply deny their support to the criminal justice system, refusing to assist the police in their efforts to apprehend the offender or the courts in their quest for reliable testimony.

In no society, except perhaps a total police state, can the criminal justice system function effectively without public participation in the different stages of its operation: crime prevention and detection, documentation of proof, trial, rehabilitation, and the provision of technical training and actual work opportunities during the sentence and the parole period after release. Public participation in the American criminal justice system is diminished to a large extent because, I submit, the legitimacy of the system is being questioned, either consciously or subconsciously.

## CONTROL-REDUCING VALUES

By raising the expectations of its citizens in various areas—economic, political, and social—and not being able to satisfy them all, the American culture inherently creates dissatisfaction, frustration, and possible aggression, which may be manifested through criminal behavior. The latter eventuality is more likely when, because of widespread discrepancy between the declared socioeconomic expectations and actual practices people in the lower social strata choose to withdraw the attribute of legitimacy and their support for the system and to visualize themselves in constant conflict with the establishment, a perception which makes law-breaking a justifiable reaction.

Another transformation has taken place in American culture, that is, the weakening of self-restraining forces in the individual citizen. Independently of the level of expectations and the chances of their fulfillment, self–control is an important factor in preventing criminal behavior; where it exists, the individual can resist the temptation to violate social norms, including those officially sanctioned as rules of law. It seems clear that the American culture in the past few decades has, on the one side, encouraged personal and material wants and desires as we have already seen and on the other, has to a large extent diminished the sense of responsibility and self-control in the individual. It has thus taken away another restraining factor, which in most other societies acts effectively to keep the average individual within the bounds of accepted morality and social awareness. The reasons for this transformation in the American culture are many.

### Weakening of Religious Beliefs

Factors of the modern age have helped transform the religious mood in many Western societies. Besides various excesses committed in the name of religion, religious beliefs in the past beclouded the reality that poverty and other social ills are created, not by God's will, as most religions had taught, but by man's own inequitable social arrangements. Marx emphasized the negative functions of religion, which had helped pacify and immobilize the masses against outrageous social inequalities. Freud regarded God and all spiritual and religious explanations and experiences as mere projections of the individual's own sense of insecurity, fear, and wishful thinking. A very long tradition of cynicism and doubt about the validity of certain religious dogmas and practices was compounded by two world wars which angered millions of people who had hoped God would prevent people from committing cruel and savage acts against others. Because of these trends it has now become fashionable, at least among the educated classes, to deny the sanctity of all religious beliefs and to oppose the acceptance of or association with absolutist religious teachings. At the same time, the various political and other secular ideologies that had become dominant in the West were often contradictory or unconvincing; they could not replace the weakening religious beliefs as viable substitute guides for action. Thus, the fear of God, damnation, or loss of His love and protection, which still acts effectively in many cultures to curb individual excesses, has in the West and especially in America lost most of its power to control human behavior.[54] On the other hand, the social ideologies that have gained dominance in the American scene tend to encourage rather than curb the actualization of various human desires and willing submission to all sorts of temptation.

## Relativism

> It all depends on where you are,
> It all depends on when you are,
> It all depends on what you feel,
> It all depends on how you feel.
> It all depends on how you're raised,
> It all depends on what is praised,
> What's right today is wrong tomorrow,
> Joy in France, in England sorrow.
> It all depends on point of view,
> Australia or Timbuctoo,
> In Rome do as the Romans do.
> If tastes just happen to agree,
> Then you have morality.
> But where there are conflicting trends,
> It all depends, it all depends...[55]

Relativism has been a powerful force in the human quest for progress but also a cause of enormous uncertainty and anxiety. Its positive effects have of course been tremendous; advance in science and technology, weakening of prejudices, and enhanced tolerance for differing ideas and ideologies. At the same time, modern people have lost belief in absolute moral values; on the basis of relativism we have reached the dangerous conclusion that everything can be explained and justified in relation to something else, which is a valid observation in science, but can lead to anarchy in social relations if carried to the extreme. We are no longer sure what distinguishes good from bad, right from wrong, even though such characterizations cannot be valid except in particular contexts. We no longer have a system of ready-made answers for every conceivable problem, and therefore, face many moral and intellectual dilemmas for which there are not commonly accepted solutions. We must grope alone in the dark, without the help of a definite value system and under constant pressure from contradictory demands and tendencies. The weakening of moral values has resulted in more intellectual and emotional freedom, but at the same time it has created a nagging feeling of uncertainty, anxiety, and spiritual vacuum.

Relativism, in its popular interpretation, is a lax state of mind; it means being uncommitted to any definite set of moral values. It means rationalizing one's actions and reactions with the convenient argument that there are no scientifically tested general guidelines for our behavior. In the realm of science, relativism has been a blessing, paving the way for further progress. In social relations, the actual application of this outlook has produced many disturbing problems.

The most influential treatment of the subject of relativism in ethics was that of Edward Westermarck, the renowned anthropologist who showed the variety of moral judgments in different societies and in different individuals.[56] Using a wealth of historical data, Westermarck demonstrated that moral standards vary from age to age and from culture to culture.

Durkheim's research on social phenomena also indicated that everything that exists in any given society, whether a social institution, belief system, artifacts, or whatever, is functional within that particular setting. Being functional for the existence and continuity of life there, it is also necessary and meaningful in the context of that society. In his study of primitive religions, where he focused his attention on the functional aspect of superstitions, rituals, and other religious practices which seemed quite bizarre and incomprehensible to Western mentality, Durkheim unraveled the relative meaning and significance of these phenomena in maintaining and perpetuating the social system in various societies.[57]

Following the same lead, American anthropologists Ruth Benedict and Margaret Mead further documented the relativity of cultural imperatives and moral values. Margaret Mead, for instance, showed that the traits and characteristics that American culture associates with sexual roles do not necessarily apply to other cultures. After living and studying in three primitive societies on the island of New Guinea for a number of years, she showed that most sexual traits and practices are created by the culture. In general, there is no such thing as a fixed, inevitable, and unchanging "human nature."[58]

Studies by other anthropologists have also indicated the relative nature of group practices and their moral values. The spread of sociology as a popular social science in the United States more than any other place in the world and the reputation it has acquired here for being a descriptive, value-free tool for analyzing the status quo have likewise facilitated the easy acceptance of relativism in America. The study of the learning process in social institutions, called "socialization" in sociological literature, indicates that the structure and contents of personality, including individual beliefs, values, and emotive perceptions are derived from the surrounding environment and hence are relative to each particular society.

The nature of social life in industrial societies, including the basic premises and requirements of the economic system, have also necessitated the rejection of the more traditional belief systems and the adoption of different ways of experiencing reality and of doing things in ways more suitable to the requirements of industrialization. Since innovation is the hallmark of every growing capitalistic system, constant change and readaptation of ways and means and flexible and relative mentality and morality are prerequisites for the survival and prosperity of the system.

### Pragmatism

A philosophy closely identified with and consistent with the American way of life is pragmatism. Like every other philosophy, it must have already existed in this society, albeit in a cruder form, in the folkways of the people before William James, the great American philosopher, gave it distinct expression and a more definite form. Rather than being obsessed by theoretical quibblings over the truth or falsity of moral ideas, proposed James, we should judge them according to their usefulness in solving practical problems. In his words:

A pragmatist turns his back resolutely and once for all upon a lot of inveterate habits dear to professional philosophers. He turns away from abstraction and insufficience, from verbal solutions, from bad a priori reasons, from fixed principles, closed systems, and pretended absolutes and origins. He turns toward concreteness and adequacy, towards facts, towards action and towards power. That means the empiricist temper regnant and the rationalist temper sincerely given up. It means the open air and possibilities of nature, as against dogma, artificiality and the pretense of finality in truth.[59]

Ideas and beliefs are meaningless to James unless they can be and are used as guidelines for action and insofar as they can help achieve our goals. They "become true just in so far as they help us to get into satisfactory relations with other parts of our existence."[60] What actually works and makes a difference in the way one lives is "true." Anything else is irrelevant and should not be pursued because it distracts us from worthier occupations.

Another great American pragmatist, John Dewey, was likewise concerned with the detrimental effects of traditional values—in his case, religious beliefs—which are supposed to help prepare the individual for life here and hereafter. Actually such values inadvertently encourage people to inactivity, so that they will not be seriously motivated to solve the concrete problems at hand. To him, too, it was futile to speculate about absolute, ultimate goals; our task was to tackle the immediate problem and then proceed to the next step. As he explains it, "Until one takes intermediate acts seriously enough to treat them as ends, one wastes one's time in any effort at change of habits. Of the intermediate acts, the most important is the next one. The first or earliest means is the most important end to discover."[61]

Dewey insisted that there are no absolute moral rules; when need be, any particular moral rule should be treated as a hypothesis and tested to see whether it fits the new experiences we face. If not, it is irrelevant to our experience and should be disregarded. The question, of course, is what in the absence of commonly accepted norms and values should guide the individual in the pursuit of private interests. James and Dewey were, no doubt, far from recommending an unbridled sway of individual whims and wishes as guides for action. They were both humanists and very much concerned about human well-being in general; they were certainly no advocates of hedonistic pursuit of one's desires. However, the popular understanding and interpretation of their philosophy has evolved into a crude pragmatism, which tries only to solve practical problems without bothering to think about the more significant issues that have beset humanity from the dawn of time. What is more interesting and alarming is the fact that this popular version of pragmatism has been praised and advocated by several serious thinkers as well as those who have used it for more down-to-earth objectives. Thus, Harvey Cox, a theologian, describes with seeming admiration the contemporary pragmatic person:

He approaches problems by isolating them from irrelevant considerations, by bringing to bear the knowledge of different specialists, and by getting ready to grapple with a new series of problems when these have been provisionally solved. Life for him is a set of problems, not an unfathomable mystery. He brackets off things that cannot be dealt with and deals with those that can. He wastes little time thinking about "ultimate" or "religious" questions. And he can live with highly provisional solutions.[62]

The ultimate stance in rejecting traditional moral values and advocating concepts consistent only with the pursuit of individual interests, was reached in the writings of Ayn Rand. She takes the economic ideology of free enterprise and capitalism one step further and applies it to concepts of morality as well. She attacks the moral code of altruism and advocates unimpaired freedom for the individual to develop his or her own standards of morality, even though she insists that this should be done on the basis of "reason," not arbitrary whims or desires. Her guideline, called "objectivism," for human action is:

An ultimate value is that final goal or end to which all lesser goals are the means—and it sets the standard by which all lesser goals are evaluated. An organism's life is its standard of value: that which furthers its life is the good, that which threatens it is the evil. . . . Ethics is not a mystic fantasy—nor a social convention—nor a dispensable, subjective luxury, to be switched or discarded in any emergency. Ethics is an objective, metaphysical necessity of man's survival—not by the grace of the supernatural nor of your neighbors nor of your whims, but by the grace of reality and the nature of life.[63]

Ayn Rand praises "selfishness" as a moral value and objects to any sacrifice if it does not befit one's own purpose.

The Objectivist ethics holds that human good does not require human sacrifices and cannot be achieved by the sacrifice of anyone to anyone. It holds that the rational interests of man do not clash—that there is no conflict of interests among men who do not desire the unearned, who do not make sacrifices nor accept them, who deal with one another as traders, giving value for value.[64]

"The proper method of judging when or whether one should help another person is by reference to one's own rational self-interest and one's own hierarchy of values: the time, money or effort one gives or the risk one takes should be proportionate to the value of the person in relation to one's own happiness,"[65] she says. We can suspect the moral indignation Ayn Rand must have felt toward the hypocrisy of some of the more exacting religious teachings. However, to follow her advice, one would be faced with a chaotic and brutish world where everyone, in order to survive and prosper, would have to wage a petty personal war against all. If one had to live in accordance with only his or her selfish needs and desires—and everyone would—then what could mitigate against the inevitable clash of individual interests? And who can believe honestly that people can be effectively taught to act always in accordance only with rational interests, whatever they may mean? And what happens to the unfortunate masses who start life with a disadvantage and can never hope to reach an equal footing with the lucky few? Are they expected to submit forever to the requirements of their lower social status, or should they also pursue their own selfish—and rational—interests, joining hands to revolt against the highly advantageous position of the few?

Even laying aside the question of the moral worth or validity of such philosophies, there can be no doubt that if people decided to live by them, social evil and conflict, including crimes of all sort, would ensue as acceptable justification for the selfish human desire for survival and success. If one is convinced that "his" ultimate moral value should be to survive, enjoy himself, and advance his personal interests at all costs and without proper regard for the happiness and interests of his fellow men, as traditional moral philosophies have always advocated, then murder, rape, mugging, embezzlement, bribery, and the like would be legitimate means of achieving various objectives. In this type of ideology they are not immoral per se but are condemned only because they may cause one to suffer possible punishment.[66] Of course, one would have to be careful not to be caught and brought to justice, but in the context of factual realities and the way the American criminal justice system works, the possibility has been reduced to a minimum.

It is fortunate that this extreme emphasis on selfishness is not widely accepted in American culture. Moreover, the popular and misguided interpretations of pragmatism and relativism are tempered by deep-seated religious and ethical convictions, which keep reasserting themselves in a cyclical manner. Nevertheless, there is no doubt that such teachings have an impact on the way certain groups of people visualize their interests and the methods that can be used to achieve them. They also influence the degree to which the individual may feel inhibited by inner sentiments and convictions to engage in deviant behavior, when that behavior can maximize selfish interests and especially when the possibility of detection or conviction is minimal.

## Lack of Respect for Laws

Aside from the question of legitimacy, which could be raised on a more conscious level, there is also a more deep-seated, culturally reinforced disrespect for laws among Americans. This lack of respect for laws may have originated in perceptions of original governments and their machinery of laws, which on the whole served the interests of the ruling class, as illegitimate; in other words it stems from particular events in American sociopolitical history. Nevertheless, it has gradually moved to an unconscious level, making the feeling of disrespect all the more natural and less accessible to rational analysis.

The reasons for this particularly American reaction to law are many. America started as a British colony, gradually resisted the rule of the king, and revolted against it. The domination of the British was justified by reference to laws and other formal arrangements. As time went by, however, Americans began to see the real function of laws made by the British. As Gunnar Myrdal observed, "A low degree of law observance already became habitual and nationally cherished in colonial times when the British Parliament and Crown, increasingly looked upon as a foreign ruler by the

Americans, insisted upon passing laws which the Americans considered unwise, impractical or simply unjust.[67]

Another important factor that has affected the Americans' view of laws is the so-called frontier mentality. The early settlers had to fight their way through dangerous situations to open new vistas for their dreams. Under these circumstances, when utter chaos dominated social relations in this country, concern for laws as such seemed superfluous. "The long encounter with the frontier has contributed to both the openness and the lawlessness of American society. . . . The whole history of the American frontier is a narrative of taking what was there to be taken," historian Joe Franz has written. "The timid never gathered the riches, the polite nearly never. The men who first carved the wilderness into land claims and town lots were men who moved in the face of danger, gathering as they progressed. The emphasis naturally came to be placed on gathering and not on procedures. . . . Forced to rely on themselves, Americans, even those who lived in the effete East, came to define manhood as freedom from restrictions of law and custom."[68] " 'We should be men first, and subjects afterwards,' Henry David Thoreau declared, adding that he knew no reason why a citizen should 'ever for a moment, or in the least degree, resign his conscience to the legislator,' or indeed to anyone else. Only a relative handful of Americans ever had any direct contact with the frontier. But the frontier ethos has had a profound effect on American consciousness, and the metaphors of the West retain their curious hold on the American imagination."[69]

These historical experiences naturally produced corresponding reactions in the psyche of the American people. "Under the influence of all these and many other factors the common American citizen has acquired a comparatively low degree of personal identification with the state and the legal machinery."[70] It is not surprising, then, that Americans conceive of law only as a means to an end, to be followed only if it serves this function, and not as an institution that has any intrinsic value in itself, something to be respected and followed whether it benefits or harms particular interests. Again, to quote the same European observer who has viewed the problem with a different perspective and as it were, from outside:

Laws become disputable on moral grounds. Each legislative statute is judged by the common citizen in terms of his conception of the higher "natural law." He decides whether it is "just" or "unjust" and has the dangerous attitude that, if it is unjust, he may feel free to destroy it. The strong stress on individual rights and the almost complete silence on the citizen's duties in the American Creed make this reaction the more natural. The Jeffersonian distrust of government—"that government is best which governs least"—soon took the form, particularly on the Western frontier, of a distrust and disrespect for the enacted laws.[71]

As a corollary of this perspective on law, Americans have also developed an ambivalent attitude toward the deviant, the lawless, the criminal. On the one hand, criminals have been treated with the least possible consideration; in many places, jail and prison conditions are unbearably dehumanizing. On the other hand, Americans are fascinated by the daredevil, the daring deviant. Not only is there a soft spot in everyone's heart for the people who transgress laws and social customs, but there is also a long and strong tradition of idolizing the renegade, the rebel, the criminal. Hollywood has made at least twenty-one movies about Billy the Kid. In one film Paul Newman and in another Kris Kristofferson played the role even though the real Billy was described as a "slight, short, bucktoothed, narrow shouldered youth who looked like a cretin."[2] Gary Cooper, the late popular star, played Wild Bill Hickok. And in one of the several versions on the James brothers, Tyrone Power played Jesse, and Henry Fonda was his brother Frank. Al Capone, the scar-faced gangster, has been filmed many times, in one version with Rod Steiger. And of course we have had Marlon Brando's admirable portrayal of the "Godfather," a personified symbol of willpower, fortitude, courage, and even love of justice.

## Lack of Self-Discipline

For various reasons, Americans have come to believe and act according to the idea that any expression of discipline and control over the child may be harmful to the full development of his potential. A partial reason for this attitude could be the nature of the American society. At least in the beginning America required the expansive and creative energy of enterprising people who could not be restricted in their tireless efforts to open up new frontiers in search of more arable land and greater fortunes. As some have suggested, perhaps the relative lack of discipline in social relations is also intentionally, though at times perhaps unknowingly, encouraged by the mass media in the service of advertising agencies who want to sell various products at all costs. Another reason may be the wholehearted and widespread acceptance and application of psychoanalysis in America. This phenomenon is certainly unparalleled in any other society, even though, of course, the adoption of analytical psychology itself has to be explained by reference to some other, prior causes. The fact remains that as of the 1920s, Americans explicitly and extensively adopted a concept of education both at home and in school that emphasizes the unquestionable wisdom of the therapeutic modes of thought at the expense of the more traditional ways of educating children.

In the family, the natural instincts of parents to take care of their children have been seriously questioned by social workers, psychologists, and psychoanalysts. Gradually, various establishments with claims to exclusive knowledge of what is best for the child and for the parents became prominent in formal and informal education. Instead of the family circle, which for centuries had more or less provided the warmth, affection, and feeling of trust that children needed, numerous therapeutic organizations appeared, which at best treated the problem child with objective detachment and unemotional understanding. Parents' confidence in their ability to provide for the various needs of their children was eroded by the concerns expressed so solicitously by the new social disciplines. Strong fears were generated that parents could ruin the children by showing too much love and affection or by not seeking professional help whenever they noticed the slightest irregularity in the behavior of their offspring. Many of the new professionals were not qualified to help; many were outrightly dishonest and in business only to make money. At any event, the result of creating serious doubts about the ability of parents to bring up their children properly on the basis of common sense and traditional American values was that the role of the parent as a natural teacher of moral values, including self-discipline and respect for the rights of others, was greatly diminished. In its place moral education of the child was in practice left mainly to television programs, which are basically motivated to make money and function under the inevitable control of manufacturers and their agents, the advertising agencies, peer group pressure, which is itself influenced by the prevailing cultural values, and other mass media which likewise reflect what is dominant in current American culture.

A similar process took place in the formal educational system. The teacher's ability to help the problem students was subjected to questioning and doubt. He had to send all such cases to a school psychologist or student counselor. He learned eventually not to interfere at all. Unlike the traditional teacher who interacted with his or her students as whole human beings and was concerned about both their intellectual and emotional development, the modern teacher's role was drastically modified to be confined only to that of the unemotional transfer of information. Thus, the moral authority of the American teacher, who in the intimate interactional atmosphere of the classroom could act as a natural transmitter of traditional American values, was also eroded. This process of undermining the teacher's authority as a moral agent of society was also facilitated by the legalistic battles waged and won on the basis of the separation of church and state clause of the Constitution against prayer and meditation in the schools and thus against school's traditional authority and responsibility to inculcate ethical values in the child.

Again, the vacuum created in the child's formal education, which in the past emphasized self-restraint and respect for authority, was filled by television and other mass media, which in the service of rich and powerful consumer products companies downgraded self-restraint and encouraged an incessant urge to buy newer products. Not only was the authority of the parent and the teacher, the people who used to act as caring and responsible human beings in transmitting the basic ethical values in a warm, personal atmosphere, eroded, but the educational and moral ideologies themselves underwent drastic transformations.

In the 1920s and 1930s behaviorism was quite fashionable among psychologists. John B. Watson and Arnold Gesell stressed the causal link between the mother's behavior toward the child and the latter's eventual development into a particular personality type. And since human society was not the ideal place people had always expected it to be, parents who exerted control over the reactions of the child became objects of severe criticism. Mothers were admonished to discard their traditional habits of doing things and adopt modern scientific outlooks. They were seriously warned that "mother love has been found by science inherently dangerous, and some of them (grew) panicky as they let the significance of the new teaching sink into their thoughts." They were given hope, however, that if they followed the new teachings, they would be able to give their children the undeniable blessing of "freedom from emotional bondage to their parents."[73]

In the 1930s and 1940s a debased interpretation of Freudian theories resulted in permissiveness in dealing with children. Repression of instincts, a word Freud used to refer to the basic human drives, produces anxiety and neurotic tendencies, and this is one of the basic principles of analytical psychology. However, Freud had not by any means advocated that to avoid neurosis, children should be given uninhibited sway to satisfy their instinctual desires at will. As a matter of fact, the whole Freudian theory of personality development by the gradual shaping of the ego and the superego from the basic life forces, though somehow short-sighted due to Freud's lack of sociological insight, makes it quite clear that to control and balance the antisocial tendencies of the id on the one hand and the exacting and threatening demands of the superego on the other, a strong and well-adjusted ego is necessary. At the same time we know that the content and relative strength of the ego are directly related to the type of interaction the child has had with his parents. If parents are lax in demanding adherence to rules and practices, the ego that develops and guides the child's actions throughout life, unless modified by psychoanalysis or extreme emotional trauma, will be likewise weak and lax. It will easily give in to demands of the id; it will come up with easy rationalizations to satisfy the superego that it is appropriate under the circumstances to follow instinctual desires. It will lack self-restraint and indeed any incentive for self-restraint.

The effects of cultural phenomena discussed in this chapter on criminal behavior are many. Their significance stems from the obvious fact that cultural values and perceptions motivate and shape human action. Only with this perspective in mind does the study of the crime problem become meaningful. Let us take just one example.

Richard A. Cloward and Lloyd E. Ohlin, in discussing the perception of legitimacy, raised an important issue: whether the individual delinquent attributes his personal failure to the social system or to his own shortcomings. How the delinquent perceives the problem is of course very important to our understanding of his motivations. As the authors explain, "It is our view that the most significant step in the withdrawal of sentiments supporting the legitimacy of conventional norms is the attribution of the cause of failure to the social order rather to oneself, for the way in which a person explains his failure largely determines what he will do about it."[74] And again:

Whether the "failure" blames the social order or himself is of central importance to the understanding of deviant conduct. When a person ascribes his failure to injustice in the social system, he may criticize that system, bend his efforts toward reforming it, or dissociate himself from it—in other words, he may become alienated from the established set of social norms. He may even be convinced that he is justified in evading these norms in his pursuit of success-goals. The individual who locates the sources of his failure in his own inadequacy, on the other hand, feels pressure to change himself rather than the system. . . . By implication, then, attributing failure to one's own faults reveals an attitude supporting the legitimacy of the existing norms.[75]

The perception of inadequacy may be of course a sub- or unconscious feeling, impervious to conscious and rational reasoning. Thus, it is quite possible that some individuals may develop a sense of inadequacy or failure in spite of all efforts by the educational system to instill a feeling of trust and confidence in them, and this, I believe, happens more frequently in America than in many European countries. Prevailing American values include high expectations, relativity of moral commands, overemphasis on the rights of the individual in the absence of any reference to social responsibilities, and finally the development of a weak ego and a weak superego incapable either of resisting the innumerable opportunities and temptations or of condemning the individual for giving in to them. In this context it is much more likely that the average individual does not accept blame for his personal failures and attributes them to a supposedly illegitimate social system. As I have argued, the current American values emphasize the validity of the fun culture ("the pursuit of happiness" interpreted in exclusively materialistic terms), relativity, selfishness, and uninhibited expression of emotions and desires. In psychoanalytic terms, this means that the contents of the superego—which Freud erroneously assumed to be always "social" and "moral"—actually support deviant behavior. They may, under certain conditions, encourage criminal behavior, which in reality means the satisfaction of socially cherished desires in an unconventional or illegal manner.[76] Add to this the disturbing fact that even when the ego perceives that a criminal act may result in the unpleasant event of punishment, it is not strong enough to curb the temptations that are constantly reinforced by the advertising agencies. Furthermore, the punishment is not certain, due to the nature and practice of the American criminal justice system. Now the reasons for the comparatively high rates of criminal activity in the United States become clearer. If the picture I have portrayed is genuine, then what would really be astonishing is that crime rates are not actually higher than they are now. And the plausible answer to this puzzle may be that the traditional American has not completely given in to the messages emitted daily in the mass media; that the majority is still basically religious and bound by traditional, ethical values. Another reason may be that Americans have developed various means of acting out and dispelling their frustrations caused by unfulfilled desires created and nurtured by their consumer society.

To summarize, we are faced with a situation where the authority of traditional agents of socialization, especially parents and teachers, is to an alarming degree diminished. On the other hand, a social outlook has developed in America that advocates permissiveness, lack of self-restraint, and incessant satisfaction of highly elevated material expectations and desires. This ideology, based at least partly on a debased interpretation of Freudian psychology, fits perfectly with the interests of a consumer society that puts the highest premium on constant production and consumption of new commodities. In this process, the responsibility for the moral education of the public has fallen mainly to advertising agencies; therapeutic professions are also supposed to provide the public with the reliable knowledge needed to create the best of all possible worlds. The former is admittedly guided by prospects of financial gain; the latter at best cannot be intimately involved as much as parents naturally were with the emotional well-being of regular and problem children. The outcome of this process then, is individuals who lack strong moral convictions, whose ego is too weak to control their impulses, and who function under the formidable urge, built into the personality structure and reinforced through various media, that one should give in to temptations; one should buy, possess, and enjoy the many beautiful things that whet the appetite on television screen and magazine pages. No wonder that the result is partial breakdown of all traditional sources of control and the very serious social problems America faces today. As Christopher Lasch, an astute observer of the American culture, has noted:

The popularization of therapeutic modes of thought discredits authority, especially in the home and the classroom, while leaving domination uncriticized. Therapeutic forms of social control, by softening or eliminating the adversary relation between subordinates and superiors, make it more and more difficult for citizens to defend themselves against the state or for workers to resist the demands of the corporation. As the ideas of guilt and innocence lose their moral and even legal meaning, those in power no longer enforce their rules by means of the authoritative edicts of judges, magistrates, teachers, and preachers. Society no longer expects authorities to articulate a clearly reasoned, elaborately justified code of law and morality; nor does it expect the young to internalize the moral standards of the community. It demands only conformity to the conventions of everyday intercourse, sanctioned by psychiatric definitions of moral behavior.[77]

## NOTES

1. Gunnar Myrdal, "An American Dilemma," in *Man in Contemporary Society* prepared by the Contemporary Civilization Staff of Columbia College, New Student Edition (New York: Columbia University Press, 1969), pp. 450–451.

2. James Q. Wilson, *Thinking About Crime*, rev. ed. (New York: Vintage Books, 1985), pp. 259–260.

3. See Michael H. Graham, *Tightening the Reins of Justice in America: A Comparative Analysis of the Criminal Jury Trial in England and the United States* (Westport, Conn.: Greenwood Press, 1983).

4. Ibid., pp. 14–15.

5. *Kuruma Son of Kaniu v. Reginam* (1955) 1 All E. R. 236, 239, quoted in Graham, *Tightening the Reins*, p. 26. See also my note in the *Brooklyn Journal of International Law* 11, no. 1 (Winter 1985): pp. 177–180.

6. *Social Surveys*, Gallup Poll, Ltd. (SOC), May 1966.

7. Jules Henry, *Culture Against Man* (New York: Vintage Books, 1965), pp. 17–18.

8. Ibid., p. 19.

9. Ibid., p. 20.

10. Ibid., p. 20.

11. Ibid., p. 21.

12. Max Weber, *The Theory of Social and Economic Organization*, ed. Talcott Parsons (New York: The Free Press, 1964), pp. 129–130.

13. Ibid., p. 131.

14. Ibid., p. 130.

15. Ibid., p. 131.

16. John Locke, *Second Treatise of Government* (Chicago: Gateway Edition, 1955), section 232, pp. 193–194.

17. Ibid., section 240, pp. 203–204.

18. For quotation and source see *The Annals of America*, vol. 1 (Chicago: Encyclopaedia Britannica, Inc. 1968), section 28, pp. 154 ff.

19. Ibid., section 61, pp. 265 ff.

20. *The Annals of America*, vol. 2, section 103, p. 432.

21. *The Annals of America*, vol. 9, section 49, p. 253.

22. *The Annals of America*, vol. 3, section 22, p 82.

23. Ibid., section 23, p. 84.

24. In the Soviet Union, for instance, in addition to the diversity of opportunities available to different groups in the enjoyment of material values, a new power elite has emerged that has exclusive control over the decision-making processes. See, for instance, Milovan Djilas, *The New Class: An Analysis of the Communist System* (San Diego: Harcourt Brace Jovanovich, 1983).

25. Ferdinand Lundberg, *The Rich and the Super Rich* (New York: Lyle Stuart, 1968), pp. 144ff.

26. Richard Parker, *The Myth of the Middle Class: Notes on Affluence and Equality* (New York: Harper Colophon Books, 1974), p. 120.

27. Michael Parenti, *Democracy for the Few* 2d ed. (New York: St. Martin's Press, 1977), pp. 9–10.

28. William J. Chambliss, *On the Take: From Petty Crooks to Presidents* (Bloomington, Ind.: Indiana University Press, 1982), p. 157.

29. *New York Times*, May 10, 1985, p. D1.

30. Ibid., September 12, 1985, p. A35.

31. Ibid., September 19, 1985, pp. 1, A28.

32. See *Statistical Abstracts of the United States* (U.S. Department of Commerce, Bureau of the Census, 1985), p. 429.

33. Ibid.

34. See *Time* and *Newsweek*, March 5, 1984.

35. *New York Times*, May 23, 1985, p. 1.

36. Michael Harrington, *The Other America*, (New York: Macmillan, 1962); reprinted with new Afterword, Baltimore: Penguin Books, 1982) Chapter One, The Invisible Land, pp. 1ff, especially pp. 3–7.

37. Ibid., p. 11.

38. Ibid., p. 203.

39. Richard Parker, *Myth of the Middle Class*, p. 92.

40. Garret and Monroe, "Police Conditions in the United States," National Commission on Law Observance and Enforcement, Report on Police 14, (Washington, D.C.: U.S. Government Printing Office, 1931), p. 45.

41. Chambliss, *On the Take*, p. 176.

42. Ibid., p. 159.

43. See *International Herald Tribune*, April 30, 1973, pp. 1, 2.

44. John B. Oakes, "The Pac-Man's Game: Eating Legislators," *New York Times*, September 6, 1984, p. A23.

45. Ibid.

46. Ibid.

47. Parenti, *Democracy for the Few*, pp. 232–233.

48. Ibid.

49. Ibid., p. 234.

50. The House of Imran, Sura 3, Verse 25, trans. A. J. Arberry (New York: Macmillan Publishing Co., 1955), p. 76.

51. June Louin Tapp and Lawrence Kohlberg, "Developing Senses of Law and Legal Justice," in June Louin Tapp and Felice J. Levine, eds., *Law, Justice and the Individual in Society: Psychological and Legal Issues* (New York: Holt, Rinehart and Winston, 1977), pp. 101–102.

52. Ibid., p. 102.

53. David Matza, *Delinquency and Drift* (New York: John Wiley & Sons, 1964), p. 102.

54. In European countries religious traditions have dominated social relations for many centuries. Thus, even when a particular religious dogma or belief is rejected, society is still religious in its overall outlook. In America, religious traditions, like others, are relatively young and therefore, less resilient.

55. Quoted in Abraham Edell, *Ethical Judgment: The Use of Science in Ethics* (New York: The Free Press, 1955), p. 16.

56. See his book, *Ethical Relativity* (Patterson, N.J.: Littlefield Adams & Co., 1960).

57. Emile Durkheim, *The Elementary Forms of Religious Life*, trans. Joseph Ward Swain (New York: Collier Books, 1961 .

58. See Margaret Mead, *Sex and Temperament in Three Primitive Societies* (New York: William Morrow and Co., 1935). Margaret Mead's observations on Samoa have come under heavy attack recently and have been rejected by some as lacking in reliable proof. Her basic premise, however, that it is the culture that creates and cultivates "proper" roles for the sexes is still a valid and accepted conclusion.

59. William James, *Pragmatism and Four Essays from the Meaning of Truth*, ed. Ralph Barton Perry (New York: Meridian Books, 1955), p. 45.

60. Ibid., p. 49.

61. John Dewey, *Human Nature and Conduct: An Introduction to Social Psychology* (New York: The Modern Library, 1930), p. 35.

62. Harvey Cox, *The Secular City: Secularization and Urbanization in Theological Perspective*, rev. ed. (New York: Macmillan Co., 1978), p. 55.

63. Ayn Rand, "The Objectivist Ethics," in *The Virtue of Selfishness: A New Concept of Egoism* (New York: The New American Library of World Literature, 1964), pp. 17, 23.

64. Ibid., p. 31.

65. Ayn Rand, "The Ethics of Emergencies," in *The Virtue of Selfishness*, p. 45.

66. As Justice Blackmun says in his concurring opinion in *Parker, Warden et al. v. Levy*, (Supreme Court of the United States, 1974, 417 U.S. 733), "Relativistic notions of right and wrong, or situation ethics, as some call it, have achieved in recent times a disturbingly high level of justification of conduct that persons would normally eschew as immoral or even illegal."

67. Myrdal, *An American Dilemma*, p. 465.

68. Quoted in Charles Silberman, *Criminal Violence, Criminal Justice* (New York: Vintage Books, 1980), p. 49.

69. Ibid., pp. 49–50.

70. Myrdal, *An American Dilemma*, p. 466.

71. Ibid., p. 463.

72. Silberman, *Criminal Violence*, p. 33.

73. Ernest R. Groves and Gladys H. Groves, *Parents and Children* (Philadelphia: J. B. Lippincott, 1928), pp. 5, 116.

74. Richard A. Cloward and Lloyd E. Ohlin, *Delinquency and Opportunity: A Theory of Delinquent Gangs* (New York: The Free Press, 1960), p. 111.

75. Ibid., pp. 111–112.

76. According to Jules Henry the collapse of parental authority in America reflects the collapse of "ancient impulse controls" and a shift "from a society in which Super Ego values (the values of self-restraint) were ascendant, to one in which more and more recognition was being given to the values of the Id (the values of self-indulgence)." Henry, *Culture Against Man*, p. 127.

77. Christopher Lasch, *The Culture of Narcissism: American Life in an Age of Diminishing Expectations* (New York: Warner Books, 1980), p. 185.

# 5

# Frustration, Crime, and the Social System

## IN SEARCH OF A COMPREHENSIVE FRAME OF REFERENCE

As long as there have been deviation and strife in human society, the curious and the concerned have tried to find their causes. In religious literature, it is the Devil or the wicked spirit that deceives and pushes man to break God's commandments. Many people still believe that criminality is basically due to the corruption of the soul.

The more scientifically minded have tried to find the seeds of criminal behavior in inherited physical qualities and more recently in flawed personality structure, psychopathology (as in involuntary aggressive outbursts), and faulty ego development in intentional violation of social norms.

Eventually, the focus of attention has been directed to social factors; poverty, slums, family break-up, unemployment, and decline in moral education have been picked at one time or another as the cause of criminal behavior. The problem is that none of these factors alone can explain the reason(s) for crime. Most poor people or people who are raised in slums do not become offenders; unfavorable family atmosphere does not always lead to ciminality. Neither can it be shown that any other single social factor inevitably causes criminal behavior, which means that all single-factor theories of crime causation have been by and large invalidated.

In their search for theoretical explanations, and hopefully practical solutions for ciminality, certain criminologists have come up with more comprehensive theories of crime. Although these theories are helpful in bringing forth sociological considerations that were missing in more traditional, one-factor explanations, they, too, fall short of providing a sufficiently comprehensive frame of reference, as we shall see shortly.

## Differential Association

First presented in his 1937 book, *The Professional Thief*,[1] the theory of differential association was further expanded and summarized by Edwin H. Sutherland and his coauthor Donald R. Cressey.

1. Criminal behavior is learned, not inherited.
2. It is learned in interaction with other persons in a process of communication.
3. The principal part of the learning of criminal behavior occurs within intimate personal groups.
4. The learning of criminal behavior includes (a) techniques of committing the crime, and (b) the specific direction of motives, drives, rationalizations, and attitudes.
5. The specific direction of motives and drives is learned from definitions of the legal codes as favorable or unfavorable.
6. A person becomes delinquent because of an excess of definitions favorable to violation of law over definitions unfavorable to violations of law.[2]

Sutherland's theory is valuable for what it purports to do: to show that the subjection of the individual to criminal norms for a long period of time, and in the relative absence of law-supportive norms, will lead him to the acceptance and practice of those norms. What it does not explain is how these criminal norms are created and reinforced in the first place, and under what circumstances the criminal tendencies thus created are likely to lead to actual criminal behavior.

## Culture Conflict

A notable effort to study the role of culture on criminal behavior is reflected in Sellin's theory of culture conflict. Sellin does not investigate the impact of commonly shared cultural values on behavior; rather, he is concerned with the impact of the conflicts among various value systems on criminal behavior. Specifically, he is interested in the effect of cultural conflicts among different ethnic groups in the United States. His basic assumption, which is quite valid, is that in more complex societies, especially if the population is heterogeneous and composed of different immigrant groups that have their own distinctive mores and norms of behavior, cultural conflicts are certainly apt to arise. The cultural diversity, in turn, will result in diverse patterns of behavior that can cause actual conflicts among the different social groups. As Sellin explains it, "The more complex a culture becomes, the more likely it is that the number of normative groups which affect a person will be large, and the greater the chance that the norms of these groups will fail to agree, no matter how much they may overlap as a result of a common acceptance of certain norms."[3]

Sellin gives the example of a Sicilian father in New Jersey, who killed the sixteen-year-old seducer of his daughter and was amazed at being arrested for his act. In his mind he had acted only according to the dictates of his culture's code of honor, which required close relatives of a seduced girl to avenge the dishonor brought upon the family by killing the seducer. Sellin explains what he means by culture conflict and its ramifications:

Culture conflicts are the natural outgrowth of processes of social differentiation, which produce an infinity of social groupings, each with its own definitions of life situations, its own interpretations of social relationships, its own ignorance or misunderstanding of the social values of other groups. The transformation of a culture from a homogeneous and well-integrated type to a heterogeneous and disintegrated type is therefore accompanied by an increase of conflict situations.[4]

He further explains that conflicts between the norms of divergent cultural codes may arise:

1. when these codes clash on the border of contiguous culture areas;
2. when, as may be the case with legal norms, the law of one cultural group is extended to cover the territory of another; or
3. when members of one cultural group migrate to another.[5]

When a person acts according to the cultural norms and values of his own group, he is only conforming his behavior to ideals of his particular social environment, although his acts may happen to have been defined as criminal by dominant social groups.

Sellin's theory is a significant contribution to our understanding of the crime problem. His is perhaps the first outside the deterministic Marxist ideology to go beyond individual factors and superficial social arrangements to focus attention on the ideological bases and cultural values that maintain and support social institutions. His theory, however, fails to explain certain essential issues. We know, for instance, that conflict is inevitable in all complex, heterogeneous, and dynamic societies. We need a theory, however, to explain the process by which cultural conflicts in norms and values are translated into actualized criminal behavior. We know that in many societies diversity, inequality, and conflict are accepted as inevitable; the masses take the existing inequalities for granted. In such societies cultural conflict is seldom activated in the form of open defiance against the ruling classes. Thus, an important element missing in Sellin's analysis is how the public perceives and reacts to existing cultural and social conflicts.

Another problem, which I shall discuss more fully in the following pages, is that by focusing attention on cultural conflicts among various groups, we may inadvertently lose sight of the more commonly accepted social norms and values which may be criminogenic in nature.

## The Study of Subcultures

In the more recent sociological writings on crime, the concept of subculture has been used to distinguish between the cultural norms and values of different segments of the population. The valid assumption is that some of the norms and values belonging to particular groups may be at odds with those that are officially supported under threat of punishment. Thus, the theory goes, a person may be acting in comformity with the expectations of his subculture though he is considered an offender and punished by the criminal justice system. After Thrasher's classic study of the gang[6] several American criminologists have used the concept in studying the ways members of a particular group with a distinct subculture develop antisocial behavior patterns that are consistent with the requirements of the subculture.[7]

The concept of subculture is useful for understanding the differential influence of various groups and organizations on the behavior of their respective members. The concept is also helpful in focusing attention on the learning processes that take place in some partly isolated institutions, where standards and patterns of behavior that are officially defined as "criminal" or "abnormal" are routinely presented to the individual in the context of close interaction with other members of his group as natural and normal. However, we should be cautious that in concentrating on the parts and components, we do not lose sight of the nature and impact of the whole social order. We should keep in mind that the various subcultures that exist in a society are not entirely alien to one another or to the more common cultural values that dominate the whole society. The different subcultures essentially embody the norms and values of the more general culture, though they may give these common phenomena different interpretations and expressions.[8] The error to be avoided is that, for instance, in attributing violence to certain subcultures and their group members, we may forget that as several social scientists have documented, violence has always been a pervasive problem in the United States. In fact, the history of many events—the Gold Rush, railroads, labor unions, political parties, and police, to name a few—has been riddled with extreme violence.[9] To be sure, certain forms of violence are tolerated and condoned while others are severely punished. The fact remains, however, that we cannot understand the violence attributed to certain groups, or for that matter any kind of violence, without reference to the more pervasive cultural values that condone and in fact encourage violence.

## Anomie

A similar theory to our anaylsis of the role of frustration in causing criminal behavior, although as we shall see much more limited in scope, is offered by Robert Merton. Taking the concept of anomie from Emil Durkheim and extending its implication, Merton constructed his hypothesis, which in brief is as follows:

1. Success, measured by the amount of money and material possessions, is a strong value in American culture.
2. Everyone is encouraged to believe that, like every other person, he has a right to be successful, and that by trying his best, he will certainly achieve his goals.
3. Nevertheless, because of social conditions and economic realities, not everyone or every group possesses the required means to succeed; hence, anomie and crime.[10]

As Merton explains, "we have considered the emphasis on monetary success as one dominant theme in American culture, and have traced the strains which it differentially imposes upon those variously located in the social structure."[11] As Weber and others have shown, the success theme, even when it is measured in terms of material possessions, is not an exclusively American trait. Merton goes on to point out, "what makes American culture relatively distinctive in this regard . . . is that this is a society which places a high premium on economic affluence and social ascent for all its members."[12]

Modifying his original formulation in terms of the actual internalization of cultural values and the individual motivation for success, which is different in different social strata, he indicates that possible reactions to anomie are innovation, ritualism, retreatism, and rebellion. The first may be linked to the problem of crime and delinquency.[13]

Merton's theory, though valid at the level of analysis he has chosen, is open to several criticisms. As he explains:

Anomie is . . . conceived as a breakdown in the cultural structure, occuring particularly when there is an acute disjunction between the cultural norms and goals and the socially structured capabilities of members of the group to act in accord with them. In this conception, cultural values may help to produce behavior which is at odds with the mandates of the values themselves.

On this view, the social sturcture strains the cultural values, making action in accord with them readily possible for those occupying certain statuses within the society and difficult or impossible for others. The social structure acts as a barrier or as an open door to the acting out of cultural mandates. When the cultural and the social structure are malintegrated, the first calling for behavior and attitudes which the second precludes, there is a strain toward the breakdown of the norms, toward normlessness.[14]

The concept of anomie is useful as a possible explanation of at least certain types of criminal activity. There are, however, a few problems with the concept. On the theoretical level, the use of the concept anomie, in the context used by Merton, is arbitrary and out of line with the accepted meaning of the word. Anomie means normlessness; it occurs when, for various reasons, there are no definite sets of norms and values to guide the individual in his social activities. Merton's theory, on the contrary, pre-supposes a set of well-defined and dominant norms in American society, specifically those of success and achievement. What causes criminality, in Merton's view, is not normlessness or anomie, but rather lack of legitimate means for certain groups and individuals necessary to achieve the desired and clearly defined cultural objectives.

Another limitation of the theory is that, if viewed in the dynamic context of social life, it loses its potential as an explanatory concept. In other words, if enough people with enough frequency rejected the "success theme" as the sure consequence of hard work and the opportunity presumably available to everybody, as happened in the 1960s among several disillusioned groups, then the outcome may be quite different. That is to say, the disadvantaged who realize they cannot possibly achieve the culturally endorsed values of success and achievement may decide to reject the values, rather than engage in criminal activity to achieve them. To use Merton's own terminology, they may react by retreatism or revolution, rather than by innovation and deviance.

Still another limitation, conceded by Merton himself, is that the striving for material success is but one instance where a host of social situations put anomic pressure on the individual. In his words:

It will be remembered that we have considered the emphasis on monetary success as one dominant theme in American culture. . . . The theory holds that any extreme emphasis upon achievement . . . will attenuate conformity to the institutional norms governing behavior designed to achieve the particular form of "success." . . . It is the conflict between the cultural goals and the availability of using institutional means—whatever the character of the goals—which produces a strain toward anomie.[15]

My contention is that by focusing on the success theme, or its more comprehensive counterpart, extreme emphasis upon achievement, we unduly limit and divert our attention from various other social situations that may also lead to criminality. We have seen, for instance, that excessive emphasis on individual rights or freedoms may be disruptive and possibly criminogenic. If we try, by the stretch of imagination, to call such overemphasis on individual rights and interests in total disregard of corresponding duties and responsibilities an emphasis upon achievement and thus within the purview of the concept of anomie then obviously the concept becomes too general to be of practical value. Besides, one can easily think of numerous situations where the individual may be motivated to break the law or fight the social system, not because he wants to succeed materially or achieve any personal goal, but simply because he is outraged by the ills that are undeservedly visited upon his fellow human beings, by the widespread existence of inequality and injustice which makes a mockery of the constitutional and other pledges for the "inalienable rights" of the citizen. To cover such situations, as well as those called anomic by Merton, I believe the concept of frustration as analyzed by psychologists is much more useful.

## FRUSTRATION AND CRIME

Our basic premise is almost self-evident; except for extreme cases of involuntary criminal acts—kleptomania, for instance, or crimes committed to quench a strong feeling of guilt and need for punishment—we should look behind the criminal act to find the mentality and the motivation that drove the offender to his crime. Unless what we call a criminal act is widely accepted as normal behavior—the way, for instance, robbery was in ancient Sparta, or massive genocide is in times of war—the individual must somehow justify or rationalize for himself the offense he is committing. For the average individual who is brought up with the moral and legal values of his society, there must be a reason, an excuse, or a pretext to commit an act that may lead to punishment. I believe the underlying cause for such an excuse or justification is a sense of frustration. Even where a whole social group considers certain criminal acts as natural and normal, I believe that under the group's norms and values one can detect a sense of frustration, perhaps originally felt some generations ago and then translated into class consciousness. One feels the symbolic but strong belief in the ongoing war among the different interest groups and the breakdown in the basic legal premises—and promises—of the social system. Psychologists have shown that frustration normally leads to an appropriate reaction aimed at alleviating the source of the frustrating experience. This reaction may be expressed in the form of aggression, but as we shall see, depending on the sociocultural system and the personality structure of the individual, there may be other alternatives. When the needs of the individual remain unsatisfied, when there are obstacles (imagined or real) in the way of their satisfaction, the individual may experience a sense of frustration.

There are of course certain physical needs that must be provided if the individual's well-being or even life is to be preserved. Hunger, sex, and immunity from excessive heat or cold are among the most basic of such needs.[16] In addition, however, there are other needs that stem from the particular sociocultural heritage of each society. Such socially created "needs" may exist in one society and be irrelevant in another. However, once they are created and transmitted to the next generations, they acquire the same compelling force and urgency as the physical needs. We have learned about the people who, under social pressure, have been willing, even eager, to give up their lives, for instance for their country, to save their honor, to save the life or reputation of a lover, or otherwise to save face, simply because they are brought up to think of these risks as socially required. In fact, physical needs are also conditioned and controlled to a large extent by sociocultural considerations. There are accepted (or rejected) ways of satisfying one's need for food, sex, and security in every culture. Hindus don't kill cows to satisfy their hunger, and many starve to death. Pork and certain types of seafood are prohibited in Judaism and Islam. Sexual needs are satisfied within the monogamous family or in extramarital relationships in the West. In some other cultures, like the Muslim world or among devout Mormons, polygamous marriages are allowed. Temporary marriages without limitations as to number are also allowed and practiced in Shiite communities while extramarital relationships are strictly forbidden. Types of clothing and shelter are also determined by the culture and social conditions of each society. The variety of social needs and the means and methods of their satisfaction seem to be limitless. As Jules Henry states:

The fact that in stable cultures whatever is produced has a complementary need suggests the existence of a vast potential of human needs. For, after all, if in stable cultures all over the world almost every object, however bizarre it may seem to us, is found to have a complementary need, it is only common sense to suppose that human beings have the potential for developing an enormous variety of needs. If the Ashanti of West Africa, for example, need golden stools, the natives of the South American jungles need curare, intoxicating drugs, dyed parrots, feather cloaks, shrunken heads, and flutes several feet long; if the Incas of Peru needed fields of flowers made of silver and gold and the Kwakiutl Indians needed totem poles, slat armor, engraved copper plates six feet square, and painted cedar boxes inlaid with mother of pearl, one can realize without even looking at Greece, Rome, Babylon, Egypt, and modern America that human beings have the capacity to learn to want almost any conceivable material object.[17]

Frustration is a function of the number and intensity of the perceived needs and the expectation that they should and can be satisfied. Here, we must take note of a basic difference between the traditional Third World countries on the one hand and Western industrial societies on the other in terms of the perception of needs and the possibility of their satisfaction. In traditional agricultural societies, the needs and desires of the people, due to the marked limitation of resources, are likewise limited. In accordance with this seemingly inevitable state of affairs, the world outlook in such societies calls for moderation, control, self-denial, acceptance of one's social position, and active assistance to those who are less fortunate. In industrial societies, on the other hand, due to the presumed limitless capacity of the economic system to produce and the promise of abundance (which in many countries has been realized), people's desires and social needs have likewise become limitless. The corresponding mentality, which is necessary for the continuous material progress of industrial societies, assumes that the boundless needs and desires of the individual can be satisfied through hard work, perseverance, and cooperation with other human beings. In such societies, people are considered masters of their own destinies, and it is firmly believed that every individual can advance material status and social standing by hard work. The actualization of this world outlook, which is premised on the idea of boundless human potentialities, has taken different shapes in different industrial societies, but the consequence has been more or less the same: on the one hand, creation of high hopes and expectations in the individual; on the other, the eventual realization that the system can never fully satisfy those hopes. In less advanced societies, where expectations are lower, people seem to be more content, a fact that is puzzling to Westerners. In such countries even a partial satisfaction of basic human needs brings about a heart-felt sense of joy and satisfaction. As Durkheim puts it:

No matter how one acts, desires have to depend upon resources to some extent; actual possessions are partly the criterion of those aspired to. So the less one has the less he is tempted to extend the range of his needs indefinitely. Lack of power, compelling moderation, accustoms men to it, while nothing excites envy if no one has superfluity.[18]

This is not the case in industrial societies where the economic system in fact forces the public to desire more and buy constantly to make the continuous material advance of the system possible.

The perception that there is no limit to the human ability to produce is, of course, not limited to material things. It is a comprehensive world view that considers every human desire as legitimate and realizable within the system. And since people come to believe in their own powers as the supreme moving force behind every event, unbounded and limitless in effectiveness, their belief in the supernatural origins of morality weakens. Religious teachings, which in essence attempt to prevent people from engaging in excessive emotions and conduct, cease to exert much influence.

In modern industrial societies, "religion has lost most of its power."[19] In other words, religious and ethical values have been interpreted to correspond with the dictates of modern production systems. In any event, people began to think of their capacities as limitless and subject not to God's will, but to rules and regulations created by people themselves. They became aware of the social causes of inequality; they also began to desire more and to tolerate fewer restrictions.

In harmony with its sociocultural structure, every society develops a set of moral concepts that by and large rationalize the existence of frustration in individual life. In less developed countries, as I have pointed out, there is the religious belief that God has willed the poverty of the lower classes and prosperity of the rich. This inequality, it is explained, will be corrected and adjusted in the next world; the rich will be sent to Inferno, while the virtuous poor will live in perpetual joy and tranquillity in Paradise. Concomitant with this belief, most Eastern cultures hold the view that the world we live in is essentially wicked and full of disappointments for the righteous. Life on this planet is an illusion, and a bad one at that, a real nightmare for those who can see the truth. Obviously, in such a world outlook, frustration is normal. Thus, frustrating experiences, even of the most basic needs of hunger, sex, and shelter, do not produce strong reactions except for perhaps pathetic expressions of gloom, usually in the privacy of one's inner self, or even exaltation for those who feel they should accept their God-willed misery with gratitude and joy.

If the individual is less of a believer and strongly feels the frustration, then because of the sociocultural values he usually directs his aggressive tendencies against his own self. He may be plagued by all kinds of psychological morbidity, self-persecution, or drug addiction. In extreme cases he may commit suicide. Because of the particular cultural perceptions, normally no external agent or agents are blamed for individual frustrations; no aggressive reaction is initiated against those who rule the country or control the riches. Thus, other factors being equal, there is less crime in such societies, because the misery of individual experience is normally attributed to the will of God and acceteped as inevitable. In this context, incidentally, the overall inertia of developing countries can be understood as well as the existence of extreme injustice and inequality and seemingly puzzling contentment of the masses.

In modern industrial societies frustration is no longer explained in fatalistic terms. As a matter of fact, it has become axiomatic in these countries that every human being has the right to be free from all needs, to develop his full potential. In the American Declaration of Independence, as was pointed out before, the right to the pursuit of happiness is also recognized. It is only natural, therefore, that in a society that stimulates endless social needs and leads the people to believe that they have an unalienable right to happiness and satisfaction of all their desires, the amount of frustration should be much greater than in more traditional developing countries. And if, as we shall see, frustration can lead to criminal behavior under certain conditions, again it is only natural that the scope and intensity of criminal activity should be much greater in Western industrial societies, especially in the United States.

American criminologists have noted that among certain ethnic groups, second-generation immigrants (children born in America of immigrant parents) commit relatively more crimes than the native-born Americans. The reason often given is that the immigrant parents, who have a low social status and are divested of their parental authority, lose control over the behavior of their children.[20] Although it is true that immigrant parents can no longer exercise as much parental authority in American society as they did in their old culture with this society's emphasis on freedom and autonomy of the individual, nevertheless the theory does not explain fully why the second-generation immigrant is more inclined to engage in criminal activity. Aside from the possible lack of parental authority which neutralizes the role immigrant parents could play in shaping the behavior of their children, there must be some positive factors that lead the immigrant children to criminal activity. The clue, I believe, lies in the highly aroused expectations of second-generation Americans. When immigrants come to this country, they are usually fleeing adverse economic or social conditions. They may suffer much hardship in America, but they are more or less content, because they do not expect too much from their new life here. In fact even the worst of conditions in this country seem preferable to what they used to put up with in their own. Immigrants as a whole are, therefore, grateful for what they get and careful not to lose these new opportunities. Under the circumstances it makes sense to abide by the laws. Children born in America of immigrant parents, however, are exposed to the same cultural values as any other child. They think of themselves as Americans and grow to develop the same type of expectations as every other person in this society. The lowly economic and social position of the parents, however, does not allow for the satisfaction of all their socially stimulated needs, or the acquisition of knowledge and skills required for success, or the display of material possessions, regarded so highly, especially in the context of their parents' previous cultural upbringing and aspirations. Hence, frustration in second-generation Americans, as compared with their parents and other Americans who may be better equipped to satisfy their needs, increases. And as we shall see later, frustration can turn into criminal activity under suitable social conditions.

## SOURCES OF FRUSTRATION

As was pointed out before, frustration occurs when our needs and desires are obstructed. Most of the needs, however, are created by society. They are also quite varied; they can be psychological as well as physical. In fact, whenever there is any strong expectation that is not fulfilled, the individual, all other things being equal, will experience frustration.

Sometimes frustration is caused by expectations associated with learning and assumption of social roles. Each social group has its own rules and procedures to initiate new members within its ranks, and some of the demands put on the aspirants to membership may be quite frustrating. Depending on the nature of the activities of each group, expectations imposed on the individual may be self-indulgent or self-restraining as regards violation of social norms and standards. There are also more permeating expectations that stem from the general structure of social relations; they, too, may involve frustrating experiences for the individual. Here we will study only a few of these experiences related to the assumption of social roles.

## Learning the Professions

In traditional societies, learning the professions, crafts, and various occupations takes place in an informal manner within the intimate surrounding of the family circle and/or village shop. A prospective baker learns the craft by watching and helping his father or mother bake bread. A blacksmith, shoemaker, tailor, and other craftsmen likewise teach their children their skills in practical situations. For the growing child the transition from a dependent member of the family to a competent breadwinner, or someone who has acquired the necessary skills to assume a productive social role, is quite smooth and takes place in gradual stages. Then, there are certain rites of passage that initiate the young members of society to the assumption of adult social roles and positions.

In more advanced industrial societies, on the other hand, because of the increasing complexity and sophistication of occupational roles, job training no longer takes place within the family circle or the village shop. It is carried out through specialized educational institutions, which are a far cry from the intimate day-to-day relationship and cooperation of the family or village life. Because the acquisition of certain more lucrative occupational skills is highly involved and desired, there is a tremendous amount of competition and with it a highly charged emotional atmosphere, tension and conflict, fear of failure, and frustration. Furthermore, in highly developed industrial societies, a person cannot after a certain age depend on continuous financial support of his parents or other members of the family. Therefore, frustrating experiences become doubly intolerable. This feeling of frustration associated with the assumption of adult roles and occupations is so strong that certain criminologists have considered it the basic cause of juvenile delinquency in America. Bloch and Niederhoffer, for example, state:

The adolescent period in all cultures, visualized as a phase of striving for the attainment of adult status, produces experiences which are much the same for all youths, and certain common dynamisms for expressing reaction to such subjectively held experiences. The intensity of the adolescent experience and the vehemence of external expression depend on a variety of factors, including the general societal attitudes toward adolescence, the duration of the adolescent period itself, and the degree to which the society tends to facilitate entrance into adulthood by virtue of institutionalized patterns, ceremonials, rites, and rituals, and socially supported emotional and intellectual preparation. When a society does not make adequate preparation, formal or otherwise, for the induction of its adolescents to the adult status, equivalent forms of behavior arise spontaneously among adolescents themselves, reinforced by their own group structure, which seemingly provides the same psychological content and function as the more formalized rituals found in other societies. This the gang structure appears to do in American society, apparently satisfying deep-seated needs experienced by adolescents in all cultures.[21]

## Masculine Identification and Crime

Another theory that attempts to explain juvenile delinquency as a consequence of frustration associated with the attainment of social roles focuses on the difficulties American boys normally feel in identifying with a masculine figure in their family. Talcott Parsons, for example, asserts that the structure of the American family and the sharp differentiation between occupational roles and kinship responsibilities of the father make it very difficult for American boys to develop masculine traits and characteristics naturally. The requirements of occupational roles, which have become much more sophisticated, keep the father preoccupied with interests outside the home and leave the mother as the most significant person in the family. She makes all the important decisions affecting every family member. The relative absence of the father from the family and the consequent weakening of his status make him an unfit model for identification, thus depriving American male children of the opportunity to develop skills, attitudes, mannerisms, and characteristics associated in American culture with the masculine image. Because of this faulty identification with a masculine model, according to a number of criminologists, some youngsters join gangs. They overreact to their basic sense of masculine ineptitude by acting tough, by engaging in fights and other types of antisocial activity, which are the identifying mark of delinquent groups in America. The process is described by Parsons as follows:

> Our kinship situation, it has been noted, throws children of both sexes overwhelmingly upon the mother as the emotionally significant adult. In such a situation, "identification" in the sense that the adult becomes a "role model" is the normal result. For a girl this is normal and natural, not only because she belongs to the same sex as the mother, but because the functions of housewife and mother are immediately before her eyes and are tangible and relatively easily understood by a child. . . . Thus the girl has a more favorable opportunity for emotional maturing through positive identification with an adult model, a fact which seems to have much to do with the well-known earlier maturity of girls. The boy, on the other hand, has a tendency to form a direct feminine identification, since his mother is the model most readily available and significant to him. But he is not destined to become an adult woman. Moreover he soon discovers that in certain vital respects women are considered inferior to men, that it would hence be shameful for him to grow up like a woman. Hence when boys emerge into what Freudians call the "latency period," their behavior tends to be marked by a kind of "compulsive masculinity." They refuse to have anything to do with girls. "Sissy" becomes the

worst of insults. They get interested in athletics and physical prowess, in the things in which men have the most primitive and obvious advantage over women. Furthermore, they become allergic to all expression of tender emotion; they must be "tough." This universal pattern bears all the earmarks of a "reaction formation." It is so conspicuous, not because it is simply "masculine nature," but because it is a defense against a feminine identification.[22]

Parsons remarks that the structure of the American family system and the relative absence of a masculine model at home results in "a strong tendency for boyish behavior to run in anti-social if not directly destructive directions, in striking contrast to that of pre-adolescent girls."[23] Parsons does not himself claim that this lack of identification with a masculine figure is the cause of juvenile delinquency. The task of assuming such a causal link has fallen on others who, on the basis of similar observations, have attempted to present a general theory of juvenile delinquency. Both Cohen and Miller, for example, claim that the problem of masculine identification can be a source of criminal behavior; both also suggest that the problem is essentially confined to lower-class boys.[24]

## FROM FRUSTRATION TO CRIME

To understand the crime problem, it is not enough to illustrate, as these theories have attempted to do, situations and processes that may engender frustration. It may be quite true, for example, that the youth in a particular society suffer from the feeling of deprivation and frustration associated with the ambiguity or difficulty of practices that are required for the attainment of social or occupational roles. However, they may or may not resort to criminal activity, depending on other sociocultural factors. In order to understand the processes that can lead to criminality, we also have to know what factor or factors cause the frustrated individual to channel his aggressive reactions into various forms of criminal activity.

Depending on personal and sociocultural factors in a society, reaction to frustration can take any of the several different forms. From one extreme where aggression is openly and violently directed against other persons or objects, to the other extreme where it is directed against the self in different degrees of self-persecution culminating in suicide, we can think of various other outlets, some of which are socially sponsored and endorsed, through which frustration can be minimized and emotional equilibrium restored. In this process of transformation of frustration into possible forms of reaction, one factor is always significant: whether or not the frustrated individual feels justified in attacking the social structure and the legal norms that support it. Certainly, the growth of personality through the process of socialization requires constant renunciation or postponement of the gratification of needs and desires. By growing up in various social institutions, we learn to maintain certain restrictions on our tendencies and wishes. But the renunciation or postponement of these needs and desires—which, by the way, is the main source of the development of attitudes consistent with the respect for law and order—is premised on the basic assumption that the social system that imposes such deprivations is just and impartial. The assumption is, of course, subjective, and the belief in justice does not necessarily correspond with what actually happens in society. It is a state of mind, which changes with the scope of social awareness. A slave may feel that his condition is just because his race is inferior to that of his master. The poor masses (as is true in many parts of the world) may accept their destiny, even be content, because they feel that it is the will of God, and that they will be amply compensated in the next world for their misery here. On the other hand, a successful businessman in an industrial society may still feel victimized because of his aroused expectations or consciousness of the existing inequalities in the distribution of wealth among different classes and individuals. To the latter, the existing social system may seem utterly unjust. In any case, the smooth functioning of the social system is based on the subjective feeling that the system is essentially just and equitable. Therefore, if the majority of the people in Western democracies for any reason cease to think that the sociopolitical system is just, then problems of all sorts, including criminal activity and even revolution, will probably arise. Without going into detail, Durkheim has the following to say about the subjective element involved in the maintenance of law and order in society:

As a matter of fact, at every moment of history there is a dim perception, in the moral consciousness of societies, of the respective value of different social services, the relative reward due to each, and the consequent degree of comfort appropriate on the average to workers in each occupation. The different functions are graded in public opinion and a certain coefficient of well-being assigned to each, according to its place in the hierarchy. According to accepted ideas, for example, a certain way of living is considered the upper limit to which a workman may aspire in his efforts to improve his existence, and there is another limit below which he is not willingly permitted to fall unless he has seriously demeaned himself.[25]

The acceptance of the existing arrangements for the distribution of values depends, then, on the tacit or explicit assumption that the social system is just. Otherwise, the enacted laws, traditions, customs, and social forces that help maintain the stability of the system cannot long withstand the pressures of discontent, of frustration turned into compensatory reactions.

When [the moral discipline which regulates desires and needs] is maintained only by custom and force, peace and harmony are illusory; the spirit of unrest and discontent are latent; appetites superficially restrained are ready to revolt. This happened in Rome and Greece when the faiths underlying the old organization of the patricians and plebians were shaken, and our modern societies when aristocratic prejudices began to lose their old ascendancy.[26]

The industrial revolution and the material progress of the West have been achieved with the corresponding rise in human social awareness that rejects God's responsibility for shaping human destiny on earth, questions the legitimacy of existing social orders, and claims equal rights and opportunity for all to realize their human potentials. It is, thus, possible to see the role assigned by many moral thinkers to the weakening of religious beliefs as a potent cause of increased criminal activity. It should be noted, however, that it is not only the question of the decline in the effectiveness of ethical rules, associated in many cultures with religion, in controlling human behavior. More importantly, it is the transformation in religious thought that does not regard God's will as the prime source of a person's social position that has caused the idea of "justness" to be measured in terms of observable, man-made social relations. In other words, the justness of the system, which in most religions is taken for granted as being willed by supernatural forces, has become open to questioning and critical doubt. This in turn has increased expectations, and with it the level of frustration.

In modern societies, the distribution of wealth, power, and other social values and the maintenance of the social system and of law and order are achieved through the machinery of government. It is through government that laws are enacted and enforced. These laws either maintain or change the distribution of social values. It is also the government that uses the police, the courts, punishment, and other official means of social control to protect and safeguard the existing socioeconomic structure of society. It is natural, therefore, that the government should be identified with the dominant interests realized through the existing social structure and blamed for all the shortcomings in the nature and practice of social interaction. Thus, it can be presumed that as long as government or the political system is conceived to be just or legitimate, criminal activity will remain at a relative minimum. But if citizens doubt the legitimacy of the political system for any reason, they may choose to direct their aggression against the apparatus of the state or any of its manifestations. Hence, as we noted before, the attribute of legitimacy of the functioning of government is important for the study and understanding of crime. We should also take note that depending on how vulnerable people have become to foreign political propaganda, especially the type that blames every conceivable evil on the imperialist or capitalist nature of government in the West, the tendency to violate the existing rules and standards in Western democracies may intensify.

Whether the individual chooses to withdraw allegiance to the political system by denying it the attribute of legitimacy, and in case of such withdrawal, whether he chooses to commit a crime or tries to find other outlets for his aggression, depend on certain other personal and social factors. We will first discuss the personal factors that may be responsible for such a choice; then we will consider the effect of the legal system on crime. Finally, we shall see how the presence or absence of other alternatives for the discharge of aggression in society can be of crucial importance in lessening the need to resort to criminal activity.

## Personality Factors

Scientists do not agree on the actual extent of the impact of hereditary factors in shaping a person's patterns of behavior. We know, however, that individuals differ in their reactions to outside stimuli in accordance with certain distinguishable characteristics. Knowledge of such characteristics can be helpful in forecasting the type of crime an individual is likely to commit. It is also useful for classification and treatment of criminal offenders. Jung's typologies of introverts and extroverts, for example, can be used in recognizing and predicting the nature and type of criminal and noncriminal activities of particular individuals. The introvert, who is more pensive and basically seeks satisfaction in his inner self, is on the whole less likely to engage in the type of activity—criminal or noncriminal—that requires human contact and deeper emotional involvement. The typical embezzler, con man, and defrauder is almost always the gregarious, outgoing, and sociable individual who is likely to enjoy the sympathy of victims before or even after the commission of the crime.

The tendency to act in a particular manner may also be socially conditioned. If we agree with Riesman that Americans are other-directed and acquire their values and standards of behavior from their peer groups, then it follows that in general Americans are affected more readily by changes in their social environment.[27] Peer groups, as carriers of constant change and innovation in this country, exert very strong pressure on their members to conform. If an American youth, for instance, finds himself in a college dormitory where smoking marijuana is widely practiced, he will be pressured to conform if he wants to gain the friendship and respect of other dormitory occupants. The same pressure to conform also applies to criminal gangs, as well as other groups. In contrast, an Indian or Japanese youth, being bound and pressured by traditions of his culture and hence being more responsive to the norms and expectations of his family and other social groups, is more likely to resist the temptations presented by deviant groups.

To understand what goes on in the mind of the offender when he ventures on the path to criminal activity, the psychoanalytic explanation of personality dynamics can be very helpful. As Freud himself pointed out, we should not consider the tripartite division of personality into id, ego and superego as definitive or rigid. We can use the concepts, however, to distinguish between the conflicting tendencies that may go on in the human mind. Among the three, the id is the unchangeable, basic driving force that pressures the individual to gratify his physical needs. It is out of this life force, through the influence of parents and other important individuals, that the other two components of personality, the ego and superego are gradually formed. The ego is the social self, the part of the personality that is in contact with the realities of the outside world and which, at the same time, tries to harmonize the conflicting demands of the superego and the id. The ego embodies the actual norms of social behavior, while the superego reflects the moral values of society as a whole. The superego, in Freud's theory, rejects the uncontrolled drives of the id, while the ego either tries to gratify them in a modified form that is acceptable to the superego, or else suppresses them altogether and forbids their actualization.

What is visible and important in the day-to-day activity of the individual is his ego or social self. How the person acts or abstains from acting depends on the strength of the ego. If a strong ego is formed in the individual, it will guard him against committing what is considered improper or wrong. With the development of a strong ego, the individual becomes to a large extent the master of his own actions and will be guided in his behavior by the demands of the outside world (the "reality principle") and of his own conscience.

What is important and has not been explicitly discussed by Freud, who uncritically regarded the ego as the embodiment only of positive, constructive norms and values, is the fact that both the contents and the process of ego development may vary from family to family according to the family's socioeconomic position and class orientations. On a more general level, the contents and structure of the ego are also created and conditioned by the cultural values and expectations of each particular society. As we saw before, American society, for example, under the influence of relativism, pragmatism, and their popular interpretations, as well as psychoanalytical teachings—which for various reasons have become more dominant here than in other countries and decry the terrible effects of suppression of instincts on the behavior and mental well-being of the individual—has adopted a much more permissive attitude toward education at home, in school, and through the mass media. The educational philosophy emphasizes the positive aspects of freedom without stressing the requirements of discipline and restraint for the development of healthy personalities. This one-sided emphasis has resulted in the creation of a family atmosphere where the child is free to do virtually anything he wants without being sufficiently guided or controlled by the parents. The same permissive philosophy is also followed in American schools where the teacher is deprived of the power and responsibility of imparting to the students the respected moral values and convictions that could serve as guidelines for individual and social action. The school prayer cases, which are laudable in preventing the forcing of any particular religious belief on the suggestible mind of the child, show at the same time the serious dilemma that American society faces in not educating the young in any system of social morality. Another problem of the educational system, like that of the family, is lack of sufficient discipline, which has come to be regarded by certain educated classes as only a tool for the regimentation of the mind and the development of authoritarian personalities. The effect of these developments, as far as we are concerned, is the emergence of a weak ego, lack of self-discipline, defiance of all authority and uncritical submission to the demands of one's own wishes and desires.

The third component of personality, the superego, is also insufficiently scrutinized in Freud's theory. To him, the contents of the superego are uniform and unchanging in everyone, incorporating and reflecting the moral values of the society at large, as if these values were a set of invariable, uniform standards. In his way of thinking, therefore, the superego is always opposed to the inclinations of the id; it pressures the ego to act in accordance with the individual's moral convictions, which in Freud's theory are synonymous with those of the family and society.

Thanks to the teachings of the New Freudians, sociologists, and anthropologists, we now realize that the structure and content of the superego vary according to life experiences of the individual, moral values of the family, school, and reference groups, and the basic teachings and assumptions of the culture. If, for instance, the individual is brought up in a family atmosphere where stealing from others is deemed legitimate and even praised as an indication of a clever mind, his superego will be formed on this basis. It will not prevent him from stealing if his ego decides that it is worth taking the risk. Again, on the cultural level, we know that the general traditions and moral values of a culture are reflected in people's conscience. Thus, an average individual living under the influence of a culture which, for instance, praises individual competitiveness or allows sexual license, will not experience remorse, other things being equal, if he indulges in such activities. It is very important, therefore, to study culture in order to understand the basic moral values which have such a strong impact on human attitudes and behavior.

Compared with American children, a European child receives much more discipline at home and school. He learns early in life that he is expected to behave in a certain manner in each particular situation, to respect rules and regulations, and will receive punishment if he does not act according to the demands and expectations of his society. The same perception is reinforced—perhaps even more severely—in school, where the demand for discipline, self-restraint, and obedience to authority is strictly enforced. The result is that as a general rule European children are much more disciplined and controlled.

The culturally imposed barriers to unfettered freedom of feeling and expression can conceivably prevent, to some extent, the development of the child's creative abilities. It should be stressed, however, that constructive creativity requires at least as much self-discipline as it does freedom of expression. No creative endeavor in the arts, literature, or science has ever come to fruition without hard work, perseverance, and discipline.

The child's experience of discipline and expectation of negative reaction in case of disobedience can play a significant role in mitigating the crime problem. However, in the child's subjective world, the association of crime (wrongful act) with punishment (negative reaction of parents and teachers) as cause and effect will be sensed only if the sequence is experienced consistently and enough times at home and in school and is further reinforced by other agencies. If this happens, then in the adult (unless he is pathological) the anticipatory sensation of punishment tends to discourage any activity associated with painful memories and identified as morally reprehensible.

It should be noted here that the introduction and teaching in schools of materials directly related to law and law enforcement (books, movies, and so on) and particularly, actual favorable contacts with law enforcement agencies (such as a visit to a police station or courts) will have a positive impact on the child's mind and encourage him to respect the law and its agents. From the time of Plato to the present, and especially with Freud's deep insights into the human psyche, the great impact of childhood training and education on adult behavior has been amply documented, and many European societies take advantage of such possibilities to educate the young to respect and observe the laws.

## The Law-Enforcement Apparatus Affecting Crime

A strong ego that has been conditioned to respect the legal norms and social arrangements still needs continuous reinforcement from outside forces to keep it immune from temptations. The law-enforcement apparatus as the most salient and powerful agent of social control, can be used to reinforce the basic attitudes needed for the spread of respect for individual rights, public safety, law, and order. To achieve this objective, however, the apparatus, which includes all law-enforcement agencies—police, courts, and penal institutions—must function in a proper manner to strengthen and reinforce the much advertised and deeply felt conviction that crime will almost invariably end in some sort of punishment. If the criminal justice system does not convey this message, it certainly does not give support to the law-abiding or alarm the deviant ego. Its impact in creating expectation of punishment for specific acts is almost nonexistent; actually it may have the opposite effect, indicating, by nonaction or inefficiency, that crime does not necessarily result in punishment. Bearing this fact in mind, it is interesting to note that Beccaria, who has had more impact than anybody else on the reform of criminal law, considered the certainty of punishment, not its severity, to be the important factor in deterring prospective offenders from engaging in criminal activity.[28]

The matter is of course more complex when considered in the light of differing social conditions. A very repressive police force, for instance, may have a stronger effect by strengthening the subjective association between crime and punishment. However, such a force will also entail the suppression of all human potentialities.

Courts, likewise, can act with haste, convicting the accused without sufficient regard for rights and arranging for quick punishment. This would shorten the interval between the commission of a crime and suffering of punishment, thus reinforcing the subjective crime-punishment association. However, legitimate concern for individual rights and realization of the enormous damage improper court practices can cause to society has compelled the judicial system in democratic countries to act cautiously, deliberately, and according to due process requirements. Between the extreme example of the police state, which is obviously repugnant to all free spirits, and the exaggerated concern for judicial technicalities that at times ignores the rights of the victim and the general public, there remains a vast margin where proper functioning of the police and the courts can have a tremendous influence on public attitudes and sentiments concerning law and order. This margin cannot be demarcated precisely; any decision as to the advantages and disadvantages of prompt judicial action against crime, with due respect for the rights of the public, will have to depend on various sociocultural factors. It is much easier, therefore, to specify the negatives, that is, some of the obstacles to an efficient criminal justice system. The police, for instance, would have a much better chance of detecting criminal activity within the bounds created by the law, if they were better trained for their official duties, were better motivated to administer those duties conscientiously (and here a host of factors, including financial considerations, but more importantly subjective and social considerations, such as the policeman's perception of his official role and the response of others to his activities, will have a strong bearing on his behavior), and if they enjoyed the emotional support, or better yet, the actual cooperation of the public.

Likewise, a court system that is plagued by an overload of cases and consequently functions with unjustifiable delays, that has a low morale (because of financial and/or psychological considerations), must labor under a system that is not conducive to the discovery of truth or labors under the influence of confused and contradictory ideologies, will certainly lose face in the eyes of the public and accordingly will not enjoy the public's understanding, support, respect, and cooperation. The same argument pertains to other areas of the law-enforcement process. If imprisonment, probation, and parole practices meet with the understanding and approval of the public, the belief in the justice of the system and the need to obey the laws will be enhanced. If, on the other hand, these institutions function, or seem to function, in an inefficient, unjust, or inconsistent manner, then their effectiveness as likely forces for the deterrence or rehabilitation of offenders will diminish.

## Sociocultural Factors: Alternative Outlets for Aggression

In every society, there are established ways of reducing the aggressive tendencies of the public caused by frustrating experiences. The nature of the means and methods for the release of aggressive tendencies varies in different societies. The following description attempts a partial listing of such alternative outlets for aggression.

*Political democracy.* In societies where the public takes part in the decisionmaking process, either directly or indirectly through election of public officials, a large amount of pent-up aggression is dissipated by means of political activity. Whether the public actually has control over the distribution of social values or casts its vote believing that it does, is mostly irrelevant to our present concern. As long as people believe that they make the choices, the result is socially positive. When the people identify a public official as the cause of some social ill or as someone who has not fulfilled his promises and vote him out of office, this act of rejection decreases the amount of their aggression and frustration. This healthy mechanism is totally lacking in totalitarian regimes and personal dictatorships where the public is forced to put up with the policies adopted by the ruler. In such societies aggressive tendencies, grown out of frustration with the political system and the bureaucracy, stay within the individual citizen who will therefore have to look for other possible outlets.

*Social outlets for release.* Many cultures have institutionalized means for the innocuous release of aggression. In such societies, people are allowed, at special times of the year, to break some of the social restrictions, to engage freely in otherwise illegal sexual acts, feasting, dancing, consumption of alcohol or drugs, and other activities that use up a great deal of suppressed aggression. The Mardi Gras festivities in Brazil, the "panty raids" in some American colleges, the 14th of July in France, and various wine and beer "fests" in most European countries come to mind as examples of such institutionalized outlets for aggression.

*Sports activities.* The physical participation in various sports—boxing, football, jogging, and many more—or the vicarious participation by means of identification with team players or other individuals who are directly involved, has the therapeutic effect of releasing pent-up energy. Thus, physical activity has been recommended by many therapists in treating psychological problems. On the same basis, some authorities have tried to defend the showing of violence on television, arguing that people who are aggressive in nature can achieve vicarious satisfaction and emotional release by watching such programs without having to commit the violent act themselves.

As a matter of fact, some have suggested that watching a person get murdered on television has the valuable function of draining off aggressive energy.[29] Many authorities, however, question the scientific validity of such assertions. Studies on modeling, for instance, have shown that children, and to a lesser extent adults, learn their behavior from models in their environment and that the effects of such learning will endure in time. Albert Bandura and his associates have shown that seeing another person behave aggressively can increase the aggressive behavior in children, even though they may have no frustrating experience themselves.[30] Psychologists Robert Liebert and Robert Baron, after surveying the available evidence in their report to the surgeon general, state that "of eighteen studies on this issue, sixteen support the notion that watching violence increases subsequent aggression among observers."[31] The social psychologist Elliot Aronson summarizes the findings:

The evidence suggests that violence on TV is potentially dangerous, in that it serves as a model for behavior—especially for children. And what do we see on TV? In the fall of 1969, George Gerbner and his associates conducted an exhaustive survey of television programming during prime time and on Saturday mornings. He found that violence prevailed in eight out of every ten plays. Moreover, the rate of violent episodes was eight per program hour. Cartoons—which are the favorite viewing matter of most young children—contain the most violence. Of the ninety-five cartoon plays analyzed in this study, only one did not contain violence.[32]

Is it possible that watching violence on televison is not a cause of subsequent aggressive behavior, that only children who already have a violent nature enjoy viewing violence on television? Controlled experiments tend to refute this possibility.

In one study Liebert and Baron exposed a group of subjects to a TV production of the "The Untouchables," an extremely violent cops-and-robbers type of program. In a control condition, a similar group of children were exposed to a TV production of a highly action-oriented sporting event for the same length of time. The children were then allowed to play in another room with a group of other children. Those who had watched the violent TV program showed far more aggression against the other children than those who had watched the sporting event.[33]

What is happening to television programs in view of the mounting evidence that confirms the destructive impact of violent films on children and adults? Is the showing of violence somehow limited? Apparently not. "(In) 1975 it was estimated that, by age 15, the average child will have witnessed more than 15,000 killings on TV."[34]

*Sublimation.* Psychoanalysis has shown that basic human drives can be

sublimated and satisfied on an elevated level. Daydreaming, wishful thinking, and all artistic activity may be used as substitutes for channeling frustration into aggressive behavior. The melancholic and neurotic life of
Tchaikovsky, for example, is reflected and expressed in his music, which
to a large extent diminished the impact of his miseries and disappointing
experiences. Aggression can be sublimated and dispersed through the medium of music as also in Shostakovitch, for instance, or Beethoven or
creative activity in the realms of painting, poetry, drama, and other arts.
Sublimation can be used fully as an alternative to physical aggression, however, where and when a culture is advanced enough to allow and encourage
artistic expression. Nevertheless, even in the so-called primitive cultures,
the process can take place as exemplified in rudimentary forms of mythol-
ogy, folklore, music, and other arts. The horror stories of gods waging
terrible wars against the Devil, or vice versa, may provide opportunities
for people to participate vicariously in aggressive behavior and thus to get
rid of some of their own aggression. The point is that in addition to the
creative artist who transforms his frustration into various art forms, the
ungifted masses can also benefit vicariously from the creative process by
watching, hearing, or imitating the art work.

In more restrictive cultures, where some artistic activities and showing
of any unfavorable sentiment toward the father figures are strictly forbidden,
people's aggressive tendencies may find outlets in other socially accepted
forms of behavior. Such acts may seem innocuous at face value but actually
convey (in a concealed manner) a great deal of frustration, bitterness, and
anger. Jokes and gossip, for instance, are favorite means of aggression
discharge in many societies. They are tolerated or even endorsed because
they have some functionally positive effects. One also learns in the culture
how to deal with them when exposed to their vicious sting. Other factors
being equal, such intricate and concealed forms of aggression obviously
play an important role in keeping the frustrated public within legal bounds
by reducing, to a large extent, the need for overt aggression.

In an insightful article first published in 1943, Hortense Powdermaker
tried to show how aggressive tendencies of American Blacks were channeled
through cultural processes into socially innocuous behavior.[35] Because of
the fear of the most severe kind of punishment—cutting of the ear, whip-
ping, castration, death by mutilation—Black slaves learned fast not to commit any act that could displease the masters. Even after their officially
announced liberation from slavery, Blacks had a very low social standing
in society, and they were still fearful of what the white population could
do to them. Thus, they realized instinctively that any direct expression of
aggression in the face of tremendous frustrations was still dysfunctional.
They therefore developed other mechanisms that were socially harmless.
By these means they could get rid of their frustrations. In fact, they sublimated both their frustrations and the consequent aggressive tendencies.

They chose one or several of the following channels for this purpose: substituting a Black object for the release of their aggression, meaning that they would commit crimes against Blacks instead of whites; retreat to an "ivory tower," cutting off from social realities (this was a difficult task and hence rarely used as a substitute); diversion of aggression into wit, a mechanism clearly observable in Black comedy stars but also in other Blacks; and finally, showing a meek and unassuming composure with the help of the Christian doctrine that preaches love and affection in the face of enmity and cruelty. The aggressive tendencies of Blacks, which were suppressed because of social pressures with the help of the religious doctrine, created an unconscious feeling of guilt toward the white population—the real objects of hate—and thus made Blacks even meeker and more accommodating toward whites. The religious doctrine was also satisfying in another way: it gave the promise of future reward for the suffering of Blacks in this world. "The last shall be first, and the first shall be last" and "The meek shall inherit the earth." Of course, increasing social awareness was reflected at first in higher rates of criminality among Blacks. This increased crime rate was an expression of the frustration-aggression sequence, frustration that was not sublimated as much as before and was directly activated in aggressive behavior. At the same time, social awareness of Blacks opened up other productive channels of creativity, a process that is still at its initial stages and should expand in scope and intensity with the passage of time.

*Work.* Certain professions—butchery, surgery, law, and literary criticism, to give just a few examples—provide other socially accepted channels for aggression discharge. Presumably, the butcher and the surgeon by cutting and the lawyer and the critic by engaging in heated arguments get rid of their frustration. As a matter of fact, however, every kind of creative work can have a therapeutic effect in discharging extra energy (physical or mental) and in maintaining psychological equilibrium in the individual. The depression caused by unemployment is not simply the result of the loss of one's security and source of income. More importantly perhaps, unemployment is also felt as a threat to the psychological integrity of the individual. A similar devastating effect can be observed in many people at the time of their retirement from active work, when their habitual means of creative activity are taken away and alternative channels for the discharge of extra energy are not readily available to them.

*Self-directed aggression.* When a considerable amount of frustration exists in a society and the resulting aggression is not dissipated through any of the socially approved alternative channels, the sufferer will have two avenues of reaction left. If his social self or ego is weak and vulnerable and especially when there are tangible exterior causes to justify the withdrawal of his allegiance to the political system, he may engage in criminal activity. If, on the other hand, he has developed a strong ego and is conscious of and responsive to positive social pressures, he may turn the frustration-induced aggression inward and gradually or quickly hurt himself. The reversion of aggression against the self may take different forms, depending on cultural values and social standards. The individual may become addicted to alcohol or drugs. Many cultures approve such addiction and in a way encourge it, because they recognize, perhaps unconsciously, its functional importance for maintaining the existing social system. In extreme cases the individual may even commit suicide. Again, because of the functional utility of suicide in strengthening the social system, many cultures have sanctioned it under special circumstances. In still other cultures, the introjected aggression may take the seemingly less harmful form of totally or partially paralyzing the creative potentials of the individual. In Middle Eastern countries, for instance, indifference, cynicism, fatalism, laziness, and similar traits may result from the great amount of frustration that is felt individually but because of the sociopolitical atmosphere cannot be directed against forces outside the individual.

Obviously, a society will be more easily subjected to criminal activity, other factors being equal, proportionally as the chances for rechanneling aggressive tendencies into socially harmless alternatives decrease. Conversely, when there are not enough opportunities for the discharge of aggression by socially endorsed means and practices, the chances for the commission of crimes will increase.

## NOTES

1. *The Professional Thief*, by a Professional Thief, annotated and interpreted by Edwin H. Sutherland (Chicago: University of Chicago Press, Phoenix Books, 1965), pp. 206–209.

2. Edwin H. Sutherland and Donald R. Cressey, *Criminology*, 8th ed. (Philadelphia, J. B. Lippincott Company, 1970), p. 75.

3. Thorsten Sellin, *Culture, Conflict and Crime* (New York: Social Science Research Council, 1938), p. 29.

4. Ibid., pp. 63–70.

5. Ibid., p. 63.

6. Frederic M. Thrasher, *The Gang: A Study of 1,313 Gangs in Chicago* (Chicago: University of Chicago Press, 1926).

7. See for example, Albert K. Cohen, *Delinquent Boys: The Culture of the Gang* (Glencoe, Ill.: Free Press, 1955).

8. See M. E. Wolfgang and F. Ferracuti, *The Subculture of Violence* (London: Tavistock, 1967).

9. See Charles E. Silberman, "As American as Jesse James," in *Criminal Violence, Criminal Justice*, pp. 27 ff.

10. See, in general, Robert K. Merton, *Social Theory and Social Structure*, enlarged ed. (New York: The Free Press, 1968), pp. 185 ff.

11. Ibid., p. 220.

12. Ibid., p. 221.

13. See, for instance, his comments on observations made by Hyman about his theory of anomie. Ibid., pp. 177, 224 ff.

14. Ibid., pp. 216–217.

15. Ibid., p. 220.

16. Kingsley Davis, *Human Society* (New York: Macmillan Co., 1953), pp. 28 ff.

17. Jules Henry, *Culture Against Man* (New York: Vintage Books, 1965), pp. 18–19.

18. Emile Durkheim, *Suicide: A Study in Sociology* (New York: The Free Press, 1951, 1966), p. 254.

19. Ibid., p. 255.

20. See S. N. Eisenstadt, "Delinquency Group-Formation Among Immigrant Youth," *British Journal of Delinquency* 2 (July 1951): 34–35; Edwin H. Sutherland and Donald R. Cressey, *Criminology*, 8th ed. (New York: J.B. Lippincott, 1970), p. 211.

21. Herbert Bloch and Arthur Niederhoffer, *The Gang: A Study in Adolescent Behavior* (New York: Philosophical Library, 1958), p. 17.

22. Talcott Parsons, *Essays in Sociological Theory*, rev. ed. (Glencoe, Ill.: Free Press, 1954), pp. 304–305.

23. Ibid., p. 306.

24. See A. K. Cohen, *Delinquent Boys: The Culture of the Gang* (Glencoe, Ill.: Free Press, 1955); W. B. Miller, "Lower Class Culture as a Generating Milieu of Gang Delinquency," *Journal of Social Issues* 14, no. 3 (1958), 5–19.

25. Durkheim, *Suicide*, p. 249.

26. Ibid., p. 251.

27. David Riesman, Nathan Glazer, and Revel Denney, *The Lonely Crowd* (New Haven, Conn.: Yale University Press, 1950).

28. See Leon Radzinowicz, *Ideology and Crime*, (New York: Columbia University Press, 1966), p. 10.

29. Joseph Klapper, *The Effects of Mass Communication* (Glencoe, Ill.: Free Press, 1960).

30. Albert Bandura, Dorothea Ross, and Sheila Ross, "Transmission of Aggression Through Imitation of Aggressive Models," *Journal of Abnormal and Social Psychology* 63 (1961), 575–582.

31. Elliot Aronson, *The Social Animal* (San Francisco: W. H. Freeman and Company, 1976), p. 159.

32. Ibid., pp. 159–160.

33. Ibid., p. 160. See also the discussions presented and authorities cited in Urie Bronfenbrenner, *Two Worlds of Childhood: U.S.A. and U.S.S.R.* (New York: Touchstone, 1972), p. 109 ff.

34. Ibid., p. 160.

35. See Hortense Powdermaker, "The Channeling of Negro Aggression by the Cultural Process," in Clyde Kluckhohn and Henry A. Murray, eds., *Personality in Nature, Society, and Culture* (New York: Alfred A. Knopf, 1949), pp. 473–484.

# Part III
# Criminal Law Aspects

# 6

# The Criminal Justice System

In traditional societies where the force of social custom binds the people, the role of law as a means of social control is relatively insignificant. By growing up in such societies, the individual learns, under group pressure and threat of ostracism, to adapt his behavior to the expectations of others, to the dominant cultural norms and values. The legal system reinforces the same basic norms and standards; however, before the individual becomes subject to the rule of law as an independent agent, he is already socialized. As a rule, he has learned to satisfy his needs and desires according to accepted norms and patterns of behavior that prevail in his society. By and large, he conforms to social expectations even without the threat of official sanctions.

In a highly industrialized society like the United States, where due to various factors including cultural and racial heterogeneity of the population, overemphasis on individual achievement, and a whole-hearted faith in the power of the sciences to solve all problems, social bonds are weakened and morality is relativistic, the potential significance of law as an instrument of social control is much greater. In such a society the individual learns to look at moral values not as absolute dicta to be observed even at the cost of deprivation and sacrifice, but simply as relative statements that can be either valid or invalid depending on the situation, personal needs and desires, and the possible material gains or losses that may result from adhering to them. Moral education or whatever is left of it in such a society is not, therefore, sufficient by itself to keep the individual within desired legal bounds. Here, what would be required as a substitute for the traditional and moral ties in traditional societies is an equitable and efficient criminal justice system that can unmistakably convey the message that whoever violates laws and regulations will be subjected to sure, clear, and definite punishment. As a long–time American judge has correctly stated:

Unless agreements can be legally enforced, unless disputes can be resolved peaceably and lawfully, unless law violators are lawfully accused, tried, and punished, no member of the community can feel a sense of assurance in the pursuit of his daily life. Indeed, it is that very lack of assurance that the law will be enforced promptly, fairly, and appropriately that is the cause of much public dissatisfaction.[1]

If the proper message is clearly sent out by the criminal justice system, the chances are that the majority of the people who normally act on the basis of a rational calculation of possible gains and losses and who have acquired a valuable stake in society that they don't want to lose will refrain from engaging in criminal activity under normal conditions.

Amitai Etzioni, the American sociologist, has developed a useful scheme to show what motivates people to act in accordance with social norms and expectations. In his view, there are two divergent sources of human motivation: "What is satisfying and what is legitimate." He defines satisfaction as a positive deferred response to a genuinely felt need. Provision of food to the hungry and water to the thirsty would be examples of such satisfying experiences. Obviously, people are motivated, even driven, to seek reduction of painful experience and enhancement of satisfaction. Another motivating force is the perception that a particular conduct is legitimate and hence morally necessary. According to Etzioni, "Legitimate conduct is carried out in response to an inner sense that the step to be taken is properly required, for instance, heeding a sign not to speed through a school zone as children rush to it in the morning."[2] Etzioni then combines the two concepts to reach four possible sources of human social action:

1. *Dictates*. Acts which are neither pleasurable nor conceived as legitimate, they "stand over the individual as something the person is coerced to do, at the point of a gun, under economic pressure, or because of powerful psychic threats."[3]

2. *Involvements*. The opposite of dictates, they are both pleasurable and legitimate. Helping out a loved family member or a close friend would be examples of such conduct.

3. *Duties*. Acts that are not satisfying but conceived as proper and legitimate are duties. Fighting for one's country or paying taxes may be given as examples.

4. *Asocial Gratifications*. Finally, acts that are pleasurable but not legitimate are defined by Etzioni as asocial gratifications. Many criminal acts and moral violations come to mind as examples, in the sense that they provide material or psychic pleasure or provide release from some repressed personal desires.

Of course, the four categories do not exist in pure form in social relations. Etzioni, however, does not discuss the various logical implications of the categories. It is possible, for instance, to think of some duties, at least in certain cultures, as being at the same time also satisfying or even pleasurable. The average Japanese or German citizen, for example, learns to derive pleasure from conscientiously performing his or her duties. Another modifying factor may be the perception of legitimacy which is developed in the individual on the basis of his personal and subcultural experiences. In this sense, the category of asocial gratifications may approach that of involvements for certain groups. The individual offender may view his transgressions not only as pleasurable but also as legitimate, for instance, because he considers the social system unjust and any attack against it as justifiable self-defense. In spite of such shortcomings, Etzioni's four categories are useful tools of analysis if we consider them as "ideal types" that closely resemble actual life situations. To complement Etzioni's scheme and make it correspond to the realitites of the criminal justice system, I am adding the independent factor of penal sanctions to his categories. Aside from the conceptions of satisfying and legitimate, the threatened or actual imposition of penal sanctions will obviously have a modifying effect on human behavior. Thus, in the light of the four categories and the added concept of penal sanctions, we can envision several possibilities.

Although one can think of social situations, especially in traditional cultures, where people may be forced to do something that is neither pleasurable nor conceived as legitimate, such situations are exceptionally rare; the individual would not normally observe an illegitimate and painful command, unless he is convinced that to do otherwise would subject him to a punishment that is considerably more painful than the required compliance.

The threatened or actual application of deprivation to shape human action seems irrelevant to situations which Etzioni calls involvement. However, several countries have tried to impose a duty of intervention and care, subject to penal sanctions, when an individual can, without danger to himself, come to the assistance of somebody else whose life is in danger.[4]

Penal law sanctions are most relevant in duties and asocial gratifications. The moral force of a positive duty can be considerably enhanced by the belief that failure to act according to one's duty will certainly result in deprivation. Finally, what may keep many people from engaging in asocial gratification, especially in cultures and periods where many forms of deviance are considered normal as is the case in the United States today, is a perceived fear of quick, certain, and effective punishment for violations of legal norms. In the light of present-day American ideologies, which as we have seen emphasize egocentrism, autonomy of personal desires as the sole basis of human action, and the relative nature of all moral values as mere reflections of class struggle, the only realistic force that could bar the average individual from asocial gratifications would be a just and efficient criminal justice system, which as we shall see does not exist in the United States today.

The role of sanctions as effective modifiers of human conduct has been documented in many social studies. In one such study by Riley and Riley, 2,500 New Jersey high school students were asked to respond to a hypothetical question: "Suppose you were taking a test and the student sitting beside you asks you the answers to some of the questions. You are sitting way back in the back of the room so most of the students won't be apt to notice what you do."

Students were asked to indicate whether they would refuse help in four different situations. Analysis of the results showed that with the additional elements of the teacher's disapproval, and especially punishment, the percentage of those who said they would refuse help increased considerably. Thus, if the teacher were out of the room and could not notice cheating, only 18 percent said they would refuse help if their best friend asked for it. If the person asking for help was not a particular friend but simply a fellow student, 47 percent would refuse help under the same hypothetical situation. If the teacher was assumed to be in the room and would disapprove if he noticed cheating, and the person asking for help was just a fellow student, 84 percent said they would not cheat. The highest percentage of refusals would come if under similar circumstances the teacher would punish the cheater, if noticed, by lowering his grades.[5]

If the criminal justice system does not convey a clear message that offenders will be definitely subjected to swift and just punishment, the incentive to commit antisocial acts, all other factors being equal, will be stronger. As Andenaes has observed, "It would be difficult to teach honesty, non-violence, and similar positive values where these rules were openly and commonly broken without punishment."[6]

We shall see that the significance of such a clear message may be even greater, not only because of its deterrent effect, but more importantly because it assures the law–abiding citizen that he has been right all along to keep the socio-legal restrictions on his heart-felt desires. The message can strengthen the average individual's confidence in the system and provide a strong impetus—other things being equal—to cooperate with police and other officials in attaining the common objectives of the criminal justice system: prevention, detection, conviction, and rehabilitation. The Japanese public interact with police, courts, and prison authorities along these lines. Take, in contrast, a system that does not function properly, that gives the image of a corrupt bureaucracy or a worn-out device that is inconsistent and preferential in the application of penal laws. Consequently, of those who commit exactly the same crime, one may never get caught, another gets away with the help of a shrewd lawyer who knows the flaws of the system, the third is convicted but gets a relatively mild sentence which is then suspended, while the fourth ends up in a devastating penal institution for quite a few years. The confidence of the public in such a criminal justice system will gradually but surely erode. In addition, the negative perception will mentally help many people rationalize any transgression that they contemplate especially in situations where detection is highly unlikely. This perception, if it is continuous and unchanging, may fill the noncriminal with deeply felt cynicism and a feeling of powerlessness, a feeling that the system works only for the rich and the powerful, that it is corrupt and unjust, and that it corresponds with the greater measure of injustice and inequality in society. As the United Supreme Court has said in the case of *Grifin v. Illinois*: "There can be no equal justice where the kind of trial a man gets depends on the amount of money he has." Such politically alarming conceptions may not occur to most people, at least consciously, but repeated experience, personal or indirect, of similar injustices will definitely lead to mistrust of government and overall apathy, if not plain aggressiveness and criminal behavior. In the words of a well-known authority:

> But if it is remembered that the prime function of the criminal law is to encourage and sustain civilized conduct, to declare and confirm the basic moral code, then the justice and evenness of its administration, the decent and civilized calm and self-consistent manner in which it is brought to bear are crucial to the attainment of its objectives, and are of a much higher order of importance than considerations of the speed and effectiveness with which we can process large numbers of cases to a successful "enforcement" conclusion.[7]

The perceptions we have of the "system" are of course formed by actual events—experiences we have had personally or learned about in the media. Our experience or accounts of other people's experiences with the police, for instance, shape our perceptions about the quality and role of the police force in our society. We notice how prosecutors handle cases, how judges formally react to crime, how sentences are handed down—by plea bargaining, for instance, or after a fair jury trial—the consistency or inconsistency of the courts in sentencing similar offenses, how many offenders who have committed heinous crimes escape punishment because of some technicality, or because the court seemed to be bent on protecting the rights of the offender, rather than or at least as much as those of the innocent victims. All these perceptions enter our consciousness and impress upon our mind and emotions the image of a system which is perceived either as just, moderately reliable, or grossly arbitrary, irrational, and unjust.

It is in the light of the signficant impact of laws, prosecutions' stance in criminal cases, police behavior, and judicial practices on the public's perceptions and reactions that we should analyze and understand the American criminal justice system. There are, of course, certain social inequalities, which in the context of free-enterprise ideologies seem inevitable. In Western democracies, for instance, wealth, which is acquired and accumulated free of many restrictions, gives certain classes of people privileged social positions. In the same way, incidentally, in Communist countries people with political power enjoy many advantages unavailable to ordinary citizens. Thus, in the West an individual who can afford to hire a highly qualified lawyer has a much better chance of winning his case or escaping punishment than a poor, uneducated citizen. Within this scheme of seemingly inevitable social inequalities, however, certain measures adopted in most Civil Law countries have made the working of the judicial system less objectionable than in the United States. Just as an example, the losing party in a civil case in a Civil Law country pays the expenses, not only his own but also those of the winning party, including lawyer's fees. The theory is that whether plaintiff or defendant, the losing party should be responsible for the litigation or its continuation and the waste of time and energy, which could have been avoided by admitting the winning party's just claims without involving the courts. The practice gives the financially weaker party a better chance to sue or defend himself, if he has a valid cause of action. Conversely, it may act as a deterrent to frivolous lawsuits. Knowing that one must pay for all the expenses of the winning party as well as his own, a potential plaintiff would think twice before filing or dragging his baseless claim in court. The same practice works to provide better legal counsel for indigent citizens. In Civil Law countries, an indigent party to a civil action is provided with free counsel. In West Germany the public treasury pays for the appointed lawyer at what are called paupers' rates. These are lower than the normal rates but still attractive enough to interest many qualified lawyers. In Italy, theoretically, a lawyer appointed to represent an indigent citizen is not supposed to receive compensation for his efforts, even though in many instances arrangements are made to compensate him. In recent years, for instance, labor unions have assumed the expenses of providing counsel for their members. The fact remains, however, that both in West Germany and Italy, as in fact in all Civil Law countries, if the lawyer wins the case, he is entitled to full compensation, on the basis of standard rates, from the losing party. Thus, the indigent can be furnished with better qualified legal assistance.[8]

Aside from the seemingly inevitable social inequalities, which are less marked in countries with social legislation for the less fortunate, there are certain other features of the American criminal justice system which further reinforce negative perceptions held by the public. In fact, judging the system from the standpoint of public perception, many of its everyday practices would seem unjust, inefficient, irrational, and arbitrary.

## THE EDUCATIVE EFFECTS OF THE CRIMINAL JUSTICE SYSTEM

As was pointed out before, official agents of social control, coming relatively late into our lives as independent human beings, have much less influence on our overall behavior than the socializing forces of the basic institutions of family and school. As a matter of fact, by the time we reach adulthood and become full-fledged subjects of legal and social rules, our basic personality and behavioral patterns have been set and solidified through the process that sociologists call socialization. It is this process of constant adaptation and readaptation in response to the expectations of important persons in our lives—parents, teachers, peers, and others—that essentially makes us what we are. The process begins from the first day of a person's life, if not indeed from the day the fetus is conceived in the womb, long before legal rules come to play any direct role in the individual's life.

Still, from among agents of social control, laws can be more effective in influencing human behavior. Laws can be stated more precisely and have the full power and authority of the state behind them. Their force is more drastically felt through the instrumentality of punishment.

Obviously when the socialization process is effective and the values it inculcates in people are consistent with those protected by laws, the role of the law and the judicial system is much less noticeable. The legal system simply reinforces sentiments and attitudes people have already acquired by growing up in various social groups. When there is defective socialization or when the values that the individual has learned are inconsistent with the legal norms, then the role of the legal system in assuring general compliance with the laws becomes much more important and complicated. In either case, however, the legal system can effectively and positively influence or reinforce social behavior only when it has certain characteristics. We shall see, in view of the learning process, what these characteristics are. For the moment it suffices to stress that with the proper use or threat of punishment the legal system can have a significant educative impact.

Relatively recently some criminologists have started to view criminal behavior not in terms of supposedly causal factors but rather as the inevitable result of the larger social structure. Considered in this light, it is necessary to study all the different factors that directly or indirectly have a significant effect on the various aspects of the crime problem. Therefore, in seeking possible solutions, we should look not only at measures needed to rehabilitate the individual offender or try only to improve the social conditions that initially drove him to criminal activity and to which he will have to return after his prison term, but also investigate how the criminal justice system deals with its subjects and affects the perceptions, attitudes, and behavior of the criminal and noncriminal public. Actually, Mayer expressed the idea quite some time ago, although it has not been heeded sufficiently. He stated, "the basic general preventive effect of criminal law does not at all stem from its deterrent but from its morality-shaping force. . . . Nothing is so convincing to man as power, provided it appears as expression of a moral order."[9] Morton repeated the same idea more recently, maintaining "the most important function of the criminal law is that of education or conditioning."[10] In another view, "Punishment expresses social disapproval, and it does this in a discriminatory way: the heavier the punishment, the stronger the disapproval. If individuals are disposed to accept the evaluations of the authorities, they will be influenced by way of suggestion."[11]

The important point, of course, is the nature of education or conditioning provided by the criminal justice system, the type of messages it directly or indirectly conveys to the public through its operations. If the system is conceived of as efficient, just, and consistent, it will generate respect and/ or fear, and by and large the public will conform to the requirements of the law. The message is confused if many people commit crimes and escape punishment or the system provides differential punishment to people who have committed similar crimes. Furthermore, if the interval between the commission of a crime and the application of punishment is so long that the necessary association between the antisocial act and the official response is lost, then the criminal justice system cannot act as the desired conditional stimuli to create the wished-for conditional reflex, that is, the feeling in the public that they should observe the laws. As an authority has observed, "For the young, underprivileged black in the ghetto, 'law' seems to be the object of much positive feeling. The National Advisory Commission on Civil Disorder in its 1968 report cited a deep hostility between police and ghetto communities as a primary cause of the riots in 1967."[12] And again:

There is much experience to show that a bad example left unpunished can be infectious. With such trivial offenses as illegal parking, lack of enforcement may easily lead to total breakdown of compliance. But the mechanism of the bad example has a much wider field of application. For example, repeatedly cases are reported of large-scale theft by employees. The more violations, the fewer qualms the individual feels. In the same way, a branch of government can be penetrated by corruption. The unthinkable becomes thinkable when comrades are doing it. Why should one be honest when others are not? The risks seem less real; moral inhibitions are broken down. This danger is probably greatest when an individual learns about offenses committed by others who are in similar situations.[13]

The long history of the failure of the American criminal justice system to detect, convict, and rehabilitate swiftly, firmly, and consistently is, therefore, one of the main causes of much disrespect for the law and thus a strong tendency to break it, especially when the chances for detection and conviction are so slim. Recent studies have confirmed the widely known fact that most criminals go unpunished. The statistics prepared by the FBI for 1,847 cities, for instance, show that in 1977, someone was arrested and charged in 37.6 percent of all the known cases of violent crime. Of these arrests, only 14.4 percent resulted in conviction, many on a much lesser charge. The statistics for property crimes show an even worse picture. In only 16.8 percent of the known cases was there an arrest and a charge. Of these, only 6 percent resulted in conviction.[14] Silberman observes:

Acceptance of the legitimacy of law is a far more effective instrument of social control than is fear of punishment. Thus the moral pedagogical role of the law is central to the functioning of any society.

Extended contact with American courts and prisons is not needed to discover that the criminal law educates badly. From the institutions of the criminal justice, there emanates a flow of propaganda that destroys, rather than encourages, respect for the law and the values it seeks to protect.[15]

As a well-known sociologist has commented, "Contemporary American conditions do not reflect an understanding of the completely self-evident fact that every violation disregarded hurts not merely the other side or the victim, but the shared rules themselves, by undermining the commitment to civility that is their ultimate foundation."[16]

In subsequent chapters we will discuss the nature and functions of American courts, police, and penal institutions and study the respective educative impact of each on public perceptions and possible reactions. But first, we should deal with a more general and essential issue: why do we punish at all? Are we consciously applying the possible objectives of punishment? Is punishment effective in realizing any of the avowed aims of penal laws?

## Philosophy and Objectives of Punishment

The stated rationale and objectives of punishment have changed several times under the influence of different theories. For a long time, people's concern in punishment was revenge, killing or inflicting pain on a person who had committed murder or caused injury to someone. Long afterwards, with the spread of psychological and sociological insights and the increasing realization that human conduct, including criminal behavior, is the outcome of a complex interaction between individual and social factors, the idea emerged that the criminal justice system can and should rehabilitate and reeducate the offender. In a similar line of reasoning, reaching another logical conclusion, the Italian School of Criminology maintained that the concepts of individual responsibility and guilt shoud not be used as the basis for punishment. We have learned, the proponents of the school argued, that people are not responsible for what is actually conditioned by more primary forces, such as family and other social institutions, over which they cannot exert any effective control. The concept of punishment, as it has existed in the West, is thus baseless and should be discarded. Instead of looking to past responsibility and guilt—concepts that are misleading in view of the social processes that condition the individual to behave in certain ways— as the basis for punishment, we should adopt proper security measures to protect society against future harmful acts. Our concern, therefore, should be directed toward the future, and in place of punishment, we should use more humane and effective methods that are better suited to the protection of society. These methods can vary from rehabilitating the individual offender, making him safe and capable of productive social life, to imprisonment and forced isolation from society, all as measures necessary for social defense. If society cannot be protected by means of these measures, for instance because the individual offender has become incorrigible, then even capital punishment would be justifiable and necessary.

Eventually all these concepts of rehabilitation, deterrence, and social defense were adopted in several American, European, and Latin American criminal justice systems and incorporated into their respective penal codes. Of these objectives, rehabilitation has by and large failed, except in a few societies. As a recent observer has commented:

No approach to rehabilitation seems to work. Whether offenders are given traditional one-to-one psychotherapy or newer methods of group therapy, they return to crime at about the same rate as those given no therapy at all. Nor are recidivism rates affected by education, vocational training, social work counseling, or any other approach that has yet been tried.

Far from eliminating punishment, moreover, an emphasis on rehabilitation simply continues punishment under another name. Whether an offender is "treated" or not, forced deprivation of liberty constitutes a punitive act. Indeed, benevolent motives have often led to more rather than less severe punishment; seeing prisoners as sick tends to remove any constraints of the length of their confinement or the nature of the "treatment" they receive.[17]

The fact is that even under the best of conditions, the methods and the approach used to rehabilitate past offenders are basically ineffective. For one thing, to assume that the causes of criminal behavior are essentially personal is to miss the mark. It is true, of course, that different individuals react differently to similar social stimuli and that the psychological makeup of each individual is a determining factor in his patterns of behavior. Nevertheless, each person learns his behavior in the larger context of social life and under conditions created and maintained by society. Thus, unless social conditions and the structure and value system of the several groups in which the offender has been raised and to which he will most probably return after his term are improved, the past offender, even if completely rehabilitated, will as a rule revert to criminal activity when faced with strong outside stimuli.

Besides, we know that even good prisons are artificially isolated institutions, separated from the everyday conditions and pressures of life. The unavoidable prevalence of deviant values and the close and exclusive interaction with other offenders which is necessitated by prison conditions in this country further reinforce the criminal tendencies of the inmate population. Thus, except for some rare cases, the offender leaves the prison more fully socialized in the ways of crime than when he entered the institution. In addition, in some American prisons there exist more aggravating conditions of violence, rape, drug abuse, and other violations of human dignity committed by inmates against each other. These traumatic experiences cause additional frustration and aggression in the average offender.

The objective of deterrence has two aspects. In specific deterrence we are concerned with the future behavior of a particular offender. The idea is that somehow by subjecting him to punishment or other measures, we discourage him effectively from engaging in any criminal activity in the future. Short of transforming the basic psychological needs and tendencies of the offender, a realistic chance of deterring him from subsequent antisocial activity would depend on his being convinced that the probable pleasure of any future crime would be strongly outweighed by the pain of a sure punishment.

General deterrence refers to the fact that the public, by learning that offenders are as a rule subjected to punishment, will feel assured that the criminal justice system works and that it is unlikely that any offender can avoid the consequence of his criminal act. The idea is that by setting the example of the convicted offender, we can convincingly and effectively discourage others from engaging in criminal activity.

Obviously, both aspects of the deterrence theory depend on certain assumptions about the nature and function of the criminal justice system. The underlying assumption is that as a general rule, anybody who commits an offense will surely be subjected to the pain and deprivations of punishment. What is important in this assumption is not so much the severity of punishment—although in many cases, especially when fines are imposed as penalty, this is a significant factor—as the certainty that commission of any criminal act will in all likelihood result in punishment. If the enforcement of penal statutes and judicial decisions strengthens this impression, then, other things being equal, the individual offender and the normally law-abiding public will think twice before venturing into criminal activity. If, on the other hand, the criminal justice system by its own deficiencies or contradictory rules and considerations creates the impression that the realistic chances of detection, conviction, and punishment are insignificant and would depend on factors that can be manipulated, then the likelihood of self-imposed restraints, especially for those who know how to work the system, becomes minimal. The possible impact of the criminal justice system is even more notable in the context of present-day American society, where, as we have pointed out, moral values and inhibitions that normally restrain people are weakened, while cultural values that encourage deviance, pursuit of individual self-interest, aggressiveness, and material success are reinforced. Under such sociocultural conditions, the incentive to engage in criminal activity is stronger if the criminal justice system repeatedly sends out the message that if one knows the deficiencies of the system, one can commit crimes with immunity.

It seems that the American system of criminal justice has also failed regarding general and specific deterrence. In the following sections, I shall argue that the failure of the system is to a large extent due to the fact that it does not convey the appropriate message to the public because the system itself does not operate under the guidance of a clear, unifying ideology of punishment. We have plagued the courts, police, and penal institutions in this country with confused ideologies and various restrictions. But before we get to that point, we have to settle the issue of whether in view of the admitted failure of the penal system to rehabilitate or deter past offenders or to have a positive educative impact on the general public, it makes any sense at all to punish the criminal. The question is particularly important when we consider the possible effect of punishment on the perceptions, attitudes, and behavior of the general, law-abiding public. My contention is that punishment still serves a very useful purpose and that its retribution aspect, which is hotly and embarrassedly negated by liberal Western criminologists, is its most potent element as a deterrent factor.

The emergence of the social self is, as we have seen, the inevitable outcome of the learning process, the introjection and assimilation of social norms and values by the individual. On the other hand, social norms and values are taught as universal commands, encompassing the behavior of each and every member of society, and as a rule, never as an exceptional demand or restriction on selected human beings. When we educate our children not to lie, steal, or curse, we impose certain expectations on them, not as our personal, idiosyncratic desires, but as universal rules of conduct to be observed by every decent, good, and respectable child. As a matter of fact, all moral values are taught in the same manner, and it is this supposed universality of shared burdens that makes the restrictions we keep on ourselves a little less onerous. We accept social limitations on our behavior because we are told repeatedly and we have grown to believe that every other person is similarly subject to the same limitations. This basic belief, which is to a large extent illusory, forms the foundation of all morality, which itself takes shape relative to specific needs and expectations of each particular society.

When an individual commits a crime, or for that matter any other deviant act, he has in reality disregarded moral commandments; he has discarded the social restrictions that everyone is suppose to observe. In short, he has done what everyone else is repeatedly tempted to do, but has denied himself through self-restraint and with the suffering of deprivation. His act, at least initially, creates the impression that after all, moral values are not universally observed, that certain individuals do in fact transgress against them. His act, then, stirs commotion, uncertainty, and anxiety among the average, conformist, law-abiding public.

In response to the sense of anxiety and uncertainty created in the average person by the offender's criminal act, two alternative reactions may occur. He or she may not be sufficiently conditioned to observe social norms and values automatically—a situation psychoanalysts would define as having a weak ego or social self. In this case he may use the example of the offender as an excuse and rationalize the unleashing of his own suppressed desires in the form of antisocial acts. The individual will act on the explicit or tacit assumption that he has been misled to believe that everyone is bound by the same moral imperatives and that he has kept control over his desires in vain while some other person has broken the rules and activated his wishes. If somehow the trust of the individual in the validity of common moral values is not restored, he will have a strong incentive to engage in criminal activity.

Alternatively, the individual may have a more integrated social self. For such a person, who normally acts under the stronghold of his own conscience, the criminal act committed by the offender can actually help to reinforce the conviction that he was justified all along in believing in the dominant moral values and keeping restrictions on his suppressed desires. However, this strengthening of moral convictions is usually effected by developing and showing strong, adverse reactions against the individual offender. The moralist and the conformist reaffirm their own beliefs and forebearance by condemning the person who has transgressed against common moral values. By their punitive reactions, these people reassure themselves that they were right after all in tolerating the restrictions and deprivations, that it is the offender who has erred in giving unbridled expression to his forbidden desires. The resulting, mostly unconscious judgment of such people is that the offender must be unquestionably punished for his act. The punishment imposed on the offender, then, acts as a useful means of reestablishing the public's sense of psychological equilibrium, which had been disturbed by the criminal act of the offender.

In this light, punishment is necessary, not only as a deterrent for the weak-egoed individual who might otherwise decide to commit antisocial acts, but also as an effective means of reaffirming the common moral values and reestablishing the mental and emotional balance in the public.[18] Again, it is in this context that the very significant role of vengeance or retribution in the long history of human society can be understood. The public's cry for punishment and vengeance is not necessarily a reflection of wickedness or the cruelty of deriving perverse pleasure from the suffering of other human beings. Rather, it has been an effective way of reinforcing the socially conditioned conviction that people must forgo the unrestrained gratification of their desires, that they must act according to the demands and expectations of their respective societies.[19]

The positive effects of the criminal justice system can be realized, of course, only if it works according to the common concepts and expectations inculcated in the individual members of society. The basic assumption that motivates the individual to stick to dominant moral values is that everybody who violates those standards will be punished, and that those who commit similar crimes will suffer similar punishments. In other words, the criminal justice system will succeed in diminishing anxiety and restoring psychological equilibrium in the public only if it demonstrates that it punishes every known transgression and that the extent of punishment is basically the same for comparable cases. In other words, the criminal justice system can play a significant sociopsychological role in reducing tension and in reinforcing moral values only if it clearly conveys the unmistakable message that the imposition of punishment on those who transgress against the law is certain, swift, and consistent. As we shall see, the American system of criminal justice operates under the heavy burden of inadequacies, misconceptions, confusion, and lopsided emphasis on the rights of the accused in almost total disregard of the rights of the victim and the general public. It gives the impression that in many cases it is incapable of apprehending and punishing offenders, and that the system is inefficient and wastes time, and that it is basically inconsistent and unfair, ineffective against the rich, the powerful, and the smart habitual offender. If this is the case—and we shall see that it is—then the alarmingly negative role of the American criminal justice system irrespective of other causes of criminality becomes clear. It seems that the system actually encourages deviant behavior, discourages cooperation with the functionaries of the criminal justice system, and spreads general apathy and dissatisfaction among the law-abiding public.

It should also be stressed here that the problem of negative messages sent by the criminal justice system is much more serious in the United States than in many other countries because of the widespread public belief in the egalitarian ideals and teachings of the sociopolitical system. By reason of basic political documents and the series of Supreme Court decisions which have upheld and extended the coverage of those documents, the average American citizen expects to be treated like everyone else. To be sure, there are subtle class differences and sometimes, as in the case of Blacks, even flagrant violations of individual rights in American society. Nevertheless, the average American learns to believe that as a fellow citizen, he should be accorded the same rights and privileges, be subjected to the same limitations and deprivations, as everyone else. In many other societies, people learn to accept differing standards of behavior and differential official reaction for the several social groups. In many societies, the ruling class is conceived of as being entitled to special privileges and immunities; the rich seem to be subjected to less stringent standards of behavior than the ordinary people; the police or other government functionaries may be considered to have the right to violate the public's rights and liberties in order to maintain law and order. A similar dichotomy of standards and expectations also exists in Communist countries, where members of the politbureau and other high-ranking party officials routinely enjoy certain exclusive rights and privileges denied to everyone else. In such societies, because the masses have accepted the social and material inequalities either as legitimate or as inevitable, they are not as outraged as people in this country by crimes and violations committed by the privileged classes. Likewise, they are less shocked or outraged if the criminal justice system treats members of the several social classes differently. The net result is that inconsistent, differential, or unfair reactions by the criminal justice system in this country potentially create a much stronger negative response in the public. This aroused sense of outrage and frustration does not, of course, always lead to more widespread criminal activity. However, it may lead to other negative means of expression or a feeling of general apathy, which in the long run is at least as harmful to society as crimes committed by some of its members.

## NOTES

1. Lois G. Forer, *Money and Justice: Who Owns the Courts?* (New York: W. W. Norton & Co., 1984), p. 50.

2. Amitai Etzioni, *An Immodest Agenda: Rebuilding America Before the 21st Century* (New York: McGraw–Hill Book Co., 1983), p. 50.

3. Ibid., pp. 50–51.

4. Article 63 of the French Code Penale, for example, provides that if a person can prevent the commission of a crime against a third person without there being any risk to himself, and does not do so, he can be convicted to from three months to five years of imprisonment and/or fined from 360 to 15,000 francs.

5. Matilda W. Riley and J. W. Riley, Jr., "Notes on a Conceptual Model," in Matilda W. Riley, J. W. Riley, Jr., and J. Toby, *Sociological Studies in Scale Analysis* (New Brunswick, N.J.: Rutgers University Press, 1954).

6. Johannes Andenaes, "The Moral and Educative Influence of Criminal Law," in June Louin Tapp and Felice J. Levine, *Law, Justice and the Individual in Society* (New York: Holt, Rinehart and Winston, 1977), p. 56.

7. Alexander M. Bickel, "The Role of the Supreme Court of the United States," *Texas Law Review* 44 (April 1966): 963.

8. See in general, Rudolf B. Schlesinger, *Comparative Law: Cases-Text-Materials*, 4th ed. (Mineola, N.Y.: The Foundation Press, 1980), pp. 342–352.

9. H. Mayer, *Das Strafrecht des deutschen Volkes* (Stuttgart: Enke, 1936), pp. 26–32.

10. J. D. Morton, *The Function of Criminal Law* (Toronto: Canadian Broadcasting Corporation, 1962), p. 43.

11. Andenaes, "Moral and Educative Influences," p. 54.

12. Ibid., p. 53.

13. Ibid., pp. 55–56.

14. U.S. Bureau of the Census, *Statistical Abstract of the United States: 1980* (Washington, D.C.: U.S. Government Printing Office, 1980), Table 319.

15. Charles E. Silberman, *Criminal Violence, Criminal Justice* (New York: Vintage Books, 1980), pp. 266–267.

16. Etzioni, *An Immodest Agenda*, p. 70.

17. Silberman, *Criminal Violence, Criminal Justice*, pp. 247–248.

18. It is theoretically possible to think of individuals who can disassociate them-

selves from the behavior of the offender and see it as a manifestation of individual or social aberration, as conduct that should not be punished but understood and, if possible, modified. There are, of course, many people who feel and react in this way. The majority, however, act according to the requirements of their repressed and mostly unconscious inclinations in the manner described.

19. As psychoanalysts have pointed out, the fact that in former times crowds gathered to see a convict hanged or otherwise executed stemmed from the same psychological need for reaffirmation of moral and individual values. It is interesting to note that as soon as the mass media were used to convey the same message by reporting the actual punishment of the convict, the need for personal presence at public executions and other forms of physical punishment diminished.

# 7

# Criminal Courts

Courts are the most important elements of the criminal justice system. They are supposed to be the final arbiters of justice in society. Any inefficiency, injustice, or violation of rights by individuals and organs of government will be more tolerable if there is a realistic likelihood that, under the watchful eyes of an impartial court system, it will be corrected and remedied. If, however, judges are deemed to lack qualifications and be unable intellectually, morally, or otherwise to decide cases according to principles of justice, the faith of the individual citizen in the system will fade, and desperation will replace the glimmer of hope for restoration when the public's rights are routinely violated. With these self-evident truths in mind, let us review some of the negative features of the judiciary which adversely influence the public's perception of the criminal justice system in America.

## CORRUPTION

The idea of justice is inseparably linked to impartiality. As a prerequisite to just decisions, the judge must be free from all undue influences such as money, personal favors, and political considerations. In Civil Law countries, all judges are employed by the Ministry of Justice. The position of judge is secure; no judge can be removed from office except for having committed and after being convicted for an enumerated crime. Although judges are government employees, they are immune from undue influence; their promotion and transfer to other assignments are decided by panels of independent justices who review their files on a regular basis. If there are complaints against a particular judge, an independent disciplinary panel of justices will review the allegations; the Minister of Justice has no influence over the decisions of these panels.

Upon completion of law school, graduates decide whether they want to become practicing lawyers or professional judges. They then take the special training program, ending with comprehensive exams, for their chosen profession. In practice, such choices are usually permanent; a law graduate who chooses to become a judge remains a judge for the rest of his life. Likewise, another person who decides to take the particular training courses and become a member of the bar as a rule remains a practicing lawyer for good. Change of profession is not impossible, but it occurs in relatively few cases. Thus, the professional judge is continuously influenced by the dictates, practices, and ideologies of his office. Of course, there are corrupt and incompetent judges in Civil Law countries, too, but on the whole, the integrity of the European judge is taken for granted. One does not hear or read about corrupt or incompetent justices there as often as in the United States.

In the United States, except for federal judges who are systematically immunized like European judges against undue influence, judges are on the whole open to various corrupting forces. For instance, in many places they are elected to office. Thus, qualities other than professional competence and moral integrity, such as physical appearance, public relations abilities, and the willingness to make various deals with powerful groups and individuals may determine their chances of becoming judges. In the absence of strong professional pressures and personal accountability to known colleagues and a civil service system on which the judge would have to depend for continued activity and promotions, it is not surprising that numerous cases of corruption have been reported among American judges. Lois G. Forer, who was herself a judge in various courts, reports the following on the judicial system:

Many judges are considered by their colleagues and members of the bar to be incompetent and/or lacking in integrity or judicial temperament. The only qualification for election or appointment to the bench is admission to the bar. Lawyers who have never tried a case or written a brief or argued an appeal are on the bench. Lawyers who have breached their duties to their clients are on the bench. Lawyers who have been convicted of crimes are on the bench.[1]

Aside from the various accounts of corrupt judges that one often reads in the press, there are also more systematic studies of judicial corruption in the United States. One such study discusses seventy–four known examples of judicial corruption. Each case is given with the name of the judge, nature of his offense, and the judicial or other action brought against him. The offenses committed include various numbers of counts of the following: murder, bribery, obstructing justice, accepting illegal fees, income tax evasion, burglary, robbery, conspiracy, receiving stolen property, extortion, profanity, fraud, use of office for personal financial profit, conspiracy to bribe fellow justices, bankruptcy fraud, selling and transporting stolen treasury bills, perjury, practicing law (while on the bench), embezzlement, forgery, false pretenses, protection racketeering, fixing traffic tickets, bailbond fraud, exploiting probates for personal loans, collection agency fraud, shoplifting, pimping, procuring pornographic films, gambling, moral turpitude, emotional involvement with divorce litigants, sexual assault, handling female court employees, drunkenness, arbitrary abuse of authority, political favoritism, fraudulently gaining admittance to the bar, filing fabricated legal opinions, incompetency, padding expense accounts, being armed while on the bench, use of judicial position for personal political advancement, voter registration fraud, improper political activity, obstructing justice for family member, illegal appointment of relatives, liquor license fraud, bias, incompetency and senility, delegating authority to court clerk, fraudulent political campaign-fraud scheme, being improperly influenced by a woman whose son was before the judge on criminal charges, verbal abuse of rape victim, prodding public defender with a dildo, use of foul language in court, mail fraud, questionable conflict of interest, and advocating revolution.[2]

The seventy–four cases of corrupt judges are only examples; they do not give an exhaustive list of such cases in the period covered by the author. As he remarks, "Unfortunately, for each case discussed there is a handful we have not included, and for each handful not included there are scores yet undiscovered."[3] The sad conclusion reached by the author, which probably echoes similar perceptions felt by the public, is:

In this country we believe, or at least claim to believe, in equality before the law. But those who have the money or the contacts, or both, exert a judicial pressure that eliminates equality and promotes a double standard of justice. For there are those who stand before the bar relying on their lawyers and their hopes. And there are those whose cases are more clandestinely and hurriedly resolved by a "fix." [4]

## INEFFICIENCY

To send the proper signals to the public, the criminal justice system must be swift in apprehending, trying, convicting, and punishing the guilty. Constant failure of the system to operate with efficiency will result in an adverse perception. If this is the case, then the following account by a former attorney general of the United States should cause a great deal of alarm.

Of the several million serious crimes reported annually to police, one in nine results in a conviction. The rate of solution varies with different crimes. Murder is usually reported, and 86 per cent of all reported murders lead to arrests. Among those arrested, however, only 64 per cent are prosecuted and but 43 per cent of the cases prosecuted result in convictions. Of persons prosecuted for murder, 19 per cent are convicted of a lesser crime, such as assault, arising from the same incident, and 38 per cent are acquitted or dismissed. Even as to murder, then, fewer than one in four of those known to the police results in a conviction.

In contrast, only 19 per cent of all the burglaries reported to the police lead to an arrest. Four out of five arrested are prosecuted and 56 per cent are found guilty. Thus for every twelve burglaries reported there is one conviction. . . .

Preventive efforts by police cannot be very effective when risks of detection, apprehension and conviction are so slim.[5]

To be effective, punishment should follow the commission of the crime in a relatively short time. Otherwise, the mental association between the two as inevitable cause and effect will not be established and/or reinforced. If a crime was committed long ago and has disappeared from the consciousness of the people, the delayed punishment—assuming of course that there is conviction and punishment for every known crime, which as was pointed out is not the case—will not have the desired effect.

We know as fact that American courts are bogged down by their heavy case loads; it is realistically impossible for them to administer justice in a swift manner. The problem is of course compounded by the weakening of social bonds and group pressure as agents of social control and by Americans' almost exclusive reliance on litigation for solving most personal problems. The result is that in "some misdemeanor courts more than 100 cases a day are heard by one judge."[6]

In many trial courts ten or twelve felony cases are heard and decided in one day by one judge. At issue is guilt or innocence, imprisonment or liberty. . . . Most juvenile court judges hear the cases of some thirty-five children in a day. The results of these hearings may be the removal of a child from his home, family and school and placement in a foster home or juvenile jail. The President's Commission on Law Enforcement and Administration of Justice aptly described the proceedings in juvenile court as the "five-minute children's hour."[7]

Given these facts and figures, the situation seems hopeless. And it is indeed hopeless unless something can be done to lessen the case load of the courts. Here is not the proper place to discuss the several effective proposals suggested by experts in the field.[8] It is certain, however, that a great deal of improvement is possible without violating any of the fundamental constitutional rights and privileges. Just to give an example, a great deal of time is usually wasted, often quite purposely, in the process of jury selection. "In the trial of Jean Harris [for instance], who was convicted of killing the "Scarsdale Diet Doctor," 550 potential jurors were questioned over a period of three weeks."[9] This whole problem could be avoided in the United States if we adopt the successful British practice of giving the judge the responsibility of selecting the jurors, by drawing lots, from among the panel of qualified people who are eligible for jury duty.[10]

Here we are caught in a vicious circle. The attributes of the whole system, including various inefficiencies and ideological inconsistencies, do not make effective deterrents. More violations and illegal practices, in turn, result in further congestion and inefficiency. My contention is that if the system were changed to work on a different conceptual basis to send out a more effective deterrent signal, we would have fewer cases in court and the courts' efficiency would also improve. In this respect, it is wise to remember that every aspect of the criminal justice system, especially the ideologies behind the practices, can have an important effect, either directly or indirectly, on the overall perceptions and reactions of the public. It is with this understanding that we study the following problems as relevant issues for the analysis of crime in America.

## BARGAIN JUSTICE

Plea bargaining or as some critics have called it, "bargain justice," involves a deal between the prosecution and the accused that the latter will agree to admit to a lesser crime in consideration for a milder punishment. Theoretically, when the state does not have enough evidence to pin down the offender in court, it enters into this kind of arrangement, which assures at least some measure of punishment for the guilty. In reality, the practice has become a routine procedure for the disposing, without trial, of the majority of criminal cases. Apparently, plea bargaining is widely used in American courts. A study showed that if the practice is considered for both felonies and misdemeanors, about 95 percent of all cases resulting in conviction are based on such bargains. In this study, the figure for felonies alone amounted to 70 to 85 percent of cases.[11] The advocates of plea bargaining have tried to justify the practice on pragmatic grounds. They argue that in many cases it would be next to impossible to prove the offender's involvement in the crime, especially in view of the exclusionary rules and other constitutional restrictions, unless he is willing to admit it himself. It makes sense, therefore, to punish him for a lesser offense than to let him escape punishment completely. The increasing number of cases which have bogged down the courts is another fact used to justify the practice. Without the possibility of a swift handling of most criminal cases by means of plea bargaining, the advocates argue, the criminal justice system will come to a halt.

Critics of the practice have attacked it mostly on legal grounds. Some have called it a travesty of justice. Others have argued that with plea bargaining the right to trial by jury, which is guaranteed by the Constitution, is in fact negated. I believe, however, that the most important negative consequence of plea bargaining in the long run is its devastating effect on the perceptions of the public. Plea bargaining and some of the other measures adopted by criminal courts on pragmatic grounds tend to undermine the fundamental assumptions that are basic to the criminal justice system. The concept of just punishment or criminal justice implies that people who have committed the same type of offense should be subjected to comparable deprivations. Variations in punishment have been allowed, of course, in most legal systems. However, the reason for giving a milder sentence to a particular offender is the existence of some mitigating circumstance in the offender or the conditions under which the crime was committed. It has never been based, at least explicitly as it is in the United States, on how shrewdly the offender or his lawyer can strike a deal with the prosecution. The clear signal sent to the public by the practice of plea bargaining is that the underlying presuppositions of the system are not observed in practice, that two people committing the same criminal act may receive different treatment solely on the basis of the deal they are able to strike with the prosecution. The principle of *nulla poena sine lege* (meaning that the extent and quality of punishment should be clearly defined ahead of time) has no place in the practice of American courts. The principle that the public should have advance notice of what constitutes a crime and how it will be punished is not followed in practice. It is not the moral sense of justice but the conditions and requirements of the market place—bargains and deals—or some other morally irrelevant consideration, that ultimately controls the fate of every offender in court. If this is the perception plea bargaining and some other court practices create for the public, as I think they do, then cynicism and disrespect for the criminal justice system and other negative reactions are only the natural results.

Let us test our own reactions and see how we would personally feel when we read about the two following episodes. "A driver who was indicted for manslaughter after his concrete-mixer truck crashed into a parked car and killed a woman and her two children last year in Manhattan has been permitted to plead guilty to reduced charges with a promise of no prison term."[12] It should be added that the driver was under the influence of drugs while driving. Doesn't it outrage you that a person takes drugs and drives his truck in a state of stupor, recklessly causing the death of an innocent woman and her two children, and then makes a deal which provides that he will not be imprisoned?

The next case is even more appalling. On March 15, 1984, the *New York Times* carried a long article about an innocent man who was convicted for having slain his former wife's stepmother and given the maximum twenty-five years, twenty-eight months of which had already been spent in prison. As it turned out, the conviction was based on certain errors caused by the false testimony of the convict's former wife, who was the actual murderer. The article expressed amazement at the fact that such a mistake could have been made. What did not seem to disturb the author, but seems more shocking to me, is the fact that the former wife who was the confessed killer and had also caused the imprisonment of an innocent man, "had been promised immunity from prosecution; she was handed $20 for bus fare and released."[13] What makes the story even more incredible is that the actual murderer was not promised immunity because she had done anything to deserve it, such as volunteering information that could have led to the release of the innocent former husband. She was actually tricked by her boyfriend, who was cooperating with the police, into admitting, while her statements were secretly recorded, that the former husband had not committed the murder.[14] Doesn't the whole approach, and as far as we are concerned, the laxity of official reaction against a real murderer and someone who had caused the baseless imprisonment of an innocent person for twenty-eight months make you outraged? Does it not negate the whole ethico-logical basis of punishment? Does it not convey a terribly negative picture of the criminal justice system? Can facts such as these generate or reinforce any sympathy or respect for the law? My assumption is that the criminal justice system, by acting inconsistently and inappropriately against various offenders, does in fact diminish the public's respect for the system and dulls its sensitivity for the need to observe the law and in some cases provides an understandable excuse for certain individuals to engage in criminal activity. We have already dealt with this subject more fully when considering the educative functions of the criminal justice system. Here, it suffices to remember that the law of causality is as applicable to human interactional relations as it is to physical phenomena. If, for a relatively long period of time, the conditional stimuli—in this case crime—is not met with comparable, proper response, that is, just, impartial, and sure punishment, then no conditional reflex—in our case, respect for and/or fear of the law—will develop in members of society. This basic truism has been repeatedly confirmed by numerous research studies on animals and human beings. For instance, Dollard and his colleagues at Yale showed, through their research and as a general law of human behavior, that "the strength of inhibition of any act of aggression varies positively with the amount of punishment anticipated to be a consequence of that act."[15] We can, therefore, maintain that if the impression created in the public because of plea bargaining and similar practices is that the nature and extent of an offender's punishment depends, not on his actual guilt, but on extraneous factors such as his ability to hide the facts or his shrewdness in striking a favorable deal with the prosecution, then obviously the control an average individual would keep over his own needs and desires would be likewise weak and inconsistent.

## SELECTIVE ENFORCEMENT AND SENTENCING

Numerous studies, including those on hidden crimes that prove criminality is much more widespread than is reflected in official crime statistics, have shown that the American criminal justice system is selective and prejudicial in the apprehension, trial, and sentencing of offenders. Dennis Chapman, for instance, using examples from court records and official statistics, has shown how the criminal justice system chooses from among the larger groups of various antisocial individuals a scapegoat group disproportionally drawn from the lower strata of society. This group, which consists of working-class, uneducated, and politically powerless people, is subjected to imprisonment for acts that are also committed by members of the middle and upper classes, who are relatively immune from punishment.[16] Selective law enforcement is practiced at the different stages of the criminal justice process: in arrests, sentencing, and conditions of confinement. Nathan Goldman in his study of police discretion in Pennsylvania found that selective biases influence the police officer's decision to process a juvenile offender through the court system. Aside from these prejudicial attitudes, other nonlegal factors, such as the policeman's concern for status and prestige in the community, make him sensitive to outside pressures. Such factors also influence his perceptions about the offense and the offender and his decision either to process or to drop charges.[17]

Another typical study of selective law enforcement relates to the disparity of punishment imposed on different classes of people. In a study of 3,475 Philadelphia delinquents, it was found that Blacks and members of other lower socioeconomic groups were likely to receive more severe punishment than the white and more affluent groups.[18] The biased and selective practice of law enforcement in the United States is keenly described:

It is common knowledge among most students of crime and delinquency that the officially designated criminal is the final product of a long process of selection. Studies of this selection process support hidden crime studies in consistently demonstrating that certain groups and certain classes of persons are overrepresented in the criminal justice system. Those caught up in the system are overwhelmingly the poor, the lower class, members of minority groups, immigrants, foreigners, persons of low intelligence, and others who are in some way at a disadvantage. Those who have a good chance of escaping the system are the affluent criminals, white-collar criminals, professional criminals, organized criminals, and intelligent criminals.[19]

Regardless of how true this assessment is, the fact remains that as long as such perceptions persist in the mind of the expert and through the mass media, various publications, and personal experience, in the mind of the public, they will have the same alienating effect as if they were based on undeniable truth. As two other authorities in the field have observed:

Aside from its manifest injustice, the principal danger of highly selective enforcement is that groups who are spared will disobey the law because no real risks exist, while target groups will perceive the enforcement as being directed against them rather than against the behavior. If such conditions persist, neither high- nor low-status groups are apt to respect the specific law, and rates of noncompliance in the group without the threat of enforcement will probably continue to be substantial.[20]

## SENTENCING

An accepted legal maxim among civilized nations is *Nulla poena sine lege*, or, there can be no punishment unless it has been provided and announced ahead of time. This principle is undoubtedly contained in the due process clause of the Constitution and it has been interpreted to mean that justice requires the legislature and the courts to inform the public about the nature and extent of the deprivation they will suffer if they engage in certain kinds of activity defined as criminal by the established authority. In other words, it implies that for each particular crime, there should be a fixed, ascertainable punishment that is proportionate to the crime's conceived danger and potential for harm. Similar offenses should, within reasonable and justifiable limits which should also be fixed by the lawmaker, receive similar punishments.

The contention is that due to peculiarities of the system and lack of a rational, explicit ideology, the American criminal justice system does not satisfy any of the implied requirements of the *nulla poena* principle. For one thing, we are dealing here not with a single criminal justice system as in most other countries, but with fifty state systems of criminal law, as well as those of the federal government and the District of Columbia. Thus, the same criminal act may be punished differently, or sometimes not punished at all, depending on where it is committed. In addition, the legislatures in the several states have enacted and accumulated through the years a large body of penal statutes that are quite disorganized and at times contradictory and unrelated to present–day conditions. A reputable authority has given us some examples.

A Colorado statute provided a ten-year maximum prison sentence for stealing a dog, while another statute in the same state provided only a six–month imprisonment and $500 fine for killing the same. In Iowa burning an empty building could bring up to twenty years imprisonment, while burning a church or school would result only in a maximum of ten. Breaking into a car to steal from the glove compartment could bring fifteen years in California. If the car itself was stolen, the maximum would be ten years imprisonment.[21] Some of these discrepancies may have been corrected by now, but our daily experience shows that there are still many laws that are contradictory or incomprehensible in view of changing public attitudes.

One recent example is the case of a Virginia man who received a forty-year prison sentence for possession and distribution of nine ounces of marijuana worth about $200. The Supreme Court of the United States, declaring that the duration of prison sentences for felonies was "purely a matter of legislative prerogative," upheld the conviction.[22] Cesare Beccaria had observed more than two centuries ago, "If the same punishment be decreed for killing a man, or for forgery, all difference between those crimes will shortly vanish. It is thus that moral sentiments are destroyed in the heart of man."[23]

The problem is more confounded in the United States, as I pointed out, because of the special nature of the American structure of government. It should also be noted that compared with European lawmakers whose traditions go back centuries, legislative lawmaking is a relatively new experience in the United States and thus more easily misused.

American law gives the judge a tremendous amount of discretion in choosing the punishment. To be sure, European judges, too, have a certain amount of leeway in determining the kind and extent of punishment for each offender. Nevertheless, the limits of such discretion are explicitly defined by the law. For one thing, for every crime there is a minimum and a maximum punishment, and the judge determines within the range fixed by the law the actual length of the sentence. For instance, theft is punishable by from six months to two years of corrective imprisonment. The judge looks into the background of the offender and the circumstances surrounding the crime. If there are mitigating factors, he can set the punishment at even less than the minimum provided by the law or give the offender a suspended sentence. The point is, however, that the mitigating circumstances are explicitly given in the penal codes or judicial decisions to limit the judge's subjectivities. For instance, some of the mitigating circumstances in many European penal codes are:

1. Age of the offender.

2. Offender's character and background.

3. Conditions under which the crime was committed; for example, whether the offender had a humanitarian or justifiable motive, whether the crime was caused, at least partly, by provocations from the victim.

4. Offender's voluntary and self-motivated confession before his crime was detected, or his cooperation with the police or the prosecution in apprehending his accomplices.

5. Offender's sincere attempt, after the commission of the crime, to restitute losses suffered by the victim, for instance, voluntary return of the stolen property or the offender's attempt to ameliorate the victim's condition. For instance, after committing assault and battery did he subsequently rush the victim to the hospital or help him otherwise? This provision seems very significant in providing the offender with a strong incentive to try and undo, to the extent possible, the harmful effects of his offense.

6. Victim's consent to drop the case. This normally happens only when the offender succeeds in establishing a close rapport with the victim, or in case he is dead, with his next of kin, either by convincing them that he is repentent for his misdeed, or otherwise, by offering an acceptable financial incentive. Either pos-

sibility signifies lessening of tension and perhaps even sincere reconciliation. The significance of this provision for the actual compensation for the victim who has suffered undeservedly for the restoration of peace and tranquility as well as a sense of justice cannot be overstressed.

The inclusion of such provisions in the penal codes of most European countries does not of course mean that there the task of judging an offender and determining his punishment is a simple matter. Nothing is automatic, and it is ultimately the judge who, using various standards and yardsticks, will have to decide whether there are appropriate mitigating circumstances in a case and how much weight they should carry. Nevertheless, three factors make the decision of a European criminal judge seem more logical, impartial, and equitable:

1. The fact that for every crime there is both a maximum and a minimum punishment provided by the law.
2. The fact that the basic examples of mitigating circumstances have been given by the code and that judicial tradition has established other types of situations that would be considered mitigating.
3. And finally, in many Civil Law countries such as Germany the judge is legally required to explain his reasons for reaching a particular decision. This undoubtedly brings the judge more within the edifying control of his own conscience and professional education, as well as the critical views and reviews of superior courts and legal scholars.

None of these factors is applicable, at least to the same extent, to American court practices. In America, many statutes fix only the maximum punishment for a particular crime. Judge Frankel gives several examples of such statutes:

1. "An assault upon a federal officer may be punishable by a fine and imprisonment for 'not more than' ten years."
2. The federal kidnapping law authorizes "imprisonment for any term of years or for life."
3. Rape, which can also be a federal crime, leads to "death or imprisonment for any term of years or for life" (U.S. Code, Title 18, Section 203).
4. Driving a stolen car across state lines may result in a term of "not more than five years."
5. Robbing a federally insured bank can result in imprisonment of "not more than twenty-five years."
6. A postal employee's theft of a letter can result in "not more than five years" imprisonment.

Within such very broad language, which provides only the maximum term—the "not more than" limit—the judge has tremendous discretion to fix any sentence he sees fit. Since he is not given concrete and intelligible guidelines, his decisions will seem arbitrary or even shocking and incomprehensible at times. As an example, James V. Bennett, the former director of Federal Bureau of Prisons said in his testimony before the U.S. Senate:

Take, for instance, the cases of two men we received last spring. The first man had been convicted of cashing a check for $58.40. He was out of work at the time of his offense, and when his wife became ill and he needed the money for rent, food, and doctor bills, he became the victim of temptation. He had no prior criminal record. The other man cashed a check for $35.20. He was also out of work and his wife had left him for another man. His prior record consisted of a drunk charge and a non-support charge. Our examination of these two cases indicated no significant differences for sentencing purposes. But they appeared before different judges and the first man received 15 years in prison and the second man 30 days.[24]

In view of the mitigating circumstances and the fact that these two offenders had no significant criminal record, a European judge would send neither of the two to prison. The Japanese system, as we shall see, provides still a better example of how the criminal justice system should work in order to achieve its attested objectives. Of course, the sociocultural traditions of a country like Japan are quite different from those prevailing in the United States. Unless we review the judicial process in Japan in the larger context of that country's social relations and cultural values, it may even seem outlandish and unbelievable to us. Nevertheless, the fact is that if we could use the same underlying principles to foster more confidence in the socioeconomic system, instead of apathy and cynicism that now prevail in the public, and apply more rational and humane penal policies in this country, it would not be impossible to approach Japan's experience of success in its fight against crime. It is estimated that in Japan about 99 percent of all the people who are tried are found guilty.

But even more astonishing to an American way of thinking, a considerable number of confessed criminals are never taken to court, and only about four percent of convicted criminals ever go to jail. The rest are left off with fines or suspended sentences and placed under the guidance of a nationwide network of volunteer parole officers. The prime objective of a Japanese prosecutor, in short, is not to send an offender to prison but to secure his confession, repentance and reform.[25]

Back to the practices of American judges:

In January the President of the United States commuted to time served the sentence of a first offender, a former army lieutenant, and a veteran of over 500 days in combat, who had been given 18 years for forging six small checks.
In one of our institutions a middle-aged credit union treasurer is serving 117 days for embezzling $24,000 in order to cover his gambling debts. On the other hand, another middle-aged embezzler with a fine past record and a fine family is serving

20 years, with 5 years probation to follow. At the same institution is a war veteran, a 39-year-old attorney who has never been in trouble before, serving 11 years for illegally importing parrots into this country. Another who is destined for the same institution is a middle-aged tax accountant who on tax fraud charges received 31 years and 31 days in consecutive sentences. In sharp contrast, at the same institution last year an unstable young man served out his 98-day sentence for armed bank robbery.[26]

Judge Frankel summarizes the inadequacies of the sentencing process in the following manner:

The sentencing powers of the judges are . . . so far unconfined that, except for frequently monstrous maximum limits, they are effectively subject to no law at all. Everyone with the least training in law would be prompt to denounce a statute that merely said the penalty for crimes "shall be any term the judge sees fit to impose." A regime of such arbitrary fiat would be intolerable in a supposedly free society, to say nothing of being invalid under our due-process clause. But the fact is that we have accepted unthinkingly a criminal code creating in effect precisely that degree of unbridled power.[27]

What perceptions can a system like this create in the public except disbelief, disrespect, cynicism, apathy, even disgust and outrage? Is it a wonder that various studies have shown a declining public trust in and growth of cynicism about the criminal justice system? A survey conducted by the *New York Times* based on interviews of 1,146 adults in all five boroughs of New York City found that:

More than two-thirds said that it was easier than it was just a few years ago to break the law in New York City and get away with it.

Fewer than one in ten had a lot of confidence that a person who tried to rob or mug them would be jailed if caught, compared with one in six four years ago. And only one in 20 had a lot of confidence that a mugger or robber would be caught at all.[28]

Another interview conducted a year later with two dozen victims who, due to fear of reprisal preferred to remain anonymous, showed a "persuasive feeling to despair" over their personal experiences and "a profound skepticism about the Criminal Justice System."[29]

## LACK OF IDEOLOGY

Perhaps because of the dynamic nature of their society, flexibility of attitudes, and openness to new ideas and practices, Americans lack a clear, ascertainable ideology in dealing with the crime problem. This lack of ideology, or rather coexistence of conflicting ideologies in the criminal justice system, can be noticed in court practices, police conduct, and functioning of penal institutions. As a former U.S. attorney general has flatly stated, "We cannot say we practice any theory of penology in America today. We do what we do. And what we do has practically no relationship to what we say we do."[30]

As a matter of fact, this lack of clear concepts is not limited to penology alone. As we have had occasion to observe, it can be noticed in all areas of social life. Americans' traditional openness to new ideas and experiments has been one of the main causes of this country's greatness, as well as of some of its tremendous human problems. Psychoanalysis and sociology, two disciplines that have revolutionized our conceptions about ourselves and our universe, have not been taken so seriously anywhere as in the United States, and they have helped, rightly or wrongly, with the development and spread of the relativistic outlook, of situation ethics. Together with other historical realities such as the lack of strong traditions that bind people together, this relativistic outlook has made Americans, perhaps more than any other nation on earth, willing to try out new ideas.

Freedom of expression and experimentation has been protected by the U.S. Constitution and the Supreme Court's interpretation of the Bill of Rights. This freedom has been used by various groups and individuals, including the people who sell new and uncommon ideas like sexual license, civil disorder, free adult-child sexual relations, and so on. The net result is that many Americans are no longer sure about what is morally or socially valid or wrong. Religious beliefs which, for better or worse, once kept a strong hold on the individual are now open to questioning and doubt and are no longer treated as authentic guides for practical living. For many people, there is nothing sacred in any of the fundamental moral principles that have kept human society together in the past.

One of the basic concepts in morality and criminal law is responsibility. We cannot logically and morally punish a person unless we can hold him responsible for his transgression. At the same time, we have learned from psychoanalysis that people act under the influence of both conscious and unconscious forces, ideas, feelings, and perceptions that have been instilled in them through the process of socialization and over which they do not have much control. In other words, there are many instances, according to this perspective, when a person cannot be held responsible for his actions. We have learned from sociology that what we are and how we react to various outside stimuli are determined by the social forces and relationships that have existed in our particular social environment. We become, by and large, what our social climate expects us to be. Free will is only a potentiality that can be developed or restricted under material and emotional deprivations. Thus, in this perspective, perhaps even more than the psychoanalytic outlook, people cannot be deemed responsible for their acts, especially if they have had to live under unsuitable social conditions.

It is within this intellectual background and also a laudable compassion for the poor, the underprivileged, and the emotionally handicapped that certain authorities express outrage that the offenders, themselves victims of the social environment, are still being punished today. A famous psychiatrist goes so far in this direction as to call society's official reaction in the form of punishment a crime in itself.[31] Lawyers and judges—and of course liberal law professors—have rightly concerned themselves with the disadvantageous position of most apprehended offenders, the discriminatory practices of police, prosecutors, courts, and parole boards, and the flagrant violation of the civil rights of poorer members of society. The result has been a widespread confusion about what to do with the offender; whether to treat him as a culprit who has unjustifiably wronged an innocent victim or, as many have advocated, as an involuntary victim of the social forces; whether to punish or, instead, to try to cure him.

Then there is the discrepancy between the declared goals of the criminal justice system and the actual practices of its functionaries. We keep talking about the rights of the accused, knowing all too well that as a rule an accused person who cannot provide bail will remain in jail even though he is innocent and may be ultimately cleared of the charge against him. The Supreme Court's concern with the right of the accused to have professional counsel has been expressed in the rule that a confession obtained without the Miranda warning is inadmissible in court. Yet, we know that normally a court-appointed lawyer for the indigent offender is not as able as a regularly paid attorney. Neither is he sufficiently motivated; thus, instead of spending the necessary time to defend the accused properly, he will make a quick deal with the prosecution. We earnestly talk about prisoners' rights. We even question whether execution by electrocution or lethal gas is not cruel and inhuman. At the same time the system allows numerous appeal proceedings to drag on for years and at the end of the long ordeal often kills the culprit. As for other rights of the prisoner, we know that rape, drug abuse, and violence are routinely committed among the inmates of many American prisons.

The cruel and demeaning treatment of offenders in American penal institutions cannot, of course, be justified or condoned. On the other hand, the sentimental and irrational approach of most American courts in their treatment of offenders does not make much sense either. It is an undeniable fact that to be effective as a deterrent and as a reassurance to the public that moral and legal rules should be observed, punishment must be swift, just, and consistent. The American criminal justice system seems to lack all these attributes. We have seen that most crimes are not detected or reported to police, that the system is overburdened with time-consuming technicalities, that sentences given by various courts are not consistent, and many times, at least as far as the public can understand, do not fit the severity of the crimes committed. Then, there is the added inability of the courts because of exclusionary rules, plea bargaining practice, or some other grounds, to treat offenders with equal justice and consistency. With the adoption of the exclusionary rules, the system has in fact chosen at times to allow an offender whose guilt has been proven beyond doubt to escape punishment simply because the police, for instance, deliberately or otherwise did not give him the Miranda warning before questioning him.[32] Instead of penalizing the police for their violations of procedural rules, the courts have given undue consideration to the offender, even when his guilt is independently established. The result has been a sense of outrage in the victim and a feeling of helplessness or complete cynicism in the public about the efficiency, justice, or rationality of the court system.

In this respect, it is interesting to note how differences in social position and perception color the arguments advanced by members of various groups. Arguments may sound rational, even laudatory, but in reality conceal certain basic flaws in the whole social system. On July 5, 1984, the Supreme Court relaxed the exclusionary rule in matters involving deportation of illegal aliens; it had recently adopted the same stance concerning some other issues. In an interview with Ted Koppel on "Nightline," Harvard professor Alan Dershowitz expressed strong reservations about the new ruling. In responding to the argument that the exclusionary rule has occasioned the release of many offenders whose guilt was established beyond doubt because of a technicality such as nonobservance of the Miranda ruling, he argued that obviously there were problems concerning such matters as the established guilt of a freed offender and the court's apparent indifference to the suffering of the victim. We should remember, he argued, that the Constitution is an expensive document and that there is a price we have to pay in order to protect our fundamental freedoms and rights.

Aside from the fact that the exclusionary rules are not part of the Constitution but were adopted by the Supreme Court in its interpretation of the document and that they are not the prerequisite or the only means of protecting individual rights, the question is what groups really pay the high cost of keeping not only the Constitution but also the Supreme Court rulings. Certainly, the Supreme Court justices don't suffer; they have all the protection they need to be safe in their offices and homes. Neither do lawyers like professor Dershowitz who have rich clients, pay the price. They can certainly afford to live in prosperous neighborhoods with all that money can buy: better police protection, effective alarm systems, safer security locks, and so on. For the keeping of the exclusionary rules, which are most often used to get the white-collar, rich offenders off the hook, the ordinary people pay, especially those who are forced to live in crime-infested neighborhoods, where they dare not come out of their homes at night. These people are repeatedly subjected to street crime and pay with their lives, well-being, and property.

The loopholes of the system, which I believe result in increased criminality in the long run—either because people may decide to revenge the injustice they suffer personally or because they become indifferent to crimes committed by others and thus do not cooperate with the police—are to a large extent due to the lack of proper perspectives in the criminal justice administration. In applying the exclusionary rules, courts have shown a lopsided concern about the rights of the accused in complete disregard of the rights of the victim and the public. They plea bargain with offenders as an expedient and necessary measure, without much awareness or regard for the long-range ill effects of the practice on the perceptions and reactions of the public toward the criminal justice system and indeed the whole social structure. Some other measures casually adopted by the criminal justice system are even more shocking, even though they are presented to the public as though they contained the most logical solution to the crime problem. For example, sometimes offenders are released from jail before they have served their time, not because they are presumably rehabilitated or present no further danger to society, but because jails are overcrowded. The long-range effects of such measures, which may sound appropriate in the context of a short-range economic, cost-benefit analysis, will be terribly negative on the perceptions of the public.

On November 2, 1983, the *New York Times* reported that 341 inmates were released from jail by the order of a federal district court in Manhattan to ease the problem of overcrowding. They were required to post 10 percent of their bail in order to be eligible for release. The mayor of New York City expressed reservations about the order, saying, "Some of these people will go out and commit crimes while they await trial." The city's correction commissioner, who oversees the jails, had similar misgivings. But the detainees were released just the same. We have the account of at least one incident involving a freed prisoner who committed rape only two days after he was released.

A Riker's Island prisoner freed last week under a program to ease jail overcrowding was ordered held on $100,000 bail yesterday after he was accused of raping a woman two days following his release. . . .

Mr. Craig was released last Wednesday, while awaiting trial on a charge of grand larceny. He paid 10 percent of the bail on the larceny charge, or $100, as required under the release program ordered by a Federal court.

According to police, Mr. Craig raped a 21-year-old woman in an abandoned building at 172d Street and Southern Boulevard on Friday. He was taken into custody Monday night.[33]

I am not arguing that bail should be set so high that all potential offenders must remain in jail while awaiting trial. As a matter of fact, many European countries routinely release accused persons without bail if there is relative assurance that they will show up for trial. My argument is that decreasing the amount of bail to such a ludicrous level and then freeing prisoners only because jails are overcrowded—acts that in fact negate the accepted principles of punishment—will generate disrespect for the law and in the long run increase antisocial tendencies. Under such circumstances, perhaps it would be more logical, and even more effective, to establish a minimum of emotional rapport with the accused as European courts try to do and set him free pending trial on his word of honor. If he does not intend to show up when he is required to—and in many societies he does show up on his own—the possibility of losing a $100 bail would not make him act differently. But imagine what the rape victim, her relatives, friends and the public feel about the criminal justice system in the case just cited.

Is it any wonder that the public should be outraged and demand far more drastic measures against all offenders? As a reporter of the *New York Times* observed:

Victims who once considered themselves "liberals" and some who still do, say they have little sympathy for their assailants or for political leaders and scholars who emphasize poverty or other environmental factors as causes of crime. . . .

If the case goes to trial, the victim hopes to read to the jury a letter in which she urges a campaign against "irresponsible judges who so indiscriminately free these muggers, rapists, killers, etc. on parole," and in which she asks for the election of a governor "who will impose the death penalty."[34]

On March 9, 1984, the *New York Post*, which has a large circulation and therefore a considerable impact on public perceptions, carried the following comments in its Page One Editorial:

New York City judges are turning the massive police war on the Lower East Side drug supermarkets into an obscene farce.

They are releasing nefarious drug dealers as fast as the cops arrest them.

Of 2,457 arrests so far in the police raids launched on January 18 most involve dealers who had been arrested at least twice, many several times. What An Insult This Delivers To Us All!

What a grim burlesque it makes of the criminal justice process.

Time after time, over the past seven weeks these base traders in human frailty have been freed to return to the empty doorways and hallways.[35]

Again, on March 9, 1984, the same paper, in trying to explain the difficulties a judge must face in dealing with drug cases, ran the headline, "The Post goes to Night Court to see why drug dealers laugh at the law. Judge shows how criminal justice system turns to junk."

The reporter explains how the judge bargains with accused persons in drug cases brought to his court knowing all too well that the more experienced offender will not accept his offer of a milder sentence in return for admission of guilt to a lesser crime. The offender knows that the district attorney (DA) cannot come up with enough evidence to prove his case in the statutory six-day period. On this particular night the judge handles "61 cases, many of them disposed of by bargaining. Each case has taken an average of six minutes, although some have taken only seconds."[36]

The dissatisfaction felt in the community is not, of course, limited to rape victims or socially responsible newspaper reporters. Even members of the criminal justice system have declared at times that they are working in an unjust and failing system. A judge of many years, who is qualified to express a noticeable opinion, describes this reality, "I believe that many judges are aware that they are presiding over a legal and legitimized system of injustice. This sense of frustration and impotence is in my opinion a major, though seldom articulated, cause of much judicial dissatisfaction."[37]

In late April 1984 the Federation of New York State Judges, the largest organization of judges in the United States, representing more than 2,000 justices at all levels, called on its members to be stricter with criminals and send everyone convicted of a serious crime to prison even if the problem of overcrowding in jails makes this recommendation difficult. The resolution of the federation stated in part:

The streets of New York have become lawless marches of robbers, rapists and felons of every kind, in part because of "true and common perception of a failing criminal justice system."

When the safety of the people of this state cannot be assured except by the severe punishment of those who brutalize them, then the prisons to which such defendants should be sent should be built. Swift and severe punishment is the only defense against predators.

The Federation has called on all judges in New York State not to be concerned with lack of space, but to sentence firmly and fairly any of those who would be a danger to society.[38]

Representing the federation, Justice Murphy said in a statement accompanying the resolution that increased imprisonment was necessary in part because society had no other remedy for crime. Rehabilitation, he maintained, has proved to be a failure. He went on:

Society is pressed to its ancient defense against the violent criminal: the fear of swift and severe punishment. . . . Either we take that road now, or we will live in the sickly twilight of a soulless people too weak to drive predators out of their own house. . . .

[Ordinary men and women] tell us that criminals have taken the city, that crime has beaten government to its knees, that the moral passion for justice has been drained out of society and, in its place, there is an overwhelming sense of helplessness.[39]

In view of the educative impact of the various aspects of law enforcement in society, the learning processes and conditioning, it is doubtful that mere "swift and severe punishment"—irrespective of what happens before, during and after detention—can solve the crime problem. As we have seen, crime is a function of various cultural and social forces much more comprehensive in their impact on individuals' perception and behavior than the possibility of detection and punishment alone, which as we have seen, is negligible under present criminal court practices. As for punishment, it is not solely the swiftness and severity of its application that produces the desired effect, but perhaps more importantly, the certainty that when a crime is committed, it will lead, in all likelihood, to punishment. Nevertheless, the resolution of the federation and statements made by its representative are significant in that they reflect the sense of rage and desperation felt by victims of crime, ordinary citizens, judges, and other public officials about the crime problem and the failure of the criminal justice system to achieve its attested goals.

## NOTES

1. Lois G. Forer, *Money and Justice: Who Owns the Courts?* (New York: W. W. Norton & Co., 1984), p. 211.

2. See Charles R. Ashman, *The Finest Judges Money Can Buy: And Other Forms of Judicial Pollution* (Los Angeles: Nash Publishing, 1973), especially pp. 270–278.

3. Ibid., p. 5.

4. Ibid., pp. 4–5.

5. Ramsey Clark, *Crime in America: Observations on Its Nature, Causes, Prevention and Control* (New York: Simon & Schuster, 1970), pp. 117–118.

6. Forer, *Money and Justice*, p. 19. Chief Justice Warren Burger of the Supreme Court declared that the nation is plagued "with an almost irrational focus—virtually a mania—on litigation as a way to solve all problems." Derek Bok, the former dean of the Harvard Law School, has pointed out that Japan graduates 30 percent more engineers than the United States and that "Japan boasts a total of less than 15,000 lawyers while American universities graduate 35,000 lawyers every year."

7. See Forer, *Money and Justice*, p. 23.

8. See, for instance, the excellent book by Norval Morris, *The Future of Imprisonment: Studies in Crime and Justice* (Chicago: The University of Chicago Press, 1974). See also Norval Morris and Gordon Hawkins, *The Honest Politician's Guide to Crime Control* (Chicago: The University of Chicago Press, 1970).

9. Forer, *Money and Justice*, p. 24.

10. See Michael H. Graham, *Tightening the Reins of Justice in America: A Comparative Analysis of the Criminal Jury Trial in England and the United States* (Westport, Conn.: Greenwood Press, 1983).

11. See Abraham S. Blumberg, *Criminal Justice* (Chicago: Quadrangle Books, 1970), p. 28.

12. *New York Times*, July 5, 1984.

13. *New York Times*, March 15, 1984, p. B1.

14. Ibid., p. B9.

15. J. Dollard, L. W. Doob, N. E. Miller, O. H. Mouirer, and R. R. Sears, *Frustration and Aggression* (New Haven, Conn.: Yale University Press, 1939), p. 33.

16. Dennis Chapman, "The Stereotype of the Criminal and the Social Consequences," *International Journal of Criminology and Penology* 1, no.1 (1973): 15–30.

17. See Nathan Goldman, *The Differential Selection of Juvenile Offenders for Court Appearance* (New York: National Council on Crime and Delinquency, 1963).

18. Trence Patrick Thornberry, *Punishment and Crime: The Effect of Legal Dispositions on Subsequent Criminal Behavior* (Ann Arbor, Mich.: University Microfilms, 1972).

19. Eugene Doleschal and Nora Klapmuts, "Toward a New Criminology," in Sir Leon Radzinowicz and Marvin E. Wolfgang, *Crime and Justice*, 2d rev. ed., 3 vols. (New York: Basic Books, 1977), 1:643.

20. Franklin Zimring and Gordon Hawkins, "The Legal Threat as an Instrument of Social Change," in June Louin Tapp and Felice J. Levine, *Law, Justice and the Individual in Society: Psychological and Legal Issues* (New York: Holt, Rinehart and Winston, 1977), p. 67.

21. Marvin E. Frankel, *Criminal Sentences: Law Without Order* (New York: Hill and Wang, 1973), pp. 8–9.

22. *New York Times*, January 12, 1982, p. B15.

23. Cesare Beccaria, *An Essay on Crimes and Punishment, 1770*, trans. J. A. Farrar (London: Chatto & Windus, 1880), p. 139.

24. Frankel, *Criminal Sentences*, pp. 21–22.

25. Robert C. Christopher, *The Japanese Mind: The Goliath Explained* (New York: Linden Press/Simon & Schuster, 1983), p. 164.

26. U.S. Senate, "Countdown for Judicial Sentencing," in *Of Prisons and Justice*, Senate Doc. no. 70, 88th Cong. 2d Sess. (1964) p. 331.

27. Frankel, *Criminal Sentences*, p. 8.

28. *New York Times*, December 22, 1981, p. B7.

29. *New York Times*, October 18, 1982, p. B1.

30. Ramsey Clark, *Crime in America*, p. 219.

31. See Karl Menninger, *The Crime of Punishment* (Baltimore; Penguin Books, 1979).

32. See Michael Graham, *Tightening the Reins*.

33. *New York Times*, November 9, 1983, p. B3.

34. *New York Times*, October 18, 1982, pp. B1, B4.

35. *New York Post*, March 9, 1984, p. 1.

36. Ibid., p. 13.

37. Forer, *Money and Justice*, p. 11.

38. *New York Times*, April 23, 1984, p. 1.

39. Ibid., p. B4.

# 8

# Police

The most visible element in the criminal justice system is the police. The average, law-abiding citizen rarely comes into contact with the courts; he is still less likely to end up in a penal institution. He meets some police officer, however, almost every day. He acquires a conception of what police functions are and how he should respond in situations where he encounters them.

Police have a number of very significant duties ranging from providing civic assistance to anyone who needs it—sick and old people, children—to detecting crime, apprehending criminals, appearing in court as prosecution witnesses, and other crime-related activities. Obviously, no matter how efficient the police are, or how diligently they try, they cannot perform their duties properly unless they have the trust and cooperation of the public. When a crime is committed police are not usually present at the scene. To solve the crime, then, they will have to depend on people in the community to report it. They will also have to depend on victims, actual witnesses, and other informants for information about the identity and possible whereabouts of the offender. If there are mutual trust, respect, and positive associations between the public and police, the needed cooperation will be more readily available. If police are conceived of as impartial law enforcers and protectors of individual rights, if in short they are viewed as true and reliable servants of the people, public cooperation and participation in all facets of the crime-control process (prevention, detection, conviction, rehabilitation) can be secured with much less difficulty. On the other hand, if police are rightly or wrongly viewed by the public as corrupt or easily corruptible by money and power, as biased agents of an unjust socioeconomic system, or as mindless instruments of discrimination, suppression, and exploitation of the majority by dominant groups, then it would be naive to expect willing cooperation of the public with the police.

## POLICE CHARACTERISTICS

The degree to which police enjoy the cooperation and effective participation of the public depends on various personal and organizational factors.

### Personal Factors

In the final analysis, it is the individual police officer who makes a postitive or negative impact on the people he is supposed to serve. The quality and extent of this impact depends to a large degree on the personal attributes of the police and their ability to establish and foster positive relations with the public. A police officer acts, however, in the larger context of historical and social perceptions about his profession. As an individual, he can try to modify the prevailing image of the police force; he cannot, however, totally transform it. For instance, even though the police perform a variety of useful social services today, the public perception of their duties, as well as their own self-image, is that of the cop chasing the robber.[1] Police image is also related to the amount of social prestige the force enjoys. It seems that compared with some European police forces, the American police enjoy a low level of prestige. As Reiss has noted, "An aspect of the prestige of any occupation is the willingness of persons to enter the occupation. Negroes have both accorded the police less prestige and have been less willing to consider it an occupational choice."[2] What is more striking is the fact that young people are less likely to consider police work as a possible future occupation. Donald Bouma found that only 8 percent of the white and only 3 percent of the Black youths "would like to be a policeman when they grow up."[3]

An authority who was himself a police officer for a number of years has the following to say about the problem:

The great stumbling block [in the way of law-enforcement occupation obtaining the status of a profession] is its traditionally low status in our culture. A warped conception of the policeman has been cultivated in the mass media. The public holds fast to the derogatory stereotypes of the grafting cop, the sadistic cop, the dumb cop, the chiseling cop, and the thick-brogued cop. There can be no profession where the public refuses to grant high status and prestige.[4]

In contrast, the British police enjoy not only a very high degree of social prestige; they also act as idealized models for proper action. Their contribution in creating the law-abiding character of the British citizen is apparently considerable. The British anthropologist Geoffrey Gorer has in fact suggested that the British incorporate a very positive image of the police, an image that becomes part of their integrated and strong superego. His observations sound convincing.

I wish to advance the hypothesis that one of the techniques by which the national character of a society may be modified or transformed over a given period is through the selection of personnel for institutions which are in continuing contact with the mass of the population in a somewhat superordinate position. . . .

I should like to suggest that, increasingly during the past century, the English policeman has been for his peers not only an object of respect but also a model of the ideal male character, self-controlled, possessing more strength than he ever has to call into use except in the gravest emergency, fair and impartial, serving the abstractions of Peace and Justice rather than any personal allegiance or sectional advantage.[5]

The consequence is, as he maintains, an internalization of a positive police image, which helps reinforce the internal policing of all antisocial tendencies in the individual. "So the bulk of the population has, so to speak, incorporated the police man or woman as an ideal and become progressively more 'self-policing.' "[6]

Police image is of course affected, directly and indirectly, by various factors, including the caliber and training of the individuals who make up the force. It is an accepted fact that in many American police forces, unsavory characters exert tremendous control over the life and property of the people. The fact was repeatedly confirmed by older studies. These studies are still valid because they represent the public's continuous conceptions about the police.

In their study of thirty candidates for the San Jose police force in California in 1916, Lewis Terman and Arthur Otis concluded on the basis of the tests they had administered that out of the thirty, twenty-one were mentally inferior, and only three had an I.Q. of 100 or more.[7] As an unexpected by-product of his work in providing a handbook on diagnostic projective tests, David Rapaport concluded that "if compared with a city population [the police] have to be considered in some degree schizoid."[8] Lois L. Kates administered standard Rorschach tests to twenty-five New York City patrolmen and found that according to the tests the more maladjusted policemen "tended to be more satisfied with their work than the less maladjusted."[9] In 1939 Read Bain, a sociologist, had prepared a report on the police in which he stated that three-quarters of policemen in the United States were mentally unfit for their work.[10] Similar misgivings about the personalities of police officers have also been voiced in more recent literature, even though there is equally reputable research that contradicts these findings. "A substantial clinical literature suggests that police officers are a special type of personality—authoritarian, aggressive, and sadistic. . . . Two studies tested the hypothesis that the police are authoritarian personalities.

Both studies conclude that policemen are less likely than the dominant population to score high on the F. scale."[11]

The F or fascism scale is a test constructed by Adorno and his colleagues that measures predispositions to hostile attitudes and actions towards certain minorities. It is composed of questions that presumably reveal the subject's potential for submission to authority, lack of introspection, superstition, stereotypical beliefs, admiration for power and sheer force, destructive tendencies and exaggerated concern with sexual mores—traits that also characterize the authoritarian personality. There is some controversy regarding the validity and capacity of the F scale to encompass the wider aspects of prejudice. McNamara found that policemen score lower on the F. scale than nonpolice people in the same class category and similar occupational settings. On the whole, however, the image of the policeman in many communities is still that of an aggressive, power-hungry, arbitrary, and perhaps even psychologically unbalanced individual. He comes from the lower class, but desiring to distance himself from his origins and seeking to get closer to the sources of power, he identifies himself with the rich and powerful. Studies summarized by Jerome Skolnick show the political profile of the policeman as a conservative, perhaps even reactionary, person of lower or lower middle–class origin, often a supporter of radical right causes, often prejudiced and repressive and extremely ambivalent about the rights of others. He works in the context of a police culture that encourages fear, suspicion, low self-esteem, and distrust of others.[12]

In contrast, observe the way some European police forces are educated and how a positive image of the police is created in the public. In Sweden, for instance, to become a police officer one has to be a citizen who is at least nineteen years old and who has a good character. He must have a driver's license and "pass a medical examination and possess minimal educational standards." In each district, the chief of police, who has access to more information about the people, reviews the local applications, and if he approves the candidate, sends his forms to the National Police Board. The board then processes the applications. If approved at this stage, candidates are sent to the police school for basic training. This training lasts forty-three weeks. After finishing the school, the candidate acquires practical experience in Stockholm where initial assignments are made according to the policeman's qualifications and abilities. Additional training is available for higher ranks of the police force at the Police College.[13] It is noteworthy that the Swedish police consider crime prevention as a significant part of their work and that to achieve their objectives, they maintain a very close relationship with the public. They have developed special programs to alert the public and show them how to deter various property crimes such as robberies, burglaries, and auto thefts. These programs are regularly presented in the mass media. "The police also give instruction in the public schools regarding law enforcement subjects, to approximately 225,000 students each year."[14]

A similar approach to recruitment and training of policemen can be observed in the practices of the West German government. There, each state has its own training school for aspiring policemen. Before an applicant is admitted to the school, it must be established that he or she does indeed possess the qualities deemed necessary for police work. He or she must have "sufficient education, high personal character, good health and other prerequisites." If the candidate is accepted, he or she is admitted to a basic police course in his or her own province. The course may last one year. But this theoretical education is supplemented by a rather long period of practical training. "The recruit must have a combination of training and approximately three years practical experience before he is recognized as a policeman." The aim is to provide the police with the basic knowledge in social sciences and to equip him with skills necessary to deal effectively with the people he is hired to serve. About 25 percent of his training time is spent in the study of psychology, government, and history.[15] "The German police have adopted the motto 'The policeman—your friend and helper,' which is in accordance with the basic German philosophy of total involvement in the community."[16]

Again by contrast, it is interesting to note what Charles Reith, a British police historian, wrote about police training in the United States, "It can be said of police training schools that the recruit is taught everything except the essential requirements of his calling, which is how to secure and maintain the approval and respect of the public whom he encounters daily in the course of his duties." The authority who quoted the preceding in his book adds: "This assessment remains applicable today, if on the generous side, since in the average police department, serving communities with less than a quarter of a million people, the police recruit now receives less than three weeks' training."[17]

## Police Perceptions about Self, Courts, and the Public

Obviously what the police think about their power and authority, image and standing with the courts and the public, and their realistic chances of properly carrying out their duties has an impact on their behavior. The American police, it seems, have on the whole a negative perception about their social image and standing with the courts and the public. Unlike most other professions, police are normally called in when there is tragedy, strife, or other unpleasant interpersonal relations. This fact, of course, affects police officers' perceptions about their role in society and their conceptions about human nature in general. The people who are involved in unpleasant crime-related situations, both offenders and victims, also develop negative attitudes toward the police. Among the less privileged, where a sense of discrimination and injustice is experienced more objectively, the negative feeling toward the police approaches concealed and at times overt animosity. Although only a small portion of police officers' daily contacts with citizens may involve antagonism between the two, an unfavorable impression remains and colors the perceptions of a much larger segment of society. "A substantial proportion of citizens who encounter the police in the long run may experience at least one encounter in which they define the police as antagonistic."[18]

In such a normally negative transactional setting, it is natural that the police should also perceive the public as uncooperative, unappreciative, or even antagonistic. As William Westley has observed:

The policeman's world is spawned of degradation, corruption and insecurity. He sees men as ill-willed, exploitative, mean and dirty; himself a victim of injustice, misunderstood and defiled. . . . He tends to meet those portions of the public which are acting contrary to the law or using the law to further their own ends. He is exposed to public immorality. He becomes cynical. His is a society emphasizing the crooked, the weak and the unscrupulous. Accordingly his morality is one of expedience and his self-conception one of a martyr.[19]

Peter Rossi and his colleagues found in their study that 54 percent of the police are dissatisfied with the respect they receive from the public.[20] Arthur Niederhoffer, for more than twenty years a police officer himself, summarizes these negative perceptions:

The police feel that they deserve respect from the public. But the upper class looks down on them; the middle class seems to ignore them, as if they were part of the urban scenery; the lower class fears them. Even the courts often appear to be against them, making it more and more difficult to obtain convictions of criminals. With bitterness, therefore, the police tend to think of themselves as a minority group in the society.[21]

Police complaints about the courts are psychologically much more significant. Theoretically, police and criminal courts have the same objectives: to bring the offender to justice. In practice, however, criminal courts have created seemingly unnecessary impediments for the police, preventing them from accomplishing their task, and have treated them with suspicion and disrespect, as if they were waging their own personal war against criminals rather than doing what is expected of them. As we shall see shortly, police are required to act under conflicting law enforcement philosophies, and they are blamed in the process no matter which ideology they follow.

It is an established fact that as police gain more practical experience, they realize that their authority is repeatedly undermined by the courts and that their competence is gradually diminished. McNamara, for instance, found that as New York City policemen go through recruitment, training, and practical experience in the field, their sense of authority appropriate to their responsibilities wanes at each stage. When presented with the statement: "The present system of state and local laws has undermined the patrolman's authority to a dangerous extent," only 24 percent of all the recruits at the beginning of their police training agreed. At the end of their training, the percentage of those who agreed with the statement rose to 34 percent. One year after the end of their training, 76 percent thought the statement was correct. Likewise 76 percent of all officers agreed at the start of their training that "Generally speaking, patrolmen today have enough legal authority to get their job done efficiently." After two years of actual experience in the field that proportion declined to 35 percent.[22]

Experienced officers thought that courts of law tended to undermine their authority. This belief became stronger with the number of years a police officer spent in the force. Police recruits generally believed that courts of law would accept them as reliable witnesses. At this stage, only 19 percent agreed with the statement: "The courts have tended in recent years to discount the testimony of patrolmen where there are other witnesses or there is no other proof regarding an alleged crime, offense, or violation." The percentage had risen to 45 percent by the end of police officers' training and to 60 percent after two years of actual police duty in the field.[23] As another known authority has aptly observed:

> When an appellate court rules that police may not in the future engage in certain enforcement activities, since these constitute a violation of the rule of law, the inclination of the police is typically not to feel shame but indignation. . . . [The] police see the court's affirmation of principles of due process as, in effect, the creation of harsh "working conditions." . . . Their political superiors insist on "production" while their judicial superiors impede their capacity to "produce." Under such frustrating conditions, the appellate judiciary inevitably comes to be seen as "traitor" to its responsibility to keep the community free from criminality.[24]

It is against this background of contradictory law enforcement philosophies and responsibilities that the police view many of the criminal courts' interpretations of the Constitution as harmful aberrations of the socially accepted standards of fair play and justice. Police feel that the impact of the exclusionary rule "has not been to guarantee greater protection of the freedom of 'decent citizens' from unreasonable police zeal, but rather to complicate unnecessarily the task of detecting and apprehending criminals."[25]

Reiss found that a substantial minority of police officers thought that prosecutors base their decision to follow a case through more on whether they can win the case in court than on any consideration for the sense of equity or justice.[26] They also thought prosecutors were too quick in reducing charges or failed to press charges without following any apparent standards or patterns of action. Similar conceptions also exist among the police about criminal courts. A Chicago survey of police opinion showed that in 1961 and 1965, 84.8 percent of sergeants thought that the courts are "too lenient" on offenders, and in 1965, 67.5 percent said that it is discouraging to be a policeman because criminal courts let so many people off with little or no punishment.[27]

## Corruption

To do a proper job as agents of the criminal justice system, police should be bound by common standards; they should treat people fairly and justly and should be above temptation and undue influences. Obviously if police are perceived to be corrupt and easily swayed by pecuniary or political considerations, they will not be trusted by the public; they cannot depend on the public's cooperation, which is so essential for successful police activity.

Unfortunately, a number of studies and too many incidents have shown that corruption is a fact of life in many American police forces. The Knapp Commission Report on Police Corruption has this to say about the problem:

We found corruption to be widespread. It took various forms depending upon the activity involved, appearing at its most sophisticated among plainclothesmen assigned to enforcing gambling laws. In the five plainclothes divisions where our investigators were concentrated we found a strikingly standardized pattern of corruption. Evidence before us led us to the conclusion that the same pattern existed in the remaining divisions which we did not investigate in depth.[28]

According to the same commission, half of the police force in New York City accepted payoffs. In 1974 widespread police corruption was found in Chicago, Philadelphia, Indianapolis, Cleveland, Houston, Denver, and New York involving illegal gambling, stolen goods, prostitution, and narcotics.[29]

The widespread use of narcotics among various social groups and the tremendous profits involved in illegal importation and sale of drugs in this country have corrupted many public officials, including police officers. When millions of dollars can be made in a big drug deal, it is not terribly difficult to buy off politicians, senators, judges, and police officers. As the same Knapp Commission Report states: "Corruption in narcotics law enforcement has grown in recent years to the point where high-ranking police officials acknowledge it to be the most serious problem facing the Department....In many cases police officers actively extort money and/or drugs from suspected narcotics law violators."[30]

In one such case, known as the French Connection, "New York City narcotics detectives diverted 188 pounds of heroin and 31 pounds of cocaine to their own use, making the Narcotics Bureau's Special Investigating Unit (SIU) perhaps the largest heroin and cocaine dealer in the city."[31] Brooklyn District Attorney Eugene Gold testified that 70 percent of Brooklyn's detectives were taking graft.[32]

Another form of corruption, usually not perceived as such due to the nature of political processes in this country, is the subservience of the police to strong interst groups. As Dan Dodson, the director of the Center for Human Relations and Community Studies at New York University has observed:

No policeman enforces all the laws of a community. If he did, we would all be in jail before the end of the first day. The laws which are selected for enforcement are those which the power structure of the community wants enforced. The police official's job is dependent upon his having radar-like equipment to sense what is the power structure and what it wants enforced as law.[33]

Although corruption is widespread among American police forces, this does not of course mean that every police officer is corrupt. The extent of corruption among American police may actually be much less than in many other places. Some of the European police forces are notorious for accepting bribes and bending the law to help the rich and the powerful. Nevertheless, since the expectations of the American public are much higher than those of many societies where people accept corruption and favoritism as inevitable facts of life, police corruption in this country may have a more devastating effect in creating frustration and possibly more criminality.

## CONTRADICTORY LOYALTIES

In every society much police work is, to say the least, very unpleasant. At times, it can result in personal injury or even death of the policeman. The task becomes even more frustrating when police have to function under contradictory standards and expectations. It is the duty of the police to detect crimes, to apprehend offenders, to bring them to justice, and to help punish the guilty. In this, there is complete harmony between police and the public. Police, however, have to work under restrictions which seem unreasonable and unnecessary at times, at least as far as the police are concerned. Nobody could advocate in a democratic society that police should be allowed unfettered autonomy in order to get every suspect convicted. Many, however, have pointed out the enormous difficulties under which police perform their duties: the inevitable frustrations they have to tolerate and hardships due to a large extent to contradictory directives they have to follow. As Jerome Skolnick has observed:

It is rarely recognized that the conduct of police may be related in a fundamental way to the character and goals of the institution itself—the duties police are called upon to perform, associated with the assumptions of the system of legal justice and that it may not be men who are good or bad, so much as the premises and designs of the system in which they find themselves.[34]

Herbert L. Packer has indicated that there are two models of law enforcement in the United States: the "due process model" and the "criminal control" model.[35] Courts assume that police should carry out their duties under the due process model. Police have learned that if they are to succeed in their war against crime, which seems to be an accepted common objective, they have to deviate from that model. Crime control entails certain adjustments and modifications of the unrealistic and unworkable due process model. Criminal courts, for instance, hold that a confession obtained without the Miranda warning is inadmissible in court. Police know that in the great majority of cases, the warning alerts the suspect and eventually makes it impossible for police to perform their duties. Stringent exclusionary rules have the same effect in making it easier for the guilty to escape punishment. Under the circumstances, the police rightly feel that if they don't violate certain judicial interpretations of the Constitution, they cannot bring criminals to justice. If they violate those rules in order to be efficient, or observe them at the price of being unproductive in their task, they will be equally criticized.

As far as police are concerned, the courts' excessive concern for the rights of the accused and disregard for the rights of the victim and the public create unreasonable obstacles for them. Worse than that, courts are not even consistent in following their own reasonings. "One year illegally seized evidence may be admitted into evidence under a legal system subscribing to the rule of law, and the next year it may not. A confession may be admitted into evidence at one time whether or not the suspect was informed of his right to counsel; at a slightly later time such a confession is found to violate constitutional protections."[36]

In the area of law enforcement police are left with restrictive and ever-changing guidelines. There are certain other areas where, due to the nature of their tasks, police are left with wide discretion but no standards to follow. It is disconcerting that when they act in such areas—as they should—they are blamed and criticized for it. James Q. Wilson, with this latter situation in mind, characterizes the two main functions of the police as law enforcement and order maintenance. Unlike particular acts which are specifically defined as criminal in penal codes, "order" is a state or condition which cannot be clearly defined. Police are entrusted with the duty to maintain peace and order. Nevertheless, what creates disorder and what degree of disorder justifies police intervention are questions left unanswered.

This . . . places the patrolman in a special relationship to the law, a relationship that is obscured by describing what he does as "enforcing the law." To the patrolman, the law is one resource among many that he may use to deal with disorder, but it is not the only one or even the most important; beyond that, the law is a constraint that tells him what he must not do but that is peculiarly unhelpful in telling him what he should do. Thus, he approaches incidents that threaten order not in terms of enforcing the law but in terms of "handling the situation." The officer is expected, by colleagues as well as superiors, to "handle his beat." This means keeping things under control so that there are no complaints that he is doing nothing or that he is doing too much. To handle his beat, the law provides one resource, the possibility of arrest, and a set of constraints, but it does not supply to the patrolman a set of legal rules to be applied."[37]

Under these ambiguous circumstances, police must act, and they must act effectively to avert challenges to their authority, danger to individuals, and threats to property. They are criticized, however, precisely for having performed their duties in an area where there are no guidelines or clarifying hints from the law.

### Police Beat

In the last analysis, effective police work depends on establishing and reinforcing positive relations with the public. As was said before, police need the cooperation of the people in the various stages of the crime–control task. If the public is willing to accord this cooperation, the task of the police in their multifaceted activities becomes manageable. To obtain public co-operation, many European police forces, as was the case in America in earlier times, cherish close contacts with the public, normally by means of police beats. By walking the beat, police learn about the people and the neighborhood; by establishing close, amicable contacts, and providing various social services, they earn the cooperation of the public. In Japan, the police walk the beat and get to know every person in the neighborhood. The country is divided into forty-five prefectures where 190,350 police officers are actively engaged in various kinds of social services. The ratio of police to population, according to a 1976 source, is 1 to 574.[38] There are 1,200 police stations in the country. There are also roughly 16,000 police boxes where police officers visibly work and interact with the public. Of this number 5,858 boxes are located in urban areas, each manned by more than three foot-patrol officers. Most of the 10,239 nonurban police boxes, located in small towns and villages, are manned by a single officer, who makes it his job, as do his urban counterparts, to patrol every inch in the neighborhood, know every single household, and become familiar with every person and every street in his jurisdiction. In a public opinion survey, 86 percent of the people interviewed said that they knew their local police box. Forty–one percent knew the face of one or more police officers, and 46 percent had talked with an officer for various reasons during the year.[39]

The public also assists the police in various aspects of their work. At one level, cooperation of the public has been effected through a citizens' organization called the Crime Prevention Association. The statistics we have for April 1, 1969, show that at the time there were 2,604 local units of the Association, one for each city, town, and village. There were also 1,200 district federations of the Crime Prevention Association that corresponded with the distribution of police stations around the country.[40]

In addition, there are smaller organizations, called liaison units, which through the Association maintain close contact and cooperate with the police in the detection, detention, and handling of criminals. In 1969 there were 410,000 such liaison units operating all over the country, working with the police in a number of ways. For instance, they organized vigilance teams to protect neighborhoods and businesses at night.

Mutual cooperation and dependence between police and the public starts at an early age, and the police become accepted and liked through this early start. On April 1, 1969, there were 2,028 school-police liaison councils. In fact, about 92 percent of all elementary, middle, and high schools in Japan have such councils, which cooperate with the police in matters of mutual interest. In the same year, there were 7,742 Vocational Unions and 886 Workshop-Police Liaison Councils, which helped with placing juveniles in productive and useful activities. For instance, the Workshop-Police Liaison Councils operated 43,045 workshops. Of these, 788 had more than 300 working juveniles.

Aside from these organizations, private citizens also help the police with juvenile guidance. In 1969 there were 126,000 volunteers for the task, 38,000 commissioned by police and the rest by other city or village officials. Those commissioned by the police would accompany them on patrol helping juveniles whenever there was need for such help. Because of the social prestige these volunteers enjoy in the community and the pressure they can exert on juveniles, the practice has been successful.

At the end of 1969, there were 350,000 Traffic Safety Voluntary Workers who controlled the traffic at school crossings. Of these, 93 percent did not receive any pay for their services. In addition, there were groups of Traffic Safety Monitors composed of 35,000 drivers, heads of transport companies, and other ordinary citizens commissioned by the police to report on accidents and submit opinions and views on traffic regulations.

Another aspect of police-public relations is carried out by telephone. People know that they can dial 110 at any time for police assistance. The following data show the variety of police activity, the many situations where they are intimately involved in the daily affairs of the citizens.

In 1973, 13 percent of all telephone calls to police consisted of requests for assistance in personal problems, 11.8 percent for nonpayment of debts, 9.7 percent for population problems, 8.9 percent for housing and land disputes, 5 percent for divorce and unregistered marriages.

In 1972, many types of cases were referred to police by the public. As we can see, most of the cases were not related to the crime problem. They were handled, however, with utmost diligence and concern. Such inter-action in a noncriminal setting certainly improves the police image and the public's willingness to cooperate with the police in crime-related situations.

Public requests for advice and counseling, the type that is normally re-ferred to psychiatrists and psychoanalysts in the United States, accounted for 220,000 cases. Other cases included 76,216 car accidents or related prob-lems, 26,539 disputes over various private contracts, the types of which ordinarily grow into lawsuits here. Cases involving divorce or inheritance disputes, again normally handled by courts in this country, numbered 22,470. There were also 17,715 cases of juvenile delinquency and 16,314 cases of poverty or unemployment. All these cases were resolved through police intervention and without further difficulty.

Compare this Japanese picture of close interaction and cooperation be-tween the police and the public with police practices in America. For one thing, the composition of the population has changed drastically in this country within a short period of time. Urban centers have grown rapidly. Social mobility has caused further anonymity; many people move to a new location before they get a chance to know their next-door neighbors. Short-age of space in big metropolitan areas has caused people to live in tiny highrise apartments with no interaction with their neighbors. Perhaps as a result of rapid urbanization and the consequent destruction of old neigh-borhoods as well as the spirit of the times police forces came to rely more and more on technological gadgets and devices. In 1931 the Wickersham Commission reported with deadly optimism that:

With the advent of the radio-equipped car a new era has come. Districts of many square miles, which formerly were officially watched by only a few men who in the very nature of the case could not watch the area, are now covered by the roving patrol car, fast, efficient, stealthy, having a regular beat to patrol, just as liable to be within 60 feet as three miles of the crook plying his trade—the very enigma of this specialized fellow who is coming to realize now that a few moments may bring them down about him like a swarm of bees—this lightning swift "angel of death."[41]

Fascination with technological inventions is not a thing of the past for the police. As Silberman has observed:

Police chiefs retain that faith in speed and mobility. Since the mid–1960s, in particular, departments have made large investments in communication centers designed to shorten the interval between the moment the switchboard receives a telephone request for service and the moment a dispatcher orders a car to the scene. . . . All this has been done on the assumption that cutting response time would increase the number of arrests and reduce the number of crimes.

It has not worked out that way. "It looks as if we asked the wrong question," Gerald Caplan, former director of the National Institute of Law Enforcement and

Criminal Justice told the chiefs attending a Police Foundation seminar. "The question should not have been, 'How long does it take the police to respond?' but rather 'How long does it take the victim to report the crime?' "[42]

Various studies have shown that on the average police cars arrive on the scene within three minutes after being notified about a crime, but it takes the victim about one hour to report it, a relatively long delay which makes police work much more difficult.

Finally, as an ill-conceived solution to the problem of police corruption many police departments have tried to cut off all interpersonal contacts with the public. The assumption was that when police do not have personal contact with people, they will not be corrupted. What was ignored was that without that close, personal touch and cooperation from the public, police will not be able to function effectively. Police departments followed a policy of "stranger policing," which Patrick Murphy calls "one of the most emotionally debilitating and intellectually puzzling theories about American policing."[43] As Silberman has noted, "Frequent rotation may help to prevent corruption, but the cure is worse than the disease, for officers develop no sense of identification with their beats, hence no emotional stake in improving the quality of life there."[44]

## Lack of Community Support

Beside the factors discussed in this chapter, Americans have a culturally cultivated mistrust of all authority and willingly accept political and economic influence as part of the democratic system. Consequently, police do not enjoy public support and cooperation to a degree comparable to that of most European and other police forces. Most victims of crime in this country are reluctant to report the incidents to police. The crime-victim surveys conducted for the National Crime Commission made it clear that at least half of all the cases involving victimization of citizens are not reported to the police. (The incidence of reporting was high where such reports were needed for insurance claims.) People gave different reasons for not reporting, but the most important reason given by victims was the belief that the "police can't do anything about it."[45]

The willingness of citizens to report to the police when they witness a crime is also negligible.[46] In response to the question why they did not report a witnessed crime to the police, most citizens stated that they did not want to get involved. For many people this meant that they were not willing to assume the financial losses that active participation in reporting and follow-up of witnessed crimes would involve.[47]

This sense of public reluctance to cooperate with the police is reflected in the latter's perception about their social image. James Wilson, for instance, found that a majority of police sergeants in Chicago thought the statement

"Civilians generally cooperate with police officers in their work" was not true.[48] McNamara found that actual police experience with the public substantially changes their perceptions about the public's willingness to give them support. While at the end of their police training only one in five patrolmen believed they would never receive the public cooperation that is needed for their success, the proportion changed to one in two at the end of two years. After two years of practical police work six out of ten felt that "it is difficult to persuade people to give patrolmen the information they need."[49]

## NOTES

1. See Charles E. Silberman, *Criminal Violence, Criminal Justice* (New York: Vintage Books, 1980), pp. 273–275.

2. Albert J. Reiss, Jr., "Career Orientations, Job Stratification, and the Assessment of Law Enforcement Problems by Police Officers," in President's Commission on Law Enforcement and the Administration of Justice, *Studies in Crime and Law Enforcement in Major Metropolitan Areas*, Field Surveys 3, vol. 2, sect. 2 (Washington, D.C.: U.S. Government Printing Office, 1967), pp. 91–94.

3. Donald Bouma, *Kids and Cops: A Study in Mutual Hostility* (Grand Rapids, Mich.: Eerdmans, 1967), p. 47.

4. Arthur Niederhoffer, *Behind the Shield: The Police in Urban Society* (Garden City, N.Y.: Anchor Books, 1969), p. 21.

5. Geoffrey Gorer, *Exploring English Character* (London: The Cresset Press, 1955), pp. 305, 310–311.

6. Geoffrey Gorer, "Modification of National Character: The Role of the Police in England," in Douglas G. Haring, ed., *Personal Character and Cultural Milieu* (Syracuse, N.Y.: Syracuse University Press, 1956), p. 337.

7. Lewis Terman and Arthur Otis, "A Trial of Mental and Pedagogical Tests in a Civil Service Examination for Policemen and Firemen," *Journal of Applied Psychology* 1 (1917): 21.

8. David Rapaport, Merton M. Gill, and Roy Schafer, *Diagnostic Psychological Testing*, Robert R. Holt, ed., (New York: The International Universities Press, 1968), p. 29.

9. Lois L. Kates, "Rorschach Responses, Strong Blanck Scales and Job Stratification among Policemen," *Journal of Applied Psychology* 34 (1950): 252.

10. Read Bain, "The Policeman on the Beat," *Scientific Monthly* 48 (1939): 452.

11. John H. McNamara, "Uncertainties in Police Work: The Relevance of Police Recruits' Background and Training," in David Bordua, ed., *The Police: Six Sociological Essays* (New York: John Wiley, 1967), p. 194.

12. See Jerome Skolnick, ed., *The Politics of Protest* (New York: Simon & Schuster, 1969), pp. 252–253.

13. See Harold K. Becker, *Police Systems of Europe: A Survey of Selected Police Organizations* (Springfield, Ill.: Charles C. Thomas, 1973), pp. 148–149.

14. Ibid., p. 148.

15. Ibid., p. 111.

16. Ibid., p. 109.

17. Norval Morris and Gordon Hawkins, *The Honest Politician's Guide to Crime Control* (Chicago: University of Chicago Press, 1970), p. 96.

18. Albert J. Reiss, Jr., "Monitoring the Quality of Criminal Justice Systems," in Angus Campbell and Philip E. Converse, eds., *The Human Meaning of Social Change* (New York: Russell Sage Foundation, 1972), p. 421.

19. William A. Westley, "The Police: A Sociological Study of Law, Custom and Morality" (doctoral dissertation, University of Chicago, 1951), pp. ii and 239.

20. Peter H. Rossi, Richard A. Berk, David P. Boesel, Bettye K. Eidson, and W. Eugene Groves, "Between Black and White: The Faces of American Institutions in the Ghetto," in *Supplemental Studies for the National Advisory Commission on Civil Disorders* (Washington, D.C.: U.S. Government Printing Office, 1968), p. 105.

21. Niederhoffer, *Behind the Shield*, p. 9.

22. See McNamara, "Uncertainties in Police Work," table 8.

23. Ibid.

24. Jerome H. Skolnick, *Justice Without Trial: Law Enforcement in Democratic Society*, 2d ed. (New York: John Wiley, 1975), pp. 228–229.

25. Ibid., p. 227.

26. See Reiss, "Monitoring the Quality of Criminal Justice Systems," p. 106.

27. See James Q. Wilson, *Varieties of Police Behavior: The Management of Law and Order in Eight Communities* (Cambridge, Mass.: Harvard University Press, 1978), p. 50.

28. Quoted in Sir Leon Radzinowicz and Marvin E. Wolfgang, eds., *Crime and Justice*, vol. 2, *The Criminal in the Arms of the Law* (New York: Basic Books, 1977), p. 162.

29. *Time*, May 6, 1974; *New York Times*, March 11, 1974.

30. See Radzinowicz and Wolfgang, *Crime and Justice*, 2: 173, 174.

31. Silberman, *Criminal Violence, Criminal Justice*, p. 312.

32. Nicholas Pileggi, *The Mafia at War* (New York: New York Magazine, 1972), p. 85, quoted in Michael Parenti, *Democracy for the Few*, 2d ed. (New York: St. Martin's Press, 1977), pp. 232–234.

33. Dan Dodson, speech delivered at Michigan State University, May 1955, reported in *Proceedings of the Institute on Police-Community Relations, May 15–20, 1955* (East Lansing, Mich.: The School of Police Administration and Public Safety, Michigan State University, 1956), p. 75.

34. Skolnick, *Justice Without Trial*, pp. 4–5.

35. See Herbert L. Packer, "Two Models of the Criminal Process," *University of Pennsylvania Law Review* 113 (November 1964): 10.

36. Skolnick, *Justice Without Trial*, p. 12.

37. Wilson, *Varieties of Police Behavior*, p. 31.

38. William Clifford, *Crime Control in Japan* (Lexington, Mass.: Lexington Books, 1976), p. 76.

39. Ibid., p. 78.

40. For these and the following statistics on Japan, see Ibid.

41. David G. Monroe and Earl W. Garrett, under the direction of August Vollmer, *Police Conditions in the United States: A Report to the National Commission on Law Observance and Enforcement* (Montclair, N.J.: Patterson Smith Reprint Series, 1968), pp. 97–98.

42. Silberman, *Criminal Violence, Criminal Justice*, p. 331.

43. Ibid., p. 281.

44. Ibid.

45. Albert D. Biderman, Louise A. Johnson, Jennie McIntyre, and Adrianne W. Weir, *Report on a Pilot Study in the District of Columbia on Victimization and Attitudes Toward Law Enforcement*, Field Surveys I. President's Commission on Law Enforcement and the Administration of Justice (Washington, D.C.: U.S. Government Printing Office, 1967), pp. 153–154.

46. Ibid., pp. 154–155.

47. Ibid., p. 154.

48. James Q. Wilson, "Police Morale, Reform, and Citizen Respect: The Chicago Case," in David Bordua, *The Police*, p. 17.

49. McNamara, "Uncertainties in Police Work," p. 221.

# 9

# Penal Institutions

Penal institutions, if organized and run according to suitable ideologies, can have a valuable effect in rehabilitating prisoners, thus reducing the incidence of crime. They can also create a positive impression on the general public, fostering confidence and trust in the criminal justice system which again, as we have seen, is a potent ingredient in successful criminal law administration. The way American prisons are maintained, however, tends to increase rather than diminish the crime problem.

In 1833 Alexis de Tocqueville and Gustave de Beaumont reported on the status of the American penitentiary system: "While society in the United States gives the example of the most extended liberty, the prisons of the same country offer the spectacle of the most complete despotism."[1]

Quoting this, a modern authority adds: "I think the anomaly must still strike us forcibly today in looking at the prison and it is the nature of this despotic regime in a democratic society which has formed the central concern of our study."[2] The President's Crime Commission, which had a much broader perspective in its study, "found overwhelming evidence of [penal] institutional shortcomings in almost every part of the United States."[3] Other studies have been more blunt in describing the overall conditions in American prisons. They have shown that in many American prisons the inmates are routinely subjected to homosexual acts, rape, drug abuse, and physical and psychological violence. This is the lot of people who have had a serious confrontation with the criminal justice system, as well as of those who end up in prison for a relatively mild transgression.

According to a report prepared for the American Correctional Association, the majority of American jails "are not properly heated, ventilated nor lighted; they do not have the necessary facilities for the preparation and service of food; proper and adequate provision for bathing and laundering are missing; sanitary arrangements are, for the most part, primitive and in a bad state of repair . . . in general, complete idleness is the order of the day. Filth, vermin, homosexuality and degeneracy are rampant, and are the rule rather than the exception." Richard Velde, the conservative administrator of the Law Enforcement Assistance Administration during the Ford presidency, described American jails as "without question, brutal, filthy cesspools of crime—institutions which serve to brutalize and embitter men to prevent them from returning to a useful role in society."[4]

Another authority, the former attorney general of the United States, offers the following comments:

Many American prisons include large dormitory rooms with a hundred beds or more where guards do not venture at night. There is no way of controlling violence in such an area. Beatings, deaths, and suicides are frequent. Rape and homosexual cultures involve most of the inmates by choice or force. . . . They are breeding places of crime, violence and despair. . . . Drug addiction is common in prison. Many become addicted there.[5]

The author summarizes his judgment on American penal institutions, "It would be difficult to devise a better method of draining the last drop of compassion from a human being than confinement in most prisons as they exist today."[6]

These facts are even more shocking when viewed in the light of the Supreme Court's excessive concern about the constitutional rights of the accused. Time and again, the Court has freed convicted offenders because of a mere technicality, for instance, because the accused was kept in police custody beyond the statutory time limitation for arraignment or because his confession, though voluntary, was not preceded by the Miranda warning. After the convicted offender is incarcerated, however, it seems everybody loses interest in him. He is confined to the hellish life in prison without any hope or prospect of a better existence. The public is apathetic to the accounts of cruelties committed in prison. The average citizen tries to ignore such accounts, and if he is exposed to them by accident, simply shrugs his shoulder. Whenever there is an attempt to upgrade the prison system, to hire more committed psychologists, social workers, or prison guards, to use better vocational facilities to rehabilitate the inmates, it is doomed to fail; the public refuses to allocate the needed funds for such reforms.

The reasons for this seemingly cruel indifference to the miserable lot of prisoners should be sought, I think, not in any aberration of national character or innate violent tendencies—Americans have shown real compassion many times even for the worst of their adversaries—but in a certain perception which is fundamentally right, albeit to some extent distorted. The average citizen is not appalled and outraged at the conditions of prison life because he intuitively believes that the inmate deserves what he is getting in prison. Of course, he is wrong in believing that everyone who ends up in prison was psychologically a responsible human being when he committed his crime, and that because of his offense—which to a large extent is socially conditioned anyway—he deserves to be treated in a most inhumane manner. Nevertheless, his basic intuition, that a person who commits an intentional wrong should be punished, is sound; it corresponds to the basic premises of morality and penal philosophy. Let us develop this concept further by reviewing the aims of punishment, methods which have been used to bring pain and deprivation to offenders.

## AIMS OF PUNISHMENT

To subject a human being who has intentionally committed a legally forbidden act to deprivation of liberty and at times even capital punishment is a serious matter. To justify it, different theories have been propounded at different times. Some of these theories have proved inapplicable in practice, even though they are still maintained to rationalize punishment. Some of the objectives of punishment are contradictory in nature. In practice it would be impossible to pursue one objective without disregarding others. Nevertheless, these contradictory aims are kept side by side and used at one time or the other to justify the punitive measures we enforce against offenders. Let us review these objectives and the related contradictions more closely.

### Revenge, Retribution, Desert

One of the oldest sentiments and concepts associated with punishment is revenge. When a person does something wrong, goes the saying, "he should pay for it"; he should be punished. To the so-called civilized person, who can easily kill people in the thousands under the pretext of war but confesses genuine concern for human rights of some others, the word revenge or vengeance is distasteful, so legal philosophers have replaced them with the word retribution. The link between the two concepts, however, is easily, though perhaps not clearly, traceable. Thus, in a reformist spirit, the 1972 edition of the Model Sentencing Act states, "Sentences should not be based upon revenge and retribution." To make the concept more palatable, some have suggested the word "desert" rather than either revenge or retribution.[7] The fact is that regardless of what we call the concept, the ordinary human reaction to criminal behavior is based on a moral sense of justice. And in this respect, all three words, revenge, retribution, and desert, are equally suitable. According to criminal law principles, we punish people for their guilt and responsibility (*mens rea*) in having committed a legally forbidden act. Because of a supposedly deliberate violation of some legal norm by the offender, we believe he or she deserves to be punished. According to Immanuel Kant, punishment of an offender is an ethical necessity. In fact he goes so far in his moralistic reasoning as to reach his famous "deserted island" allegory. Even if the whole population of an island decides to leave it forever, he argues, the last murderer should be hanged before the people are dispersed. Such punishment may not serve any useful purpose—the criminal could simply be left behind. Nevertheless, he should be punished in order to emphasize the moral convictions of the people.

The ethical ideals propounded by Kant and others, which for a very long time formed the exclusive basis for punishment, are in fact derived from the broader ethical teachings of most religious faiths. We grow up with the belief that a person is rewarded for good deeds and punished for sins. Rightly or wrongly, the same premise is still applied to the way we convict and punish offenders.

Most societies, including our own, reward those who have done deeds of special merit. Rewards may serve utilitarian ends . . . but, even disregarding such utility, a case for rewarding merit can be made simply on the grounds that it is deserved. Good work and good acts ought to be acknowledged for their own sake, and rewards express that acknowledgment. A parallel argument might be made for punishment: those who violate others' rights deserve to be punished. . . . A system of punishment is justified, the argument runs, simply because it is deserved.[8]

The point is, as I have argued before, that the concept of retribution is essential to criminal law administration not only because it is morally relevant but also because by applying the concept and punishing those who break the socially imposed restrictions to satisfy their selfish desires, we help restore the psychological equilibrium which has been upset by the commission of the criminal act. As Herbert Morris has put it:

A person who violates the rules has something others have—the benefits of the system [of mutual noninterference with others' rights] but by renouncing what others have assumed, the burdens of self-restraint, he has acquired an unfair advantage. Matters are not even until his advantage is in some way erased. . . . Justice—that is punishing such individuals—restores the equilibrium of benefits and burdens.[9]

The matter is expressed more eloquently by Salmond when he says:

Indignation against injustice is . . . one of the chief constituents of the moral sense of the community, and positive morality is no less dependent on it than is the law itself. It is good, therefore, that such instincts and emotions should be encouraged and strengthened by their satisfaction; and in civilized societies this satisfaction is possible in any adequate degree only through the criminal justice of the state. There can be little question that at the present day the sentiment of retributive indignation is deficient rather than excessive, and requires stimulation rather than restraint. . . .

We have too much forgotten that the mental attitude which best becomes us, when fitting justice is done upon the evildoer, is not pity, but solemn exultation.[10]

If punishment of the offender is required to reestablish the public's shaken belief in the prevalence of justice, if it is necessary to restore the psychological equilibrium of the people, then certain conditions should prevail.

*Equality of punishment.* It is essential for the sense of justice that people who commit the same offense should receive the same punishment. In the light of this basic premise, the negative impact of disparities in judicial sentences was discussed before. It should be noted here that the practice of indeterminate sentences, which as we shall see shortly is a precondition for another goal of punishment, is equally harmful to the public's sense of justice. In the system practiced presently in the United States, in addition to the judge who enjoys wide discretion in determining the limits of punishment, the parole board also has unlimited and unbridled power in deciding which prisoners should be accorded or denied release on parole. Some authorities have argued that the exercise of such wide discretionary powers has in practice worked to punish those who are considered threats to the established social order and to free or lessen the punishment of those who have money, power, and influence. Thus, it is stated in the Report on Crime and Punishment in America prepared for the American Friends Service Committee:

Leaders in the fields of penal policy, education, and welfare, who were deeply concerned about how to assimilate immigrants, blacks, Indians, and other cultures, recognized that theft, deception, vice, and violence were not the monopoly of these groups but existed throughout society. What was required, therefore, was a rationale of criminal justice that would justify a sharp distinction between deviance that symbolized a threat to the established order and that which did not. The developing concept of criminality as individual pathology, the evolution of individualization, the rationalization of broad discretion as a legally legitimate technique, and "treatment" geared not to the crime but to the "total needs" of the offender provided the policy basis for developing a dual system of law enforcement.[11]

Unless one is willing to accept uncritically the widely refuted Marxist dictum that all ideas, beliefs, and practices are shaped by the underlying mode of production in a society, it is doubtful that the devices referred to have been consciously adopted by the American elite to perpetuate the domination of one social class over the others. As a matter of fact, some of these ideas and practices were taught long ago by the Italian School of Criminology and adopted in several European penal codes. The fact remains, however, that indeterminate sentences—especially if awarded at the unexplained and uncontrolled discretion of the judge or the parole board—will lead to the weakening of the sense of justice—"like deserts for like moral wrongs"—and the foundations of psychological equilibrium in the public.

*Certainty of punishment.* If the sense of justice is to prevail and flourish, the public must be assured not only that like offenders receive like punishment, but also that at least a large number of offenders are caught, tried, convicted, and punished. The feeling must be widespread that there is indeed a substantial difference between people who stay within legal bounds—with all the deprivations this implies—and those who break the law for their own benefit and that the latter group will most likely suffer punishment. Thus, when the judicial system for whatever reason—lack of manpower, outdated procedures, or exaggerated concern for the constitutional rights of the accused—does not function efficiently to satisfy the public's need to see justice served, a feeling of frustration, anger, and/or apathy will develop. When a murderer is freed because of a mere technicality, the public feels betrayed and cheated. And the laudatory language of the Supreme Court which sounds so wise and righteous to us who are relatively immune from violent crime, that to protect the rights of every citizen we may have to free a few criminals who were convicted without the due process, cannot soothe the tragic pain of a father whose son was stabbed to death or a mother whose daughter has been battered and raped.

It is also in view of this underlying sense of justice, which is so essential in maintaining the fabric of a democratic and orderly society, that we criticize the practice of plea bargaining in American courts. The basic assumption for the sense of justice is that a forbidden act will invariably and certainly lead to a predefined punishment. When we allow the accused or his lawyer—and depending on his financial assets, this could mean the most or the least qualified attorney—to strike a deal with the prosecution as to what the punishment should be, we in fact abnegate the very concept of justice, of inevitability of "desert" for intentional transgressions. Whatever the objective of punishment is in our view, it must be already doomed when the prisoner and the public know that the outcome of his case depends not on any principle of justice but on the shrewdness and bargaining skills of the lawyer or himself. As an authority has pointed out:

[Prisoners] are aware that the most effective defense counsel is not the counsel who can obtain the best defense but is rather that counsel who can obtain the best deal. The more experienced in crime the prisoner is, the more he has come to appreciate the negotiative quality of the American criminal justice system. "Get me Agnew's lawyers," they all plead.[12]

The result, as the same authority sees it, is, "Our present sentencing practices are so arbitrary, discriminatory, and unprincipled that it is impossible to build a rational and humane prison system upon them."[13]

## Prevention and Incapacitation

In a prevention or incapacitation perspective, the focus of attention is shifted from just punishment for the individual offender to that of social defense, protecting society against the harmful acts of offenders. The suggested solution for the crime problem is to keep the convict in prison for as long as he is dangerous. If there is no hope that we can modify his behavior to make him safe for society, then we can even kill him as a necessary measure for the protection of other human beings. The underlying rationale is to safeguard the good of the people. Theoretically, it makes sense to deprive a person of his liberty or even life if this is necessary to protect the rights of other citizens. However, we are faced with two problems here, one practical, the other logical. No society has the means, were this morally and legally permissible, to keep every person who is deemed dangerous in confinement for an unlimited time. Besides, we contend that we punish the offender for past behavior. We give him what he deserves for the wrong he has intentionally committed. We cannot punish him for a condition which may exist in him unless he commits an illegal act. This, however, is precisely what some advocates of the prevention objective have recommended. The Model Penal Code has likewise provided that an offender may be confined if the sentencing judge finds "there is undue risk that during the period of a suspended sentence or probation the defendant will commit another crime."[14]

As yet it is impossible to predict with any degree of certainty which prisoners will be a menace to society after they complete their sentence. Thus, the adoption of a scheme such as the one suggested by the Model Penal Code would be inherently dangerous; it would open the door to possible abuse of power, making it possible to subject the unpopular or unsubmissive prisoner to unjustified extended punishment.[15]

## Deterrence

Cesare Beccaria and Jeremy Bentham argued that in punishing the offender, we prove to him that crime does not pay. We also set an example for the rest of the public; we deter them from committing the same offense. To produce such results, Bentham argued, the amount of pain inflicted by punishment should outweigh any possible pleasure that may be derived from committing an offense. If these conditions are met, the argument went, punishment could prevent both the particular offender (special deterrence) and the rest of the public (general deterrence) from engaging in the same type of activity in the future.

Some authorities have doubted the presumed effectiveness of punishment as a deterrent. They have rightly argued that criminal behavior is the outcome of numerous sociocultural forces that initially drove the offender to criminal activity and continue to exert the same crimogenic influence after he leaves the prison. Punishment, if not coupled with essential changes in the social environment of the inmate, is powerless to change these realities. It is pointed out that 80 percent of all felonies are committed by repeaters, and four-fifths of all major crimes in the United States are committed by people who are known to the criminal justice system.[16]

In view of the prevailing conditions in certain American prisons today, it seems certain not only that the penal institutions do not deter the inmates from future crimes, but that they actually reinforce their criminal proclivities. Of course, the fact that for various reasons punishment is only an uncertain eventuality further diminishes its chances of acting as a strong deterrent.

Some authorities, however, have argued that if administered judiciously and efficiently, punishment will certainly have a considerable deterrent effect, if not on a particular offender, then on the average, law-abiding citizen. They maintain that people are certainly affected by the account of punishment suffered by the offender. As H. Lawrence Ross has pointed out:

A possibility for obtaining such evidence [of deterrence exists] through the use of the quasi-experimental technique known as interrupted time-series analysis. This technique has been used successfully to demonstrate the validity of the belief that the British Road Safety Act of 1967 initially did produce deterrence of drinking and driving. The technique is based on the expectation that if a cause-and-effect relationship exists between two variables, such as law and crashes, a change in the causal variable will be associated with a simultaneous change in the effect variable. In Britain it was shown that a significant drop in motor-vehicle casualties occurred precisely at the time of introduction of the new legislation. Furthermore, the drop in casualties was greatest on weekend nights, when alcohol is usually heavily involved in serious crashes, and not present during weekday commuting hours, when alcohol is less often a cause of such crashes.[17]

Another kind of evidence, perhaps more problematic, is gathered from natural experiments, instances where some event, such as a police strike, makes the impact of the criminal justice system as a means of social control negligible. One such natural experiment occurred when the entire Copenhagen police force was arrested by the Nazis during World War II. Immediately thereafter crime rates rose considerably; the highest increases were in robberies, burglaries, and larcenies, offenses which without the presence of the police had become almost sanctionless.[18]

Punishment can also have an indirect deterrent effect. This effect is less amenable to actual, scientific scrutiny; nevertheless, it may be a highly important phenomenon. As we have argued before, in punishing the offender, the criminal justice system reinforces the sense of justice; it restores the psychological equilibrium which is so essential for the overall maintenance of law in a democratic society.

It should be stressed again that to create the deterrent effect, punishment should be perceived by the public as the inevitable consequence of criminal behavior, a perception that is not borne out by the actual functioning of the present-day criminal justice system in America.

## Rehabilitation

In recent decades, the concept that has predominated in the field of penology is rehabilitation. The premises of the concept are quite valid, especially in the light of modern teachings in the fields of psychology and sociology. If the offender is really a victim of social forces and circumstances over which he has no control, the argument goes, it is only fair and prudent that while he is being punished for his offense, we should also try to modify his behavior, to equip him with some knowledge and skill that may be profitably put to use after he leaves prison. We should also help him find an honest job to support him financially and emotionally. Such endeavors are desirable also from a utilitarian point of view. We will minimize the potential danger of the prisoner when he is freed to return to regular social life. In practice, however, most American prisons, like penal institutions in most other countries, have failed to achieve these desired objectives.

To begin with, there is an unresolved contradiction between the requirements of the rehabilitative model and those of the retribution or desert perspective. In rehabilitation, we are no longer concerned about the past of the offender; our interest lies in his future. We want to reeducate him, to cure him of his former sociopsychological maladjustments. For this purpose, the concept of guilt or responsibility is irrelevant in the same way it would be to the treatment of a physical ailment. Also, as in the case of any other treatment, the concept of time is irrelevant to our objective. We have to spend as much or as little time as necessary to "cure" the offender, and this, again, is incompatible with the traditional idea of determinate punishment, which should be proportional to the degree of guilt and social harm caused by a particular crime. Using the rehabilitative model, we would be forced to have indeterminate rather than fixed sentences. The 1972 edition of the Model Sentencing Act states, "Persons convicted of crime shall be dealt with in accordance with their potential for rehabilitation, considering their individual characteristics, circumstances and needs. . . . Dangerous offenders shall be identified, segregated, and correctively treated in custody for as long terms as needed."[19] Indeterminate sentences that are theoretically determined according to the personal needs of each offender are also subject to possible abuse of discretion by the administrative officials who are entrusted with determining the actual length of the sentence, and who, in many cases, are rightly accused of administering partial justice.[20]

Aside from these valid legal considerations, it is all but impossible to rehabilitate inmates under present-day prison conditions. American prisons are total institutions; they are isolated from the rest of the community; they control all aspects of the inmate's life; they are composed almost entirely of convicted offenders and guards who, after many years of close contact with criminal elements, tend to only reinforce the criminal image in the inmate. Prisons are, in a word, dominated by criminal values and influence the inmate population accordingly. The net result of constant interaction with other convicted offenders in the essentially abnormal and all–pervasive atmosphere of prison life is the strengthening of the criminal tendencies of the prisoner. The damage wrought on the personality and identity of the inmates in total institutions is of course much more devastating. Perhaps no one can summarize this demeaning process better than Erving Goffman who says:

The recruit comes into the institution with a self and with attachments to supports which had allowed this self to survive. Upon entrance, he is immediately stripped of his wonted supports, and his self is systematically, if often unintentionally, mortified. In the accurate language of some of our oldest total institutions, he is led into a series of abasements, degradations, humiliations, and profanations of self. He begins, in other words, some radical shifts in his moral career, a career laying out the progressive changes that occur in the beliefs that he has concerning himself and significant others.

The stripping processes through which mortification of the self occurs are fairly standard in our total institutions. Personal identity equipment is removed, as well as other possessions with which the inmate may have identified himself, there typically being a system of nonaccessible storage from which the inmate can only reobtain his effects should he leave the institution. As a substitute for what has been taken away, institutional issue is provided, but this will be the same for large categories of inmates and will be regularly repossessed by the institution. In brief, standardized defacement will occur. In addition, ego-invested separateness from fellow inmates is significantly diminished in many areas of activity, and tasks are prescribed that are infra dignitatem. Family, occupational, and educational career lines are chopped off, and a stigmatized status is submitted. Sources of fantasy materials which meant momentary releases from stress in the home world are denied. Areas of autonomous decision are eliminated through the process of collective scheduling of daily activity. Many channels of communication with the outside are restricted or closed off completely.[21]

The little professional help and vocational training that are offered in some prisons are forced on the inmates and thus meet with their resistance. "As experienced by the prisoner, imprisonment with treatment is identical with traditional imprisonment in most significant aspects. In both situations there is depersonalization, loss of autonomy, separation from family, denial of privacy, and the imposition of all the restrictions inherent in any institution."[22]

By the time an offender is tried and convicted to a prison term, his personal traits and characteristics are already set. Even if it were possible to change the personality structure of the prisoner while he is confined, which is highly unlikely in view of the fact that in the normal world outside the prison walls, it sometimes takes years of extensive psychoanalysis to effect noticeable changes in a person, most prisoners are not really interested in changing.[23] Furthermore, rather than preparing the inmate for eventual reentry and readjustment to normal conditions of life in society, most prisons sever any possible ties the inmate may have had with social groups, thus subjecting him or her to the total, isolated, and abnormal atmosphere of the prison community. Furthermore, by labeling and depriving him from any meaningful personal contact with the outside world during his confinement, prisons make it even more difficult for released former convicts to live and work within the legal bounds. There is reliable evidence that of offenders who have committed the same offense and have similar prior records, "those . . . who serve the longest terms in prisons tend to do less favorably on parole than those who serve the shortest terms before first release."[24]

The net result of what American prisons accomplish is perhaps best summarized by the report prepared for the American Friends Service Committee. It says:

> For those who are caught in the cycle of arrest, prosecution, and "treatment," and those who share their cultures, the impact of the criminal justice system is profoundly dysfunctional. Instead of encouraging initiative, it compels submissiveness. Instead of strengthening belief in the legitimacy of authority, it generates cynicism and bitterness. Instead of stimulating a creative means of changing the intolerable realities of their existence, it encourages "adjustment" to those realities. This is the keystone of the "rehabilitative" process. Instead of building pride and self-confidence, it tries to persuade its subjects (often all too successfully) that they are sick. Criminal justice, which should strengthen cohesion through a reaffirmation of shared basic values, is serving instead as a conduit for an increasingly dangerous polarization of conflict.[25]

Past experiences of failure in the rehabilitative ideal in American prisons do not of course mean that the ideal itself is unsound. What is needed is a different approach and different practices. Since the inmate will have to reenter the larger society after release from prison, positive contacts with the outside world should be established and developed while he is still in prison, and as early as possible. In other words, rehabilitation and reeducation of the inmate should be effected within conditions of normal social life as soon and as far as possible in each individual case. Thus, for example, halfway houses, if administered under suitable conditions and used at the earliest possible time, can act as an excellent vehicle for rehabilitation. Another way of realistically trying to prepare the inmate for future constructive life is through meaningful employment at prison or preferably in outside workshops. To be able to sustain himself, both financially and emotionally, the prisoner will certainly need a job after his sentence is ended. Prison can play a significant role in teaching the inmate useful skills and also in helping him find a suitable job outside the prison. This objective should be achieved in progressive stages, of course, and the experience of Japan in helping prisoners find useful employment can be most helpful. In that country, punishment of many crimes includes labor as well as incarceration. If a prisoner is sentenced to "imprisonment with labor," he must definitely work during his term. Only those who are not able to work because of illness are excused temporarily until they regain their health. If the sentence does not include labor, or if the accused is awaiting trial, he can still request to be given a job. As of December 31, 1973, 91.8 percent of those sentenced to "imprisonment with labor" were given assigned tasks. In addition, 90.5 percent of those sentenced to "imprisonment without labor" had asked for and were given a job.

Inmates who work are paid less than regular laborers. Still, the pay is decent. It provides a sufficiently strong incentive to work and a good financial start for the time the inmate is released from custody. The work assigned to inmates is sponsored not only by the government; many private industries cooperate with prison authorities in employing inmates in various industries, mainly shipbuilding, electronics, and agriculture. The system has worked so efficiently that Japanese prisons have become financially profitable.[26]

In fact, public cooperation in the whole criminal justice process is quite widespread in Japan. Article 1 of Japan's Offenders' Rehabilitation Law states the principle that works as the guideline for public participation in the process: "The objective of this law is to protect society and promote individual and public welfare by aiding the reformation and rehabilitation of offenders ... and facilitating the activities of crime prevention. All the people are required to render help according to their position and ability."

To implement this requirement, various organizations have been created to maintain and strengthen normal interaction between the inmates and the larger society in such a natural way that by the time the prisoner is released from prison, he is already accepted and to a large extent assimilated.

Family courts in Japan can use the valuable services of the Voluntary Guidance Hostels for Juvenile Delinquents. Before a case is finalized and settled by the court, the juvenile delinquent is sent to one of these hostels for observation and diagnosis of his problems. In 1976 there were eighty Voluntary Guidance Hostels across Japan, each taking five to thirty youths. In addition, there were about 3,000 individuals selected and approved on the basis of their social and moral integrity to work closely with family courts. Instead of sending the delinquent to a hostel, such trusted individuals would take him under their charge, and help with his readjustment. In 1966 out of 231,990 cases of juvenile delinquency handled by family courts in Japan, only 5,000 youths were committed to hostels. The rest kept their liberty while being helped emotionally and socially by concerned individuals. The government subsidized 70 percent of the expenses incurred by such hostels and individuals.

Many people volunteer to visit and help inmates with different problems while they are still in prison. These voluntary visitors are approved and appointed for one or two years by the director of the District Correctional Headquarters. They have access to the files of the convict and can learn more about him in case of need. They can visit the inmate and discuss various matters with him in confidence. At the end of 1968, for example, there were 1,640 voluntary visitors, of which 18 percent were clergymen.

As noted above, private enterprises also contribute effectively in the rehabilitation of Japanese inmates. Various businesses make contracts with prison authorities to employ inmates for production activities. Trade unions do not object to this arrangement, and about 90 percent of the whole prison population works in Japanese industries. Aside from the fact that these contracts between private industry and penal institutions provide additional funds for Japanese prisoners, they also facilitate the eventual reentry of the inmate into normal social life.

Private concerns send engineers and technicians to train the inmates, who then live in open dormitories and work in different workshops along with regular workers. Many work in shipyards and agricultural farms. Others produce electronic and electrical equipment.

Japan's system of open dormitories has been a success. From 1961 when the first group of inmates were sent to work in a shipyard, to 1976, only four prisoners took the opportunity to escape. And out of 995 prisoners who were trained to work and later reentered social life completely, only 102 had been reconvicted by 1973, a success rate of almost 90 percent.

Even after the prisoner is discharged with or without probation, the Japanese public is involved in his future activities and progress. This is certainly a very significant fact, because it is after the release from prison that the former convict faces the most difficult task in his attempt to readjust himself to normal social life. It is at this time that he should be accepted by law-abiding groups and citizens who are willing to treat him, not as an ex-convict on his way back to a life of crime, but rather as an individual who has erred but has paid his debt to society and should be readmitted to normal social life without reservation. He should be able to dissociate himself from former groups and associates who were to a large extent responsible for his criminal activity in the first place; he should establish new, positive relationships. He needs a job that is materially and emotionally satisfying. In all these needs and trials, the compassionate understanding and help of a few concerned individuals are certainly most significant. In Japan a large number of volunteers working in accord with the Voluntary Probation Officer help the released inmate to readjust to normal social relations, to find a job, to establish new, positive contacts, and to become a useful, constructive individual. These volunteers are chosen from among respected, distinguished, older citizens; their average age is sixty. There are altogether some 56,000 volunteers, only 500 of whom are full-time professional probation officers. The organization of volunteers is divided into 746 local units of probation volunteers, 46 prefectural federations, and eight regional federations, all working in cooperation with the National Federation of Volunteers. There are 130 other organizations, some working to coordinate the different aspects of the program, the majority running hostels for both the probationers and discharged prisoners.

Women volunteers have their own organization called Women's Association for Rehabilitation Aid. The association has about 500,000 members and 800 local units throughout Japan. They work mostly with released female inmates and try to make their reentry into society smoother.

## NOTES

1. Gustave de Beaumont and Alexis de Tocqueville, *On the Penitentiary System in the United States and Its Applications in France* (Philadelphia: Carey, Lea and Blanchard, 1833), p. 47.

2. Gresham M. Sykes, *The Society of Captives: A Study of a Maximum Security Prison* (Princeton, N.J.: Princeton University Press, 1974), p. 130.

3. *Struggle for Justice: A Report on Crime and Punishment in America*, prepared for the American Friends Service Committee (New York: Hill & Wang, 1971), p. 7.

4. Charles E. Silberman, *Criminal Violence, Criminal Justice* (New York: Vintage Books, 1980), pp. 351–352.

5. Ramsey Clark, *Crime in America: Observations on Its Nature, Causes, Prevention and Control* (New York: Simon & Schuster, 1970), pp. 213–215.

6. Ibid., p. 214.

7. See Andrew von Hirsch, *Doing Justice: The Choice of Punishments, Report of the Committee for the Study of Incarceration* (New York: Hill and Wang, American Century Series, 1981), pp. 45–55.

8. Ibid., p. 53.

9. Herbert Morris, "Persons and Punishment," *The Monist* 52 (1968): 475, 478.

10. John William Salmond, *Salmond on Jurisprudence*, 11th ed. (London: Stevens and Haynes, 1957), pp. 120–121.

11. *Struggle for Justice*, pp. 29–30.

12. Norval Morris, *The Future of Imprisonment: Studies in Crime and Justice* (Chicago: University of Chicago Press, 1974), p. 52.

13. Ibid., p. 45.

14. Model Penal Code, #7.01(1)(a).

15. For objections to "predictive restraint," see Andrew von Hirsch, *Doing Justice*, pp. 19–26.

16. See Ramsey Clark, *Crime in America*, p. 215.

17. Von Hirsch, *Doing Justice*, pp. 41–42.

18. See Franklin E. Zimring and Gordon J. Hawkins, *Deterrence* (Chicago: University of Chicago Press, 1973), pp. 167–169.

19. Council of Judges, National Council on Crime and Delinquency, "Model Sentencing Act," 2d ed. Reprinted in *Crime and Delinquency* 18 (1972):335.

20. See, in general, Willard Gaylin, *Partial Justice: A Study of Bias in Sentencing* (New York: Vintage Books, 1975).

21. Erving Goffman, "Characteristics of Total Institutions," in Abraham S. Goldstein and Joseph Goldstein, eds., *Crime, Law and Society* (New York: The Free Press, 1971), pp. 244–245.

22. *Struggle for Justice*, p. 25.

23. See Morris, *The Future of Imprisonment*, p. 20ff.

24. Donald Gottfredson et al., *Four Thousand Lifetimes: A Study of Time Served and Parole Outcomes* (Davis, Calif.: National Council on Crime and Delinquency Research Center, 1973), p. 25.

25. *Struggle for Justice*, pp. 9–10.

26. For this and the following data on Japan, see William Clifford, *Crime Control in Japan* (Lexington, Mass.: Lexington Books, 1977).

# 10

# Conclusions

What can be suggested as practical recommendations to ease the crime problem in the United States has been already implied in our discussions in the preceding chapters.It is nonetheless useful to highlight some of the main issues and possible improvements of the system in these concluding remarks.

We have noted that a combination of highly raised expectations, which are not confined to any particular social group, and the nonavailability of the necessary means for everyone to achieve culturally endorsed objectives results in frustration, which under suitable conditions can lead to criminal behavior. The individual feels the pressure more strongly, of course, at times of economic depression and decline when the sense of personal insecurity and inadequacy is highest. But the pressure is always there and should be confronted squarely.

For one thing, there is nothing in American culture, at least at the present stage of economic prosperity, to necessitate the pursuit of material values as the sole object of individual endeavor. There is an equally strong trend in American culture that encourages group affiliation and genuine concern for the well-being of other human beings. I believe this aspect of the culture can and should be stressed without weakening any of the incentives for achievement and productivity. It will create a stronger sense of social responsibility, social cohesiveness, and ultimately an even deeper sense of fulfillment as individuals participate in the social scene and develop a sincere sense of belonging to other human beings. After all, there is nothing in the concept of pursuit of happiness to make it an exclusively selfish idea. Individuals can learn to see happiness as at least partly based on fulfilling one's social responsibilities, being concerned about the good of other people, cooperating with other human beings in creating a better world, and in giving of oneself for the welfare of the community at large.

As long as we think of crime and other social problems as consequences of individual or isolated social causes, our vision is, by necessity, limited and distorted. We cannot blame heredity, family upbringing, poverty, urban living, and so on as the ultimate or exclusive causes of criminality. All these factors, even inherited qualities of the individual, become effective only in the context of the larger society, which operates under a particular socioeconomic setup and its corresponding ideologies. These ideologies are both the historic result and the actual support of a particular social system. It is time we realized that the curse of crime, drug addiction, impersonal relationships, prostitution, separated families, child abuse, various veneral disease epidemics, as well as the many superlative achievements of the American society, are explainable not as individual aberrations or malfunctions of certain social institutions, but in terms of the overall American value system, which, as we have seen, is rooted in the concepts of free enterprise, individual achievement, personal pursuit of happiness, relative indifference to the problems of other human beings, permissiveness, and almost total lack of discipline in child rearing and educational practices.

Changing our perspectives about crime and redirecting our attention to the more comprehensive sociocultural forces that operate in society will not result in an instant utopia. Nonetheless, it will give us a more realistic outlook, which may in turn help reduce the brunt of crime and other social problems. The change of perspective will also open up new vistas and possibilities for improvement that are not discernible within our present, limited outlook.

By studying the crime problem within the larger context of cultural values, I have already discussed the deeper causes of the problem. In the following pages, I shall try to explain more explicitly some of the possibilities I see for improvement.

## IN THE CULTURAL REALM

As we have seen, the same cultural values that are basically responsible for the crime problem have contributed to the great achievements of this society. It should be noted once more that these achievements are not only material, but scientific, artistic, social and spiritual as well. Thus, it is very difficult to suggest a drastic change in the values that advocate individual rights, high aspirations, and need for achievement. It is possible, however, to visualize a value system that pursues these same goals but stresses group, as opposed to individual, activity. This is not the place to indulge in extensive educational discussions. Suffice it to say that what, for example, Dewey suggested for the reform of the educational system—emphasizing group participation and productivity instead of individual competitiveness—can be duplicated in other social institutions with the aim of making individual behavior more group-directed, and reinforcing social integrity and cohesiveness.[1] These values of mutual concern and assistance have already existed in American history and folklore and exist today, on a large scale, in rural America. They can be fostered in big urban centers as well if the need is felt strongly and if we put our minds to it. People can be taught to alter their behavior if the proposed changes are somehow rewarded by the sociopolitical system.

It is difficult to weigh with certainty the beneficial and the harmful effects of the traditional American values (individualism, pragmatism, pursuit of happiness, and so on); but the destructive nature of the present-day belief in total freedom from social restraints is becoming increasingly evident. It is true that drastic suppression of human needs and desires can only lead to pathological conditions and possible reappearance of the same impulses in a more assertive manner. It is also true, however, that the unrestrained expression of all human drives and desires will lead to personal and social problems. The American highly exaggerated concern with rights in the absence of a corresponding regard for responsibilities, both individual and social, has resulted in the dysfunction of social relations in many areas. For instance, the almost total lack of discipline at home and school and the excessive liberty in experimentation with sex, drugs, and so on which is encouraged by groups that have a big financial stake in them, are responsible, I believe, for the relative decline in creative urges, work consciousness, and a self-disciplined productive life in present-day America. It is also obvious that an individual with a weak social self, who has not learned to control or postpone gratification of his desires, will succumb much more easily to the strong temptation of committing various criminal acts. An almost total lack of discipline, itself the outcome of permissive upbringing and education, is at the roots of many other social problems as well, such as the high rate of divorce, child neglect, venereal diseases, and the fragile loyalties to moral principles and national interests. It is the partial cause of the present slowdown in creativity and productivity and lack of commitment to one's work, family, and personal aspirations. The proverbial American land of opportunity could not have been built if past generations had the same characteristics and attitudes that exist today.

It is fortunate that Americans are not bogged down, as many other countries are, by centuries-old traditions that make any social change a difficult and painful process. Americans experiment with new ideas, learn from their past mistakes, and correct their ways in a relatively short period of time. Thus, all social problems will hopefully be noted, analyzed, and corrected with the passage of time. The problem of lack of discipline, however, is a serious one that should be more consciously and energetically faced and treated by all concerned.

## CRIMINAL JUSTICE SYSTEM

I believe that major reorientation and reform are required in all aspects of the criminal justice apparatus. For one thing, we should realize that to be effective, the criminal justice system should always follow rational and consistent standards. We should punish the convicted offender on the basis of his past illegal act, and this should be our main consideration in deciding how to treat him. We should be able to reduce or increase the actual amount of punishment, but again, this should be done on the basis of rational, clear, and predefined criteria, not because our jails are overcrowded or because we think we cannot produce enough evidence against the guilty offender to convict him.

Misplaced concern for the offender is another problem which requires clear rethinking. It is certainly true that in a real sense the offender is himself the victim of the social forces and arrangements over which he does not have any real control. But it is also true that if we want to punish people on the basis of this understanding, we have to undermine the essential premises of the criminal law administration. We cannot hope that by being lenient to those who have violated the rights of others, we somehow balance the evil effects of social injustice and inequality which push certain groups of people toward criminal behavior. Besides, we will create more social evil by sending out the clear message that the criminal justice system does not really work according to the principles it professes. To cure the malady, we have to get to the roots of the problem. We should try to eradicate social inequality and injustice as much as possible to minimize some of the most potent crimogenic forces in society. In dealing with offenders, however, especially if we are to create the type of public attitude and perception which is conducive to trust in the system and avoidance of criminal activity, we should be certainly firm, consistent, and most judicious in punishing them.

As I have argued, in the absence of strong sociocultural values that support and strengthen the existing social and legal norms, the task of safeguarding law and order in society falls mainly to the criminal justice system. For various reasons, discussed before, the American system of criminal justice seems to have failed in playing its assigned role effectively. The following are the main areas where basic changes seem necessary.

### Penal Laws: Their Overreach and Underreach

It is a fact that in America various attempts have been made to regulate morality through law. We also know that such attempts have backfired, especially in areas where the "criminal" act cannot be easily detected, such as the so-called victimless crimes, or where the demand for or propensity to commit a criminal act is strong among the public, such as the use of narcotics among certain groups of people. The sale and use of drugs is also supported at present by the enormous profits involved in drug deals.

It would seem obvious that we should stop this futile overreach of penal laws. We should decriminalize the acts which are either victimless or otherwise immune to punitive threats. By decriminalizing such acts as drug abuse we do not of course condone or encourage them. We simply redirect our energy to alternative channels which are certainly more effective than the threat of punishment, in bringing about the desired behavior changes. Cigarette smoking, for instance, is not a crime; however, because of a comprehensive educational and advertising campaign that raised the level of public awareness and the subsequent social pressure that is present everywhere, the number of people who smoke cigarettes has dropped considerably in America. Sexual permissiveness and promiscuity have been tolerated both between heterosexual and homosexual people as a natural reaction against some rigid religious teachings which required the suppression of all extramarital, non–family-oriented expressions of love. The public is wising up, however, without the passage of any criminal laws. Because of the rapid spread of venereal diseases as well as the gradual realization that solely physical and unemotional sex is not as pleasurable as that which is combined with love and tenderness, more people are convinced today that they should revert to the more traditional American values, modifying them to some extent to fit the ideals of freedom of expression and personal autonomy. None of these transformations could be effected by the use of criminal law measures. Any interference of the criminal justice system in such areas would not only create strong negative feelings in the public, but would also make the system less capable of discharging its own, valid responsibilities. On the other hand, by divesting itself of the overreach which has been imposed on it piecemeal, criminal law can use the extra resources that will become available to fight the serious crimes that threaten the very fabric of social life. By decriminalizing these undetectable and uncontrollable acts, we will also neutralize many people who commit them and thus identify themselves with the criminal elements in society.

Another aspect of criminal law coverage, which unfortunately has not been seriously noted so far, is what I would like to call its underreach. As I have discussed before, a belief in the legitimacy of the sociopolitical system and its official representatives—laws, courts, the government—is an indispensable ingredient of the rule of law and order in a democratic society. If we believe that we live in an essentially just and legitimate socioeconomic system, it would be easier to resist the ever-present temptation to break the law. To foster this belief in the legitimacy of the system, laws should punish all those who illegally cause injuries and punish them according to the magnitude of the harm they cause and the extent of their responsibility. And this should be done irrespective of what group the offender belongs to. The type of message we get from the criminal justice system unfortunately does not support such a belief. We know, for example, that a murderer can end up in the electric chair, and a desperate man who writes a check without having the funds may get up to forty years of imprisonment. We know, at the same time, that many industrial concerns intentionally dump toxic waste in our lakes, rivers, and farmland and otherwise pollute the precious irreplaceable environment, causing incurable illnesses and death to thousands of people every year, without being accountable at all for their serious crimes. I have already referred to the SmithKline Beckman case and the mild treatment it and its managers received.

Another typical case mentioned in the Introduction was that of E. F. Hutton. But these are only examples. One reads about such offenses by corporate managers and other highly placed individuals almost daily in the papers. And the mild treatment they receive, in view of the enormous harm they cause not only to public safety and health, but equally to public morale and trust in the system, is astonishing indeed. It is high time we enacted new laws or changed present penal statutes to make it easier to convict the fortunate minority who enjoy all the available social privileges at the highest extent when they abuse their power and prestige to make more money. Commensurable to their power and privilege, they should be held more responsible, not less, for creating unnecessary hazards and risks for the public. Those who spread toxic waste, those who fail to disclose the dangerous side effects of a drug they sell, whether they do it intentionally or otherwise, should be accountable and punished for their harmful acts. Their responsibility toward the public should be presumed, because they are in a position to know and control. They should have a stricter responsibility to care for the welfare of the general public who by necessity will have to depend on their goodwill and good intentions.

And of course it is not enough that we should have laws that punish people who enjoy a higher position of public trust when they violate their duties; we should also equip and require the system—police, courts, the Justice Department—to take the necessary measures, in practice, to bring such offenders to justice.

## Penal Laws: The Problem of Equality and Consistency of Treatment

Inexplicable discretion on the part of police, judge, and parole boards should be diminished as much as possible. I believe we can follow the example of European penal codes in this respect by providing the maximum and minimum punishment for every offense, the mitigating and extenuating circumstances that can affect the nature and duration of punishment, and the scope of the judges' discretion in awarding the sentence. In any event, it should be required that the sentencing judge explain the reasons for setting the punishment within the limits provided by the law. Such required conscious thinking in the application of predefined standards will certainly lead to a more rational and consistent approach in the application of penal statutes.

## Professionalization of the Judiciary

It is high time we realized that the democratic process, as exercised through popular votes, is not necessarily applicable in all areas of social life, especially if we are also interested in the quality and capabilities of the candidates for office. The practice of law, like medicine, is a profession that requires highly developed skills and abilities. We do not choose a doctor on the basis of his popularity or ability to win an election; in many states, however, we elect judges by popular vote and sometimes bring unqualified and/or dishonest people to the bench simply because they had the capacity and the money to dupe the public to vote for them. We can avoid all this by requiring standardization of qualities and skills that every judge should have and by making judges subject to professional supervision. Professionalization of justice, aside from subjecting the judge to the close scrutiny of professional groups and committees of higher judges, has the advantage of fostering systematic thinking and consistency in the application of legal norms and standards.

Time and again, qualified legal authorities have suggested that we should have a Ministry of Justice. The idea is noteworthy because by creating such an agency, we could require that every person who wanted to be a judge should be employed by the ministry and would be subject to its qualifying criteria and professional standards of conduct. The independence of judges could be safeguarded, as in Civil Law countries, by appropriate measures that would entrust the decision in all such matters as job location, transfer, and promotion of judges to independent committees composed of and elected by judges themselves.

## Police: Elevating Their Qualifications and Image

As we have seen, in the last analysis the success of the criminal justice system depends to a large extent on the quality and commitment of police forces. If they are able and willing to establish positive contacts with the public and earn its respect and cooperation, the task of crime prevention and detection will be relatively less onerous. Of course they should be able to do this without violating the law. As we have seen, police have to work under conflicting expectations, which should be understood and resolved once and for all. If it is more important for them to observe the rights of the accused than to bring offenders to justice, this should be expressed unequivocally. They should not be blamed but praised if, due to their real concern for such constitutional guarantees and despite their ardent efforts, they fail to bring criminals to justice. Otherwise, the courts and the law-abiding public should try to understand their plight and sympathize with them. In any event the relation between criminal courts and the police, on the one hand, and police and the public, on the other, should be based on mutual understanding, respect, and cooperation. For this reason, the image of the police force should be improved. Police should receive better education and higher salaries. There should be more extensive police involvement in the everyday affairs of the public, not as unsolicited intrusion in the private affairs of the citizen—which is rightly abhorred—but as providing easily available help whenever the public needs it. There should be more educational programs in schools, television, and elsewhere to introduce police services and responsibilities to the public and foster police-public cooperation in mutual areas of concern.

## Judicial Procedures

The Supreme Court's concern with the constitutional rights of the accused, which in reality means protection of the public against any possible official violation of these rights, is of course laudatory and essential to the American system of government. This concern, however, seems exaggerated at times, so that the rights of the accused are protected at the expense of the victim's and the public's suffering. Involuntary confessions, for instance, should of course be inadmissible. But why should we exclude a voluntary confession which is made without the Miranda warning? If the warning is regarded as essential, as it is from a particular perspective, then we should indicate this explicitly to the police, and we should not expect miracles from them or be disappointed if their rate of detection and apprehension of criminals seems very low. On such premises, we should also punish them if they violate the law.

The same observation can be made about search and seizure. If the observance of procedural rules related to search and seizure is so important, we should, in the interest of fairness to police, try to maintain the same lenient attitude toward their failure to produce convincing evidence and punish them whenever they violate the rules. In this way we can use the results of a voluntary confession without the Miranda warning and the illegal search and seizure, while at the same time punishing the police for their violations. Logically, such an eventuality will be short-lived. After police realize that they will be punished for their transgressions against the law, they will stop acting illegally to obtain the evidence in this manner. In the meantime, the public will not feel that it is being victimized because of an error on the part of the police.

I pointed out that in English criminal trials, the judge chooses the jury from among a list of qualified candidates, a list which has been prepared ahead of time. We know that in the United States, numerous hours, even days are wasted in the selection of the jury because defense attorneys try to select only jurors who will be more sympathetic to their cause. What would happen if we followed a similar procedure selecting the jury in each case by drawing lots from a prearranged list of qualified candidates?

The accused is logically the first person to know about his possible involvement or noninvolvement in a charged offense. Reason would require that he cooperate with the court, especially if he is innocent, to clear the matter. We cannot of course force him to make any self-incriminating statements. On the other hand, if he is silent and unresponsive to valid questions that could clarify the issues, why not allow an adverse inference to be made from his silence?

When we are required to make our reasoning explicit, we tend to be more objective. The sentencing judge should be required to give reasons for setting the punishment for each particular offender. This decision and the reasoning should be also explained to the offender in person, to create an element of personal contact and care, which can be psychologically significant for the convict. The same idea of making valid and clear explanations whenever possible should be observed in prison. The convict should know the extent of his punishment ahead of time; he should be also advised as to what is expected of him in prison and under what circumstances and for what kind of behavior he may get an earlier release. Whether the inmate will decide to observe the rules and take advantage of the opportunities is another matter. We should try, however, to be as explicit and clear as possible, at least to give him the understanding and opportunity for rehabilitation, a realistic hope and motivation for reform if he decides to do so.

## Penal Institutions

Whenever politicians want to convince the public that they are concerned about the crime problem, thus asking for more votes, they make the claim, seemingly based on the wisdom of the ages, that in order to keep society safe from all criminal elements, more prisons should be built. However, when such a proposal is actually put to popular vote, it is usually rejected, as if the public somehow knows that the crime problem cannot be solved by putting more offenders in jail. A better proposal may be the exact opposite: to destroy most of the existing prisons and to incarcerate fewer people. I suggest this not in the spirit of the reformist anarchist or the impassioned revolutionary who sees the destruction of most existing social institutions as prerequisite to the emergence of a better world order, but rather as a reasoned and practical solution for some of today's seemingly insoluble crime-related problems.

As we have noted, most American prisons, at least the way they are administered now, do not rehabilitate the offender. In fact, they create and reinforce stronger criminal tendencies in the inmate. It is thus a clear mistake to send any offender to penal institutions who does not pose any real danger to society. In many cases, the need for retribution or desert in the public, which as we have argued is the strongest possible reason for punishment, can be satisfied by realizing that the offender will be suffering a considerable financial loss by making him pay a high fine or work a certain number of weeks or months to pay off the fine. In this way the public benefits from his services, which can also be rendered on some community project; meanwhile, the offender is not exposed to strong criminal stimuli of the prison; society saves by not having to pay for his confinement in an institution; and the available prison space will be used for more dangerous, repeat offenders. If the proposal is accepted as sound and practical, the details, conditions, and limits of its application can be easily worked out. One possible procedure, which has been utilized in most Civil Law countries, is to require the consent of the crime victim and the satisfaction of the damage he has suffered before an offender can be eligible to receive a fine or security measures instead of punishment.

More dangerous criminals should of course be sent to prison, but they should not be forgotten either. We should try to rehabilitate and readjust their behavior. However, any program that is offered for this purpose and for teaching the offender a useful craft or other practical knowledge should be voluntary. Our main objective is to punish the offender for his past illegal act; it should be up to him to decide whether or not to take advantage of available opportunities.

Prisoners should be offered the opportunity of a paying job, which, depending on the condition of the inmate, could be located outside prison walls from the beginning or moved there gradually, under the competent supervision of prison authorities.

The unusual atmosphere of the prison affects not only the lives of convicted offenders but also the perceptions and attitudes of the prison guards. Each component of the system becomes conditioned to support and maintain the total institutional setup, values, and expectations. To avoid this natural process, more frequent contacts with the outside world should be encouraged and arranged. The inmates should be brought into regular, meaningful contact with outside elements, not in the artificial and demeaning form of visiting hours, but in a more productive atmosphere of work or social contacts outside prison walls. The possibility and extent of such outside contacts should be determined in practice in the light of individual needs and abilities of each inmate. The point is, however, that prison guards also need regular contacts with the outside world, a process that can hopefully remind them that what they perceive in existing American prisons is only one possible perspective which can and should be modified; that there are other possibilities of influencing the inmate to adopt a more constructive way of life. For this reason, more extended cooperation between outside citizen groups and corporate entities on the one hand and prison authorities on the other should be encouraged in arranging and executing various programs both inside and outside the prison.

## NOTE

1. Paraphrasing Froebel, Dewey says, "the primary business of school is to train children in co-operative and mutually helpful living; to foster in them the consciousness of mutual interdependence; and to help them practically in making the adjustments that will carry this spirit into overt deeds." See John Dewey, *The School and Society* (Chicago: University of Chicago Press, 1965), p. 117.

# Selected Bibliography

Albanese, Jay S. *Myths and Realities of Crime and Justice: A Citizen's Guide*. Niagara Falls, N.Y.: Apocalypse Publishing Co., 1984.

Alper, Benedict S. *Prisons Inside-Out: Alternatives in Correctional Reform*. Cambridge, Mass.: Ballinger Publishing Co., 1974.

Ashman, Charles R. *The Finest Judges Money Can Buy: And Other Forms of Judicial Pollution*. Los Angeles: Nash Publishing, 1973.

Becker, Harold K. *Police Systems of Europe: A Survey of Selected Police Organizations*. Springfield, Ill.: Charles C. Thomas, 1973.

Becker, Howard S. *Outsiders: Studies in the Sociology of Deviance*. New York: The Free Press, 1966.

Becker, Howard S., ed. *The Other Side: Perspectives on Deviance*. New York: The Free Press, 1967.

Bersani, Carl A. *Crime and Delinquency: A Reader*. London; Macmillan Co., 1970.

Bloch, Herbert, and Arthur Niederhoffer. *The Gang: A Study in Adolescent Behavior*. New York: Philosophical Library, 1958.

Blumberg, Abraham S. *Criminal Justice*. Chicago: Quadrangle Books, 1970.

Bouma, Donald. *Kids and Cops: A Study in Mutual Hostility*. Grand Rapids, Mich.: Eerdmans, 1967.

Bronfenbrenner, Urie. *Two Worlds of Childhood: U.S.A. and U.S.S.R.* New York: Touchstone, 1972.

Buchholz, Erich, et al. *Soviet Criminology: Theoretical and Methodical Foundations*. Saxon House, Lexington Books, 1974.

Campbell, Angus, and Philip E. Converse, eds. *The Human Meaning of Social Change*. New York: Russell Sage Foundation, 1972.

Casper, Jonathan D. *American Criminal Justice: The Defendant's Perspective*. Englewood Cliffs, N.J.: Prentice-Hall, Inc., 1972.

Chambliss, William J. *On the Take: From Petty Crooks to Presidents*. Bloomington, Ind.: Indiana University Press, 1982.

Christopher, Robert C. *The Japanese Mind: The Goliath Explained*. New York: Linden Press/Simon & Schuster, 1983.

Clark, Ramsey. *Crime in America: Observations on Its Nature, Causes, Prevention and Control*. New York: Simon & Schuster, 1970.

Clifford, William. *Crime Control in Japan*. Lexington, Mass.: Lexington Books, 1976.

Cloward, Richard A., and Lloyd E. Ohlin. *Delinquency and Opportunity: A Theory of Delinquent Gangs*. New York: The Free Press, 1966.

Cohen, Albert K. *Delinquent Boys: The Culture of the Gang*. New York: The Free Press, 1971.

Conklin, John E. *Illegal But Not Criminal: Business Crime in America*. Englewood Cliffs, N.J.: Prentice-Hall, Inc., 1977.

Cressey, Donald R. *Theft of the Nation: The Structure and Operations of Organized Crime in America*. New York: Harper Torchbooks, 1977.

David, Rene, and Brierly, John E. C. *Major Legal Systems in the World To-day: An Introduction to the Comparative Study of Law*, 2d ed. New York: The Free Press, 1978.

Dollard, J., L. W. Doob, N. E. Miller, O. H. Mouirer, and R. R. Sears. *Frustration and Aggression*. New Haven, Conn.: Yale University Press, 1939.

Domhoff, William. *Who Rules America?* Englewood Cliffs, N.J.: Prentice-Hall, Inc., 1967.

———. *Who Rules America Now? A View for the 80s*. Englewood Cliffs, N.J.: Prentice-Hall, Inc., 1983.

Durkheim, Emile. *The Rules of Sociological Method*. New York: The Free Press, 1966.

———. *Suicide: A Study in Sociology*. New York: The Free Press, 1966.

Etzioni, Amitai. *An Immodest Agenda: Rebuilding America Before the 21st Century*. New York: McGraw-Hill Book Co., 1983.

Forer, Lois G. *Money and Justice: Who Owns the Courts?* New York: W. W. Norton & Company, 1984.

Frankel, Marvin E. *Criminal Sentences: Law Without Order*. New York: Hill and Wang, 1973.

———. *Partisan Justice: Too Much Fight? Too Little Truth? Equal Justice?* New York: Hill and Wang, 1980.

Gardiner, John A., and Michael A. Mulkey. *Crime and Criminal Justice: Issues in Public Policy Analysis*. Lexington, Mass.: D. C. Heath and Company, 1976.

Gaylin, Willard. *Partial Justice: A Study of Bias in Sentencing*. New York: Vintage Books, 1975.

Gilsinan, James E. *Doing Justice: How the System Works—As Seen by the Participants*. Englewood Cliffs, N.J.: Prentice-Hall, Inc., 1982.

Goldman, Nathan. *The Differential Selection of Juvenile Offenders for Court Appearance*. New York: National Council on Crime and Delinquency, 1963.

Goldstein, Abraham S., and Joseph Goldstein, eds. *Crime, Law and Society*. New York: The Free Press, 1971.

Graham, Michael H. *Tightening the Reins of Justice in America: A Comparative Analysis of the Criminal Jury Trial in England and the United States*. Westport, Conn.: Greenwood Press, 1983.

Harrington, Michael. *The Other America*. 1962; Reprinted with new Afterword, Baltimore: Penguin Books, 1982.

Henry, Jules. *Culture Against Man*. New York: Vintage Books, 1965.

Hentig, Hans von. *The Criminal and His Victim: Studies in the Sociobiology of Crime*. New York: Schocken Books, 1979.

Hirsch, Andrew von. *Doing Justice: The Choice of Punishments*. New York: Hill and Wang, 1981.

Hofstadter, Richard, and Michael Wallace, eds. *American Violence: A Documentary History*. New York: Vintage Books, 1971.

Kelly, Delos H. *Delinquent Behavior: Interactional and Motivational Aspects*. Belmont, Calif.: Dickinson Publishing Co., Inc., 1978.

Krisberg, Barry. *Crime and Privilege: Toward a New Criminology*. Englewood Cliffs, N.J.: Prentice-Hall, Inc., 1975.

Lasch, Christopher. *The Culture of Narcissism: American Life in an Age of Diminishing Expectations*. New York: Warner Books, 1979.

Matza, David. *Delinquency and Drift*. New York: John Wiley & Sons, Inc., 1979.

Menninger, Karl. *The Crime of Punishment*. New York: Penguin Books, 1979.

Monroe, David G., and Earl W. Garret, under the direction of August Vollmer. *Police Conditions in the United States: A Report to the National Commission on Law Observance and Enforcement*. Montclair, N.J.: Patterson Smith Reprint Series, 1968.

Morris, Norval. *The Future of Imprisonment*. Chicago: The University of Chicago Press, 1974.

————, and Gordon Hawkins. *The Honest Politician's Guide to Crime Control*. Chicago: The University of Chicago Press, 1970.

National Commission on Law Observance and Enforcement, 6 vols. and 13 reports. Washington, D.C.: U.S. Government Printing Office, 1931.

Niederhoffer, Arthur. *Behind the Shield: The Police in Urban Society*. Garden City, N.Y.: Doubleday & Co., 1969.

Packer, Herbert L. *The Limits of the Criminal Sanction*. Stanford, Calif.: Stanford University Press, 1968.

Parenti, M. *Democracy for the Few*, 2d ed. New York: St. Martin's Press, 1977.

Parker, Richard. *The Myth of the Middle Class: Notes on Affluence and Equality*. New York: Harper Colophon Books, 1974.

President's Commission on Law Enforcement and Administration of Justice. *Task Force Report: Crime and Its Impact—An Assessment*. Washington, D.C.: U.S. Government Printing Office, 1967.

Quinney, Richard. *Criminal Justice in America: A Critical Understanding*. Boston: Little, Brown and Company, 1974.

————. *Critique of Legal Order: Crime Control in Capitalist Society*. Boston: Little, Brown and Company, 1974.

————. *The Problem of Crime*. New York: Dodd, Mead & Company, 1975.

Radzinowicz, Leon. *Ideology and Crime*. New York: Columbia University Press, 1966.

————, and Marvin E. Wolfgang, eds. *Crime and Justice*. 2d and rev. ed., *The Criminal in Society* (vol. 1), *Criminal in the Arms of the Law* (vol. 2), *The Criminal in Confinement* (vol. 3). New York: Basic Books, 1977.

Reckless, Walter C. *The Crime Problem*. New York: Appleton-Century-Crofts, 1967.

Rubington, Earl, and Martin S. Weinberg. *Deviance: The Interactional Perspective.* New York: Macmillan Co., 1972.

Sagarin, Edward, and Fred Montanino, eds. *Deviants: Voluntary Actors in a Hostile World.* Morristown, N.J.: General Learning Press, 1977.

Schlesinger, Rudolf B. *Comparative Law: Cases-Text-Materials,* 4th ed. Mineola, N.Y.: The Foundation Press, 1980.

Schur, Edwin M. *Crimes Without Victims: Deviant Behavior and Public Policy.* Englewood Cliffs. N.J.: Prentice-Hall., Inc., 1965.

———. *Our Criminal Society: The Social and Legal Sources of Crime in America.* Englewood Cliffs, N.J.: Prentice-Hall, Inc., 1969.

Sellin, Thorsten. *Culture, Conflict and Crime.* New York: Social Science Research Council, 1938.

Silberman, Charles E. *Criminal Violence, Criminal Justice.* New York: Vintage Books, 1980.

Skolnick, Jerome H. *Justice Without Trial: Law Enforcement in Democratic Society.* New York: John Wiley & Sons, 1966.

*Struggle for Justice: A Report on Crime and Punishment in America,* prepared for the American Friends Service Committee. New York: Hill and Wang, 1971.

Sutherland, Edwin H., annotator and interpretor. *The Professional Thief, by a Professional Thief.* Chicago: The University of Chicago Press, 1965.

Sutherland, Edwin H., and Donald R. Cressey. *Criminology,* 8th ed. New York: J. B. Lippincott Co., 1970.

Sykes, Gresham M. *The Society of Captives.* Princeton, N.J.: Princeton University Press, 1974.

Tapp, June Louin, and Felice J. Levine, eds. *Law, Justice and the Individual in Society: Psychological and Legal Issues.* New York: Holt, Rinehart and Winston, 1977.

Thrasher, Frederic M. *The Gang: A Study of 1,313 Gangs in Chicago.* Chicago: The University of Chicago Press, 1926.

Usdin, Gene, ed. *Perspectives on Violence: Essays on Concepts of Aggression and Related Behavior.* Secaucus, N.J.: The Citadel Press, 1976.

Vetter, Harold J., and Leonard Territo. *Crime and Justice in America: A Human Perspective.* St. Paul, Minn.: West Publishing Co., 1984.

Weinberg, Martin S., and Earl Rubington, eds. *The Solution of Social Problems.* New York: Oxford University Press, 1973.

Wilson, James Q. *Thinking about Crime.* New York: Vintage Books, 1983.

———. *Varieties of Police Behavior: The Management of Law and Order in Eight Communities.* Cambridge, Mass.: Harvard University Press, 1978.

Wolfgang, Marvin E., Leonard Savitz, and Norman Johnston, eds. *The Sociology of Crime and Delinquency,* 2d ed. New York: John Wiley & Sons, 1970.

Wolfgang, Marvin E. and F. Ferracuti. *The Subculture of Violence.* London: Tavistock, 1967.

Wright, Erik Olin. *The Politics of Punishment: A Critical Analysis of Prisons in America.* New York: Harper Colophon Books, 1973.

Zimring, Franklin E., and Gordon J. Hawkins. *Deterrence.* Chicago: The University of Chicago Press, 1973.

# Index

## About the Author

PARVIS SANEY is a Visiting Professor of Law at Brooklyn Law School, New York. He is the author of *Law and Personality* and *Criminal Law*.